CRIMINAL JUSTICE ILLUMINATED

Essentials of the Reid Technique
Criminal Interrogation and Confessions

Fred E. Inbau
The Late John Henry Wigmore
Professor of Law Emeritus
Northwestern University
Chicago, Illinois

John E. Reid
Late President
John E. Reid and Associates
Chicago, Illinois

Joseph P. Buckley
President
John E. Reid and Associates
Chicago, Illinois

Brian C. Jayne
Director
Research and Development
John E. Reid and Associates
Chicago, Illinois

JONES AND BARTLETT PUBLISHERS
Sudbury, Massachusetts
BOSTON TORONTO LONDON SINGAPORE

World Headquarters
Jones and Bartlett Publishers
40 Tall Pine Drive
Sudbury, MA 01776
978-443-5000
info@jbpub.com
www.jbpub.com

Jones and Bartlett Publishers Canada
6339 Ormindale Way
Mississauga, ON L5V 1J2
Canada

Jones and Bartlett Publishers International
Barb House, Barb Mews
London W6 7PA
United Kingdom

Production Credits
Publisher—Public Safety Group: Kimberly Brophy
Acquisitions Editor: Chambers Moore
Production Manager: Amy Rose
Production Assistant: Carolyn F. Rogers
Marketing Manager: Matthew Bennett
Marketing Associate: Laura Kavigian
Cover and Interior Design: Anne Spencer
Photo Research: Kimberly Potvin
Cover Images: photo © Jones and Bartlett Publishers;
column © Ron Chapple/Thinkstock/Alamy Images
Chapter Openers: © Masterfile
Composition: Carlisle Publishers Services
Printing and Binding: Malloy, Inc.
Cover Printing: Malloy, Inc.

ISBN-13: 978-0-7637-2728-4
ISBN-10: 0-7637-2728-8

Library of Congress Cataloging-in-Publication Data

Essentials of the Reid technique : criminal interrogation and confessions / Fred E. Inbau ... [et al.].— 1st ed.
p. cm.
An abridged version of Criminal interrogation and confessions / Fred E. Inbau ... [et al.], 4th ed.
Includes index.
ISBN 0-7637-2728-8 (pbk. : alk. paper)
1. Police questioning—United States. 2. Confession (Law)—United States. I. Title: Criminal interrogation and confessions. II. Inbau, Fred Edward.
HV8073.E83 2005
363.25'4—dc22
2004011536

6048
Printed in the United States of America
10 09 10 9 8 7

Contents

Preface vii

Part I What You Need to Know About Interrogation

1 Distinctions Between Interviews and Interrogations 3

Perspective 3
Characteristics of an Interview 4
Characteristics of an Interrogation 5
Benefits of Conducting an Interview Before an Interrogation 6
Exercises 8

2 The Importance of Obtaining and Evaluating Factual Information 11

Before the Interview 11
Gathering Information from Others Through Interviews 17
Exercises 21

3 Privacy and the Interview Room 25

The Importance of Privacy 25
Minimize Reminders of Consequences 27
Suggestions for Setting Up the Interview Room 28
Exercises 35

4 Qualifications, Attitude, and General Conduct of the Investigator 37

Interviewer Traits 37
Interviewer Qualifications 38
Initial Interview Procedures 38
Investigator's Demeanor During an Interview 41
Exercises 45

5 Preparation and Starting the Interview 47

Perspective 47
Formal Versus Informal Interviews 48
Arranging the Formal Interview 48
Preparing for the Interview 50

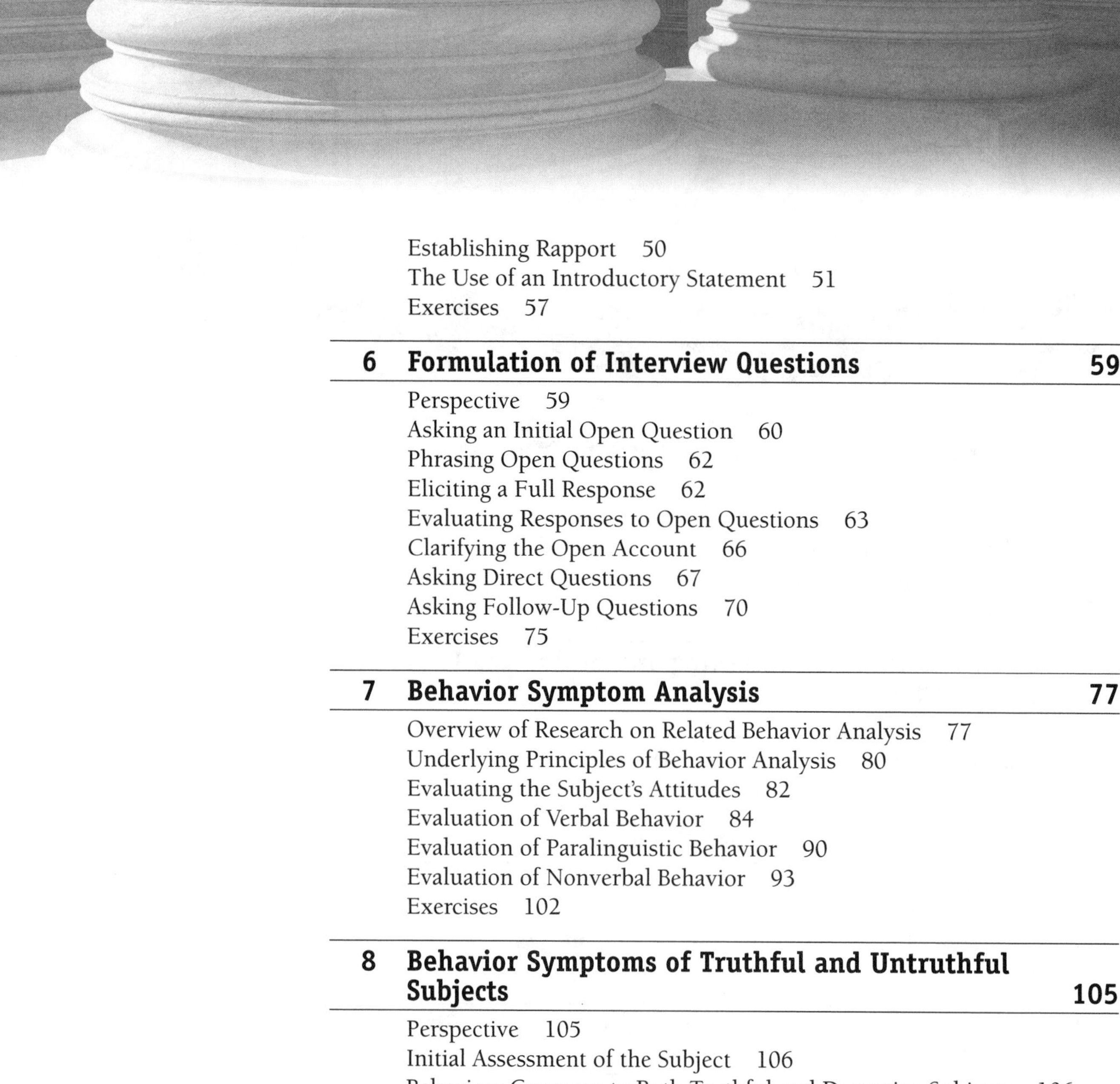

Establishing Rapport 50
The Use of an Introductory Statement 51
Exercises 57

6 Formulation of Interview Questions 59

Perspective 59
Asking an Initial Open Question 60
Phrasing Open Questions 62
Eliciting a Full Response 62
Evaluating Responses to Open Questions 63
Clarifying the Open Account 66
Asking Direct Questions 67
Asking Follow-Up Questions 70
Exercises 75

7 Behavior Symptom Analysis 77

Overview of Research on Related Behavior Analysis 77
Underlying Principles of Behavior Analysis 80
Evaluating the Subject's Attitudes 82
Evaluation of Verbal Behavior 84
Evaluation of Paralinguistic Behavior 90
Evaluation of Nonverbal Behavior 93
Exercises 102

8 Behavior Symptoms of Truthful and Untruthful Subjects 105

Perspective 105
Initial Assessment of the Subject 106
Behaviors Common to Both Truthful and Deceptive Subjects 106
Factors That May Lead to Misinterpretation of Behavior Symptoms 108
Conclusion 113
Exercises 115

Part II Employing the Reid Nine Steps of Interrogation

9 Overview of and Preparation for the Reid Nine Steps 119

Perspective 119

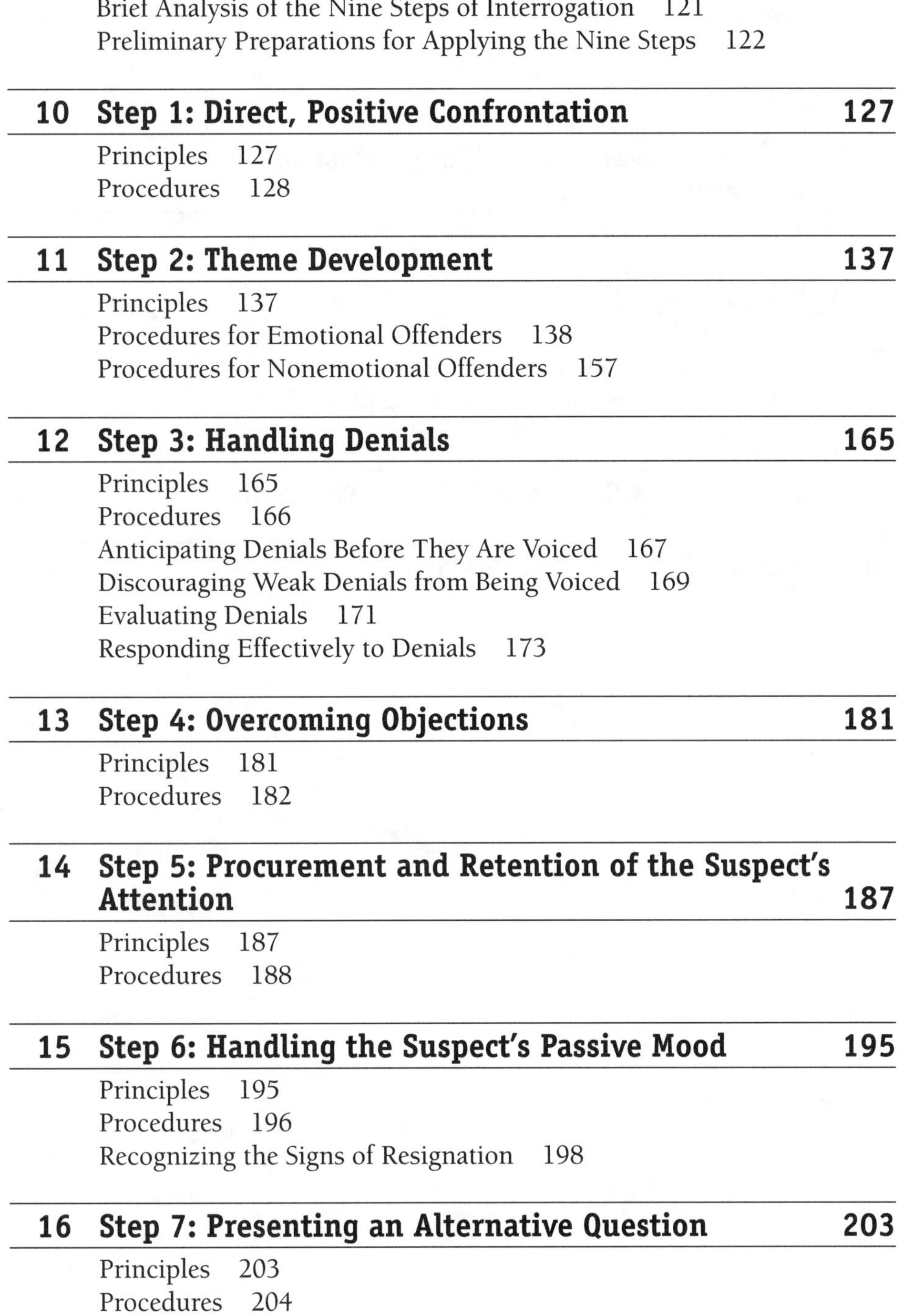

General Classification of Offenders 119
Brief Analysis of the Nine Steps of Interrogation 121
Preliminary Preparations for Applying the Nine Steps 122

10 Step 1: Direct, Positive Confrontation 127

Principles 127
Procedures 128

11 Step 2: Theme Development 137

Principles 137
Procedures for Emotional Offenders 138
Procedures for Nonemotional Offenders 157

12 Step 3: Handling Denials 165

Principles 165
Procedures 166
Anticipating Denials Before They Are Voiced 167
Discouraging Weak Denials from Being Voiced 169
Evaluating Denials 171
Responding Effectively to Denials 173

13 Step 4: Overcoming Objections 181

Principles 181
Procedures 182

14 Step 5: Procurement and Retention of the Suspect's Attention 187

Principles 187
Procedures 188

15 Step 6: Handling the Suspect's Passive Mood 195

Principles 195
Procedures 196
Recognizing the Signs of Resignation 198

16 Step 7: Presenting an Alternative Question 203

Principles 203
Procedures 204

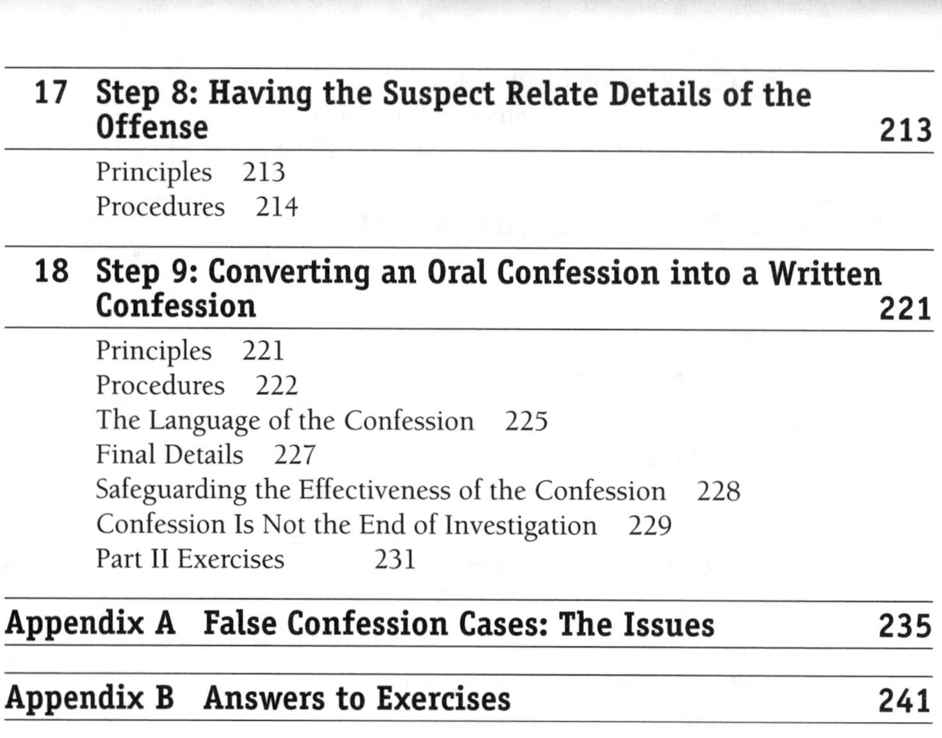

17 Step 8: Having the Suspect Relate Details of the Offense **213**

Principles 213
Procedures 214

18 Step 9: Converting an Oral Confession into a Written Confession **221**

Principles 221
Procedures 222
The Language of the Confession 225
Final Details 227
Safeguarding the Effectiveness of the Confession 228
Confession Is Not the End of Investigation 229
Part II Exercises 231

Appendix A False Confession Cases: The Issues **235**

Appendix B Answers to Exercises **241**

Index 249

Preface

The process of interviewing and interrogation that has come to be known as the Reid Technique was initially developed in the 1940s and 1950s and was described in the first edition of this text, published in 1962. A year after the Supreme Court handed down its *Miranda* decision, a second edition was published to incorporate the mandated warnings. The third edition, published in 1986, represented basically an entirely new book with improved techniques and an expanded legal section. Also, at that time, an appendix on the psychology of interrogation was incorporated to address the growing interest in interrogation techniques by academicians in the fields of psychology and sociology.

During the next fifteen years, John E. Reid & Associates, Inc. continued to refine The Reid Technique and, since 1987, has taught this material in its Reid Technique seminars across the United States, Canada, Europe, and Asia. With hundreds of thousands of investigators having received this training, it was felt that an updated authoritative text describing the proper and improper applications of the technique was needed. In addition, over the past several years, investigators were being asked in court, on a more regular basis, to describe specific interrogation tactics and the underlying principles surrounding the tactics involved in The Reid Technique. To address these issues, a fourth edition of the text was arranged. Tragically, during early stages of the project, the senior author, Professor Fred Inbau, died from injuries sustained in an accident. Joseph Buckley, coauthor of the third edition, continued with the revisions. He enlisted the assistance of Brian Jayne, who authored the psychology appendix in the third edition. Both Mr. Buckley and Mr. Jayne were fortunate enough to have studied under the late John Reid and to have worked closely with Professor Inbau on various publications.

The fourth edition, published in 2001, provides the investigator with not only updated information describing the interviewing and interrogation process, but also the underlying explanations for various aspects of the technique. This insight should assist the investigator, prosecutor, and judge in their understanding of the interrogation process and circumstances that lead to the proper admissibility of a confession. To further enhance an understanding of interrogations and confessions in court, additional chapters were written to offer guidelines in distinguishing between true and false confessions, as well as testifying about a confession.

This abridged version of the fourth edition is a concise description of the essential elements of the Reid Technique of Interviewing and Interrogation. It is designed as a refresher text for investigators who have received training in the Reid Technique of Interviewing and Interrogation or as a primer for students or other individuals who have a general interest in interviewing and interrogation. The abridged version is limited to interviewing and interrogation techniques, and some of the original information within those topics was excluded.

Consequently, this abridged version does not represent a complete description of the Reid Technique. The information that we were not able to cover in this abridged version includes chapters on case solutions, initial precautionary measures for the protection of the innocent, the behavior analysis interview, the use of specialized questioning techniques, distinguishing between true and false confessions, testifying about a confession, interrogation law, and confession law.

Due to the special nature of this book, with its discourse between interrogator and suspect, the words *he* and *him* are used generically in order to avoid redundancy.

I

What You Need to Know About Interrogation

1

Distinctions Between Interviews and Interrogations

Chapter Objectives

Upon completion of this chapter you will be able to:

- Identify the characteristics of an interview
- Identify the characteristics of an interrogation
- Explain the benefits of conducting an interview before an interrogation

Perspective

For the sake of brevity, the title of this text refers to "criminal interrogations" without mention of the interviewing process that often precedes an interrogation. Indeed, the terms interview and interrogation are often used interchangeably by investigators, depending on the audience being addressed. While testifying in court, the investigator inevitably describes his conversation with the defendant as an "interview." This is so even if it lasted four hours and clearly involved repeated accusations of guilt. Conversely, a rookie police officer may be overheard telling a fellow officer about a traffic stop he made the night before: "Yeah, this guy initially claimed he didn't know he was speeding but after a little 'interrogation' he came up with some lame excuse for going over the limit—I got him to confess." At the outset of the book, we would like to describe some of the essential differences between an interview and interrogation so the reader will have a clear understanding of what we mean by these terms as they appear in this text.

interview a free-flowing, nonaccusatory meeting or discussion used to gather information.

interrogation an accusational interaction with a suspect, conducted in a controlled environment, designed to persuade the suspect to tell the truth.

Characteristics of an Interview

nonaccusatory not indicating wrongdoing; not blaming or accusing.

The investigator should remain neutral and objective during the interview process.

- **An interview is nonaccusatory.** This should be the case even when the investigator has clear reason to believe that the suspect is involved in the offense or has lied to him. By maintaining a nonaccusatory tone, the investigator is able to establish a much better rapport with the suspect, which will assist in any interrogation that might follow the interview. A guilty subject is more likely to volunteer useful information about his access, opportunity, propensity, and motives if the questions are asked in a nonaccusatory fashion.

  In addition, the suspect's behavioral responses to interview questions can be more reliably interpreted when the questions are asked in a conversational, rather than challenging, manner. The investigator should remain neutral and objective during the interview process.
- **The purpose of an interview is to gather information.** During an interview the investigator should be eliciting investigative and behavioral information. Examples of investigative information include establishing the relationship between the suspect and the victim, the suspect's alibi, and the suspect's access to the crime scene. During an interview the investigator should closely evaluate the suspect's behavioral responses to interview questions. The suspect's posture, eye contact, facial expressions, word choice, and response delivery may each reveal symptoms of truthfulness or deception. Ultimately, the investigator must make an assessment of the suspect's credibility when responding to investigative questions. This is primarily done through evaluating the suspect's behavioral responses during the interview, along with independent assessment of factual information.
- **An interview may be conducted early during an investigation.** Because the purpose of an interview is to collect information, it may be conducted before evidence is analyzed or all of the factual information about an investigation is known. Obviously, the more information the investigator knows about the crime and the suspect, the more meaningful the subsequent interview of the suspect will be. However, on a practical level, the investigator should take advantage of any opportunity to conduct an interview, regardless of sketchy facts or the absence of specific evidence.
- **An interview may be conducted in a variety of environments.** The ideal environment for an interview is a room designed specifically for that purpose. Frequently, however, interviews are conducted wherever it is convenient to ask questions—in a person's home or office, in the back seat of a squad car, or on a street corner.
- **Interviews are free-flowing and relatively unstructured.** While the investigator will have specific topics to cover during the interview, the responses a suspect offers may cause the investigator to explore unanticipated areas. The investigator must be prepared to follow up on these ar-

eas because the significance of the information may not be known until later during the investigation.

- **The investigator should make written notes during a formal interview.** Note-taking during a formal interview (one conducted in a controlled environment) serves several important purposes. Not only will the notes record the subject's responses to interview questions, but also, by taking notes, the investigator will be more aware of the subject's behavior. Note-taking also slows down the pace of the questioning. It is much easier to lie to questions that are asked in a rapid-fire manner. By creating silence between each question, the deceptive subject experiences greater anxiety when given time to think about his deceptive response, and is more likely to display behavioral symptoms of deception. Furthermore, an innocent suspect may become confused or flustered when a rapid-fire approach to questioning is used.

  Note-taking can inhibit the gathering of information if it is done sporadically. For example, if the investigator has not taken any notes during the early stages of the interview but then suddenly writes down something the suspect has said, the suspect will attach significance to that statement and is likely to become much more guarded in subsequent answers. However, if at the outset of the interview the investigator establishes a pattern of writing a note following each of the suspect's responses, note-taking will not inhibit the disclosure of relevant information.

controlled environment an environment that is private and free from distractions.

Characteristics of an Interrogation

- **An interrogation is accusatory.** A deceptive suspect is not likely to offer admissions against his self-interest unless he is convinced that the investigator is certain of his guilt. Therefore, an accusatory statement such as "Joe, there is absolutely no doubt that you were the person who started this fire" is necessary to display this level of confidence. On the other hand, if the investigator merely states, "Joe, I think you may have had something to do with starting this fire," the suspect will immediately recognize the uncertainty in the investigator's confidence, which reinforces his determination to deny any involvement in committing the crime.
- **An interrogation involves active persuasion.** The fact that an interrogation is being conducted means that the investigator believes that the suspect has not told the truth during nonaccusatory questioning. Further nonaccusatory questioning of the suspect is unlikely to elicit the presumed truth. Therefore, in an effort to persuade the suspect to tell the truth, the investigator will use tactics that make statements rather than ask questions. These tactics will also dominate the conversation; for someone to be persuaded to tell the truth, that person must first be willing to listen to the investigator's statements.
- **The purpose of an interrogation is to learn the truth.** A common misperception exists that the purpose of an interrogation is to elicit a confession. Unfortunately, there are occasions when an innocent suspect is

interrogated, and only after the suspect has been accused of committing the crime will the suspect's innocence become apparent. If the suspect can be eliminated based on behavior or explanations offered during an interrogation, the interrogation must be considered successful because the truth was learned. Often, of course, an interrogation will result in a confession, which again accomplishes the goal of learning the truth.

- **An interrogation is conducted in a controlled environment.** Because of the persuasive tactics utilized during an interrogation, the environment needs to be private and free from distractions.
- **An interrogation is conducted only when the investigator is reasonably certain of the suspect's guilt.** The investigator should have some basis for believing a suspect has not told the truth before confronting the suspect. The basis for this belief may be the suspect's behavior during an interview, inconsistencies within the suspect's account, physical evidence, or circumstantial evidence coupled with behavioral observations. Interrogation should not be used as a primary means to evaluate a suspect's truthfulness—in most cases, that can be accomplished during a nonaccusatory interview.
- **The investigator should not take any notes until after the suspect has told the truth and is fully committed to a position.** Premature note-taking during an interrogation serves as a reminder to the suspect of the incriminating nature of his statements and can therefore inhibit further admissions against self-interest. Only after the suspect has fully confessed, and perhaps after the confession has been witnessed by another investigator, should written notes be made documenting the details of the confession.

Benefits of Conducting an Interview Before an Interrogation

The majority of interrogations are conducted under circumstances in which the investigator does not have overwhelming evidence that implicates the suspect—indeed, the decision to conduct an interrogation is in an effort to possibly obtain such evidence. Frequently, prior to an interrogation, the only evidence supporting a suspect's guilt is circumstantial or behavioral in nature. Under this condition, conducting a nonaccusatory interview of the suspect is indispensable with respect to identifying whether the suspect is, in fact, likely to be guilty. Furthermore, the information learned during the interview of a guilty suspect, when there is sparse incriminating evidence linking him to the crime, is necessary to conduct a proper interrogation.

In those instances where there is clear and convincing evidence of a suspect's guilt, it may be tempting for an investigator to engage directly in an interrogation, bypassing the interview process. This is generally not advisable for the following reasons:

- The nonaccusatory nature of the interview affords the investigator an opportunity to establish a level of rapport and trust with the suspect that cannot be accomplished during an accusatory interrogation.
- During an interview the investigator often learns important information about the suspect that will be beneficial during an interrogation.
- There is no guarantee that a guilty suspect will confess during an interrogation. However, if that same guilty suspect is *interviewed,* he may lie about his alibi, possessing a particular weapon, knowing the victim, or having access to a certain type of vehicle. During a subsequent trial, the investigator may be able to demonstrate that statements made during the interview were false and thus provide evidence contributing to the finding of the suspect's guilt.
- There is a psychological advantage for the investigator to conduct a nonaccusatory interview before the accusatory interrogation. For the interrogation to be successful, the suspect must trust the investigator's objectivity and sincerity. This is much more easily accomplished when the investigator first offers the suspect an opportunity to tell the truth through conversational questioning.

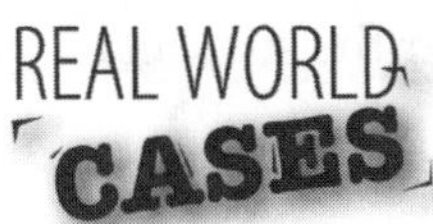

Interrogation on the Street

A car recently reported stolen is pulled over after a brief chase. In this circumstance, conducting a nonaccusatory preliminary interview of the driver makes little sense. If the suspect waives his *Miranda* rights, the arresting officer would certainly be wise to confront the suspect immediately—perhaps with a statement similar to the following: "We know you took this car. Did you take it just for a joy ride or were you going to use it as a get-away car for a robbery?"

An exception to the foregoing suggestion may be a situation in which a suspect is caught in an incriminating circumstance or clearly evidences a desire to tell the truth during initial questioning. Under this circumstance, an immediate interrogation may be warranted (see Interrogation on the Street).

Traditionally, investigators have made little or no distinction between interviewing and interrogation. However, advancements in these specialized techniques suggest that clear differences exist and ought to be recognized. As will later be presented, some investigators are inherently good *interviewers* but lack the same intrinsic skills during an *interrogation,* and vice versa. An effective investigator will gain skills in both of these related, but distinctly different, procedures.

KEY POINTS

- It is usually advisable to conduct an interview with a subject before conducting an interrogation. This allows the investigator to gather more information and determine whether the subject is likely to be guilty.

Characteristics of an Interview

- An interview is nonaccusatory.
- The purpose of an interview is to gather information.
- An interview may be conducted early during an investigation.
- An interview may be conducted in a variety of environments.
- Interviews are free-flowing and relatively unstructured.
- The investigator should take written notes during a formal interview.

Characteristics of an Interrogation

- An interrogation is accusatory.
- An interrogation involves active persuasion.
- The purpose of an interrogation is to learn the truth.
- An interrogation is conducted in a controlled environment.
- An interrogation is conducted only when the investigator is reasonably certain of the suspect's guilt.
- The investigator should not take any notes until after the suspect has told the truth and is fully committed to a position.

KEY TERMS

controlled environment An environment that is private and free from distractions.

interrogation An accusational interaction with a suspect, conducted in a controlled environment, designed to persuade the suspect to tell the truth.

interview A free-flowing, nonaccusatory meeting or discussion used to gather information.

nonaccusatory Not indicating wrongdoing; not blaming or accusing.

EXERCISES

Identify whether the following statements or behaviors would be associated with an interview, an interrogation or would apply to both interviewing and interrogation:

1. "John, if you are making up a story about being robbed, our investigation will clearly indicate that so before we go any further. Let me ask you, last Saturday night did someone steal $1500 in money from you?"

   ____

2. The only people present in the room are the suspect and the investigator.

3. "Joe, did you plan this thing (robbery) out months in advance or did it just happen on the spur of the moment? It was the spur of the moment wasn't it?"

4. The investigator takes a written note following each verbal response the subject offers.

5. The subject is advised of his *Miranda* rights prior to a conversation with the investigator.

6. The conversation between the investigator and subject occurs at the subject's home with the subject's wife and two children present.

2

The Importance of Obtaining and Evaluating Factual Information

Chapter Objectives

Upon completion of this chapter you will be able to:

- Describe how to prepare for an interview
- Explain the importance of gathering and reviewing all known facts
- Discuss the order in which people are to be interviewed
- Understand the significance of circumstantial evidence
- Discuss cautions when interviewing other investigators
- Discuss cautions when interviewing people reporting crimes

Before the Interview

Prior to conducting any interview or interrogation, the investigator must obtain the necessary background information upon which to proceed. This information will come from a variety of sources: records and documents, victim and witness interviews, and a review of the investigative findings. Collectively, this information is referred to as the case facts.

An important skill an investigator develops is fact analysis (**Table 2-1**). By fact analysis, we mean the ability to identify from factual information the probable motivation for a crime, unique access requirements (e.g., access to a particular type of weapon or vehicle, knowledge of a security code, possession of keys), the window of time during which the crime was committed (to establish opportunity), and the propensity characteristics of the person who committed the crime (e.g., highly intelligent, emotional, a drug user). Ultimately, this information is utilized in such a way as to locate possible suspects and to help

case facts information from a variety of sources that is used by an investigator to gain a solid background about a case before conducting an interview or interrogation.

fact analysis the ability to identify from factual information the probable motivation for a crime, unique access requirements, window of time during which the crime was committed, and propensity characteristics of the person who committed the crime.

identify which one probably committed the crime. Research has demonstrated that training and experience in the area of fact analysis significantly enhance a person's ability to accurately predict who is guilty or innocent of a crime.[1]

Table 2-1 Fact Analysis

The ability to identify the following from factual information:

1. The probable motivation for a crime
2. Unique access requirements
3. The window of time during which the crime was committed
4. Propensity characteristics of the person who committed the crime

investigator the person who actually conducts the interview and possible interrogation of a suspect.

fact-giver any person who provides information about a case.

The following suggestions with respect to collecting and analyzing factual information refer to the **investigator** as the person who actually conducts the interview and possible interrogation of a suspect. A **fact-giver**, on the other hand, is any person who provides information about the case, whether that person is a witness, informant, victim, employer, or another investigator who has worked on the case.

Fact Gathering

Prior to an interview, and preferably before any contact with the suspect, the investigator should attempt to become thoroughly familiar with all the known facts and circumstances of the offense. This information will be essential not only to conduct an effective interview of possible suspects, but also to demonstrate the trustworthiness of any confession given in the case. In this regard, it is important for the investigator to withhold key information about the crime from the media and all suspects. A suspect who is able to provide "**dependent corroboration**" within his confession has offered information that only the guilty person should know.

dependent corroboration information withheld from the suspects and media that is used to verify a guilty person's confession.

The case information should be obtained from the most reliable available sources, because any inaccuracies will seriously interfere with the effectiveness of the interview or subsequent interrogation. If, for example, the investigator is misguided by another investigator's preconceived theory or by an erroneous piece of information procured during the course of the investigation, the use of such information may place the investigator at a considerable disadvantage. The suspect who is guilty and who realizes the inaccuracy of the investigator's information will be more confident about lying; conversely, the suspect who is innocent may feel insecure because of a lack of confidence in the investigator's demeanor.

Case 2-1: The Evidence Tells a Story demonstrates the difficulty that can result when an investigator receives inadequate factual information or misconceived impressions from other investigators.

Case 2-1: The Evidence Tells a Story

A triple murder occurred one winter some years ago in a state park. The three victims were married women, each about 50 years of age, who were vacationing together and staying at the park's lodge. They had gone for a walk along a pathway not frequently used at that particular time of year. When all three were found dead, their bodies bore evidence of severe beatings, their hands were tied in "chain" fashion (a hand of each victim tied to a hand of another one), and their underclothing was torn, with consequent exposure of the genital areas.

As a result of the absence of any observable evidence indicative of possible robbery, the investigators settled upon a sexual motivation as the only plausible explanation. However, after a six-month lapse and no solution to the crime, a different law enforcement agency began its own investigation. Only then was it discovered that among the clothing discarded at the scene was a glove that had been worn by one of the victims. Inside the glove were two rings, one an engagement ring and the other a wedding ring. This finding gave rise to the probability of a robbery rather than a sex-motivated offense because it revealed that one victim probably had attempted to save her rings by pulling them off along with her gloves to demonstrate to the robber that she had no jewelry on her person.

A 20-year-old dishwasher in the park's lodge had originally been questioned but was dismissed as a suspect primarily because of age: He was much younger than the victims and therefore presumably unlikely to be interested sexually in them. Once the motivation for the crime was shifted from sex to robbery, the dishwasher was interrogated again. This time, he confessed the triple murders, confirming that the motive was robbery. He said he had killed the lodge guests and had torn their clothing to simulate evidence of sexual molestation, for which he thought he would not be considered a suspect. This decoy proved to be successful temporarily, as demonstrated by the erroneous surmise of the original investigators.

Another example of the difficulty experienced by investigators because of a misinterpretation of certain evidence is a case where the murder victim's body was found with his trousers and underwear below his knees. The assumption of sexual motivation was dispelled when the offender confessed that he had killed the victim as a result of an argument in a car, and then had dragged the body through a field to the place where it was discovered. During the dragging process, the pants and underwear had become dislodged. There had been no sexual involvement.

The investigator should first interview those suspects who are *least* likely to be guilty and work toward the suspect who is most likely to be involved in the offense. The more information an investigator knows about the guilty suspect, the better his chances will be to elicit the truth during an interrogation. Truthful suspects can provide valuable information about the guilty suspect. Because of their innocence, truthful suspects generally speak openly about other suspects' possible motives, propensities, or opportunities to commit the crime. Even when such information is not learned, the guilty suspect, aware that others have been interviewed, is concerned about what these people may have revealed to the investigator.

Case 2-2: Bad Habits, Bad Associates is illustrative of the benefits of interviewing suspects believed to be innocent before conducting the interview of the suspect believed most likely to be guilty.

Case 2-2: Bad Habits, Bad Associates

A restaurant reported a break-in and theft of $4,600 from a safe. Crime scene evidence suggested that the person responsible staged the burglary and had the combination to the safe. Six managers were considered suspects because each of them had the combination to the safe. One manager stood out as the most likely to be guilty because he resigned shortly after the theft. Consequently, he was the last manager interviewed. During interviews with the other five managers, it was learned that the suspected manager was a regular user of marijuana and also that he hung around with an ex-employee of the restaurant who had a prior conviction for auto theft. During the suspected manager's interview, he denied any recent use of illegal drugs and a close relationship with the ex-employee.

The information learned from the innocent suspects was used to good advantage during the interrogation of the suspected manager. The investigator pointed out the suspect's earlier lies about his marijuana use and his relationship with the ex-employee, explaining that they were seen together the night before the theft. These tactics reduced the suspect's confidence in offering further denials. The manager eventually confessed when the investigator presented the possibility that his friend, the ex-employee, suggested the staged break-in and that the theft was not solely the manager's idea.

In cases involving a living victim, such as a robbery or assault, the victim should be the first person interviewed. The information a victim provides is essential to the investigation. In those instances when a victim's account is unsupported by physical evidence of trauma or when there are no witnesses to corroborate the event, the victim's statements become the sole basis for the questions asked of a possible suspect.

In some situations the victim does not report the complete truth, and in other cases the victim may completely fabricate the crime for various reasons. We have seen many investigations in which hundreds of hours of investigative time were wasted because the victim was never formally interviewed, and the alleged robbery, rape, stalking, or harassment was totally fabricated. In other cases, although the victims were legitimately robbed or assaulted, they initially lied about their actions so as to minimize any negligence on their part that might have contributed to the robbery, or in cases of assault, they may have exaggerated the offender's statements or actions. This type of inaccurate information can greatly reduce the effectiveness of the subsequent interview of the guilty offender, as Case 2-3: Getting the Full Story illustrates.

Case 2-3: Getting the Full Story

A college student reported to her school that one of her instructors had made unwelcome sexual advances toward her. In her harassment complaint she identified six specific incidents of sexual harassment occurring at the school over the last several months. The instructor was suspended and "interviewed" by attorneys representing the school. He was never actually questioned concerning any of the specific allegations, but rather was asked if he could think of any reason why a student would file a sexual harassment charge against him, to which he answered, "No."

Fortunately, when we got involved in the case we requested to interview the student before the instructor. During the complainant's interview we learned that she initially had a crush on the instructor and, in fact, voluntarily had sexual intercourse with him at his home on one occasion. Following that incident she realized that he was only interested in a sexual relationship, and she told him that she no longer wanted to date him. In truth, only the three most recent sexual advances occurred after she had broken off the relationship, and were, thus, unwelcome. Armed with this knowledge, we were able to conduct an effective interview of the respondent to the extent that he acknowledged the sexual relationship and subsequent conversation in which the relationship was terminated. He maintained his innocence of engaging in any sexual advances toward the student following that conversation. During a subsequent interrogation, he acknowledged two of the referred-to incidents as an attempt to "renew his relationship with the student." Had we conducted his interview with the original information provided in the student's complaint, it is unlikely that we would have ascertained the truth.

Reliance on Experts

Do not rely upon a physician's estimate of the time of death of the victim or of the time when the fatal wound was inflicted. All too frequently, such reliance leads to a futile interrogation of a suspect. Even the most competent of trained forensic pathologists report that it is very difficult, and even impossible in many

Even the most competent of trained forensic pathologists report that it is very difficult, and even impossible in many instances, to accurately estimate the time of death or of the infliction of the fatal wound.

instances, to accurately estimate the time of death or of the infliction of the fatal wound. Unfortunately, the ordinary physician who has not received specialized training in this field is the one who usually indulges in unwarranted speculations. In one case, for example, a physician who worked part-time on a coroner's staff estimated that an elderly woman found murdered in an alley behind her home had been killed between 11:00 P.M. and midnight. Persons who knew her reported that she never would have been out alone at that time of night, and her son, who lived in the victim's residence, acknowledged being home during that time period. Based on this information, the son became a prime suspect and was questioned persistently, without success, by a series of police investigators.

Finally, an experienced investigator who was called into the case became convinced that the son was innocent. The investigator suggested the possibility that death had occurred at an earlier time and that other suspects should be sought. Eventually the perpetrator was discovered and he made a confession, which was thoroughly verified by details of the occurrence that would have been known only by the killer himself. The crime had occurred hours before the physician's estimate.

Most Likely Suspect

Remember that when circumstantial evidence or especially physical evidence points toward a particular person, that person is usually the one who committed the offense. This may become difficult for some investigators to appreciate when circumstantial evidence points to someone they consider highly unlikely to be the type of person who would commit such an offense—for example, a clergyman who is circumstantially implicated in a sexually motivated murder. By reason of his exalted position, he may be interviewed only casually or perhaps not at all, and yet it is an established fact that some clergymen do commit such offenses.[2]

An additional illustration of the unfavorable consequences of assuming that a person of a certain status or good repute "could never do such a thing" is the case of the wife of a business executive who had accepted a job as a part-time bank teller and who, for various reasons, seemed to be the one most likely to have embezzled $6,500 from a customer's bank account. It seemed incongruous to the investigators that a person with her personal financial assets, including $10,000 in her own savings account at the same bank, would have committed such an act. Nevertheless, an experienced, effective investigator elicited a confession from her in which she revealed a very unusual explanation. Her mother, whom her husband despised, needed money for surgery. Under no circumstances would the husband have allowed a contribution to be made to assist her. If his wife had withdrawn the necessary money from her own account, that fact would have come to the husband's attention. As an alternative source, she diverted $6,500 from the bank account of a depositor, who was a friend of hers and whose savings account could well stand a withdrawal of that amount without it being discovered soon or even noticed at all. As the foregoing case demonstrates, no one should be eliminated from suspicion solely because of professional status, social status, or any other comparable consideration when there exists strong circumstantial evidence of guilt.

Gathering Information from Others Through Interviews

After obtaining information from an investigator, consider the possibility that the investigator may have become so convinced of the suspect's guilt and so anxious to obtain a confession himself, that he may have prematurely confronted the suspect with an accusation or may have indulged in some verbal abuse. These actions can, of course, severely hinder a subsequent interview by a competent investigator, particularly in a situation where an impulsive investigator already has threatened physical abuse of the suspect. The trained investigator should recognize the immediate resentment and anger displayed by the suspect and spend the time necessary to diffuse the suspect's emotional state of mind, even to the extent of chiding the earlier investigator for his treatment of the suspect.

Consider that an investigator may have worked so many hours or days on a case that, without any malicious intent, he may have withheld relevant information or even supplied unfounded information to another investigator. When an initial investigator becomes emotionally involved in solving a case, it is not uncommon to lose the perspective of a truth-seeker and assume the adversarial role of a prosecutor, attempting to "build a case" against the person he believes responsible for the crime.

In our role as consulting investigators, we conduct stipulated polygraph examinations during which the prosecution and defense both agree to accept the results in court. In gathering factual information, we meet separately with the two attorneys. In some instances, after listening to both versions, it sounds like the two sides are talking about different cases. The astute investigator should anticipate such possible biased reporting and ask questions regarding information that may speak too favorably or unfavorably of the suspect.

Consider the possibility of rivalry between two or more investigative agencies—for example, a local police department and a sheriff's office. In such cases, the investigator should conduct *separate* interviews with the case investigators affiliated with each agency. In this way, there is more likely to be a full disclosure of relevant details. The same may be true on occasions where two or more of a single agency's investigators on the same case have been working more or less independently of each other. Understandably, there is an ego factor that may discourage a full exchange of information between the two investigative units or between individual investigators.

While listening to a fact-giver's report of the incident in question, jot down notes regarding dates, time, and nicknames of participants or witnesses, and fill in the complete details later rather than interrupt the fact-giver who is giving the report. Otherwise, an interruption may result in a break in the continuity of the investigator's thoughts or memory, and he may inadvertently fail to disclose some significant information. An effective technique, when obtaining initial facts, is for the investigator to *reiterate* what the fact-giver has told him and to *follow up* on missing or illogical information. Often, the act of verbalizing an account in this fashion will stimulate questions that would not have otherwise occurred to the investigator had he merely mentally absorbed the other person's statements.

In appropriate situations, encourage the person relating the details of a case to sketch the place of the occurrence and to note on it any relevant points. If crime scene photographs are available, they, of course, can be used, along with a freehand sketch, to trace the sequence of events. Usually a sketch that is supplemented with notations is better for the investigator's purpose than photographs alone, even though the sketch may be drawn crudely. Photographs unaccompanied by a full explanation from the investigator may be inadequate or even misleading because usually they cannot, by themselves, fully portray a situation or event.

When interviewing a person regarding the facts of a case, ask what he believes may have happened, who he believes to be the chief suspect, and why. The fact-giver, whether it is an employer, a loss prevention specialist, or a relative of the victim, is often much more familiar with the possible suspects than the investigator. In one case, for example, a fact-giver made the following observation that proved to be of considerable value: "Jim was in love with Amy, and Joe was fooling around with her and that's why I think Jim shot Joe." In another case, an investigator's inquiry of this nature drew the following response: "The word on the street is that Frank did it because he flashed a lot of money around right after the robbery." In still another case, the fact-giver said, "That guy Mike was so damn nervous he couldn't stand still!" referring to the suspect's behavior soon after the crime. In each of these cases, the information obtained proved to be very helpful to the investigator in formulating interrogation tactics and techniques.

Regard cautiously the reliability of information submitted by a paid informer. There are times when such information is based only upon the informer's conclusions rather than upon actual facts or observations. Then, too, on many known occasions, false information is deliberately furnished by an informant in order to obtain payment or to receive favorable consideration regarding his or her own criminal activities. Most certainly, many informers do reveal accurate and reliable information. However, the authors merely wish to urge a cautious evaluation.

View with suspicion any anonymous report implicating a specific person in a criminal offense. This is particularly true in instances in which the person making the report has experienced a personal problem, such as having been jilted or deserted by her spouse. Such a person might send the police an anonymous letter suggesting that the man who offended her committed a certain crime. This may be done out of spite, or for the purpose of getting the man into a situation where he may need her help or be required to delay a planned departure from the city or country—all for the purpose of "getting him back again." In summary, it is always a good practice for an investigator to view with suspicion a "tip" or accusation based on an anonymous report. To be sure, there are occasions when the report is well founded, but in the vast majority of instances, there is some ulterior motive. (A male, of course, is capable of being just as vengeful with respect to a woman who has jilted or deserted him, but his vented feelings are usually exhibited in a more blatant manner, such as damaging her property or physical abuse.)

Ask a child victim of a sex offense involving a stranger to describe the scene of occurrence. For instance, if the crime is alleged to have occurred in the home of a particular individual, the child should be asked to describe the room—its curtains, wall colors, floor rug, bed, and other such objects. If the description is accurate, that fact will serve to corroborate that the child was, in fact, in the room. Often in these situations the molester will deny that the child was ever inside his car or apartment; when the child's revelation of such details are disclosed to the suspect, it will have a very desirable impact during interrogation.

During an interview with the presumed victim or other reporter of a crime that involves money or property rather than physical offense, a skillful investigator may ascertain that no crime was in fact committed. For instance, an interview with the person who reports as a theft the disappearance of money, jewelry, or other property may reveal information that will subsequently establish that the missing item was either misplaced or perhaps deliberately disposed of by the owner in order to perpetrate a fraud on an insurance company. A "victim," upon being skillfully interviewed, may admit or otherwise reveal the claim to be false by reason of revenge, an extortion attempt, or some other purpose.

When full credibility has been established regarding the victim, the accuser, and the crime discoverer, the facts that are learned may be extremely helpful in determining the procedure to be followed in the subsequent investigation, leading to the interview and interrogation of the suspects themselves. In certain types of cases where the victim of the occurrence is in a position to influence the disposition to be made of a case solution, as in the case of a theft by an employee, the investigator should inquire about the victim's attitude with respect to what action, if any, he expects to take toward the perpetrator. The investigator should be mindful, however, that in some jurisdictions it is a criminal offense to condition a restitution or compensation agreement upon a promise not to seek or participate in a criminal prosecution. Legally permissible, however, is the settlement of a civil claim for the loss or injury incurred by the victim.

One basic principle to which there must be full adherence is that the interrogation of suspects should *follow,* not precede, an investigation conducted to the full extent permissible by the allowable time and circumstances of the particular case. The authors suggest to investigators, therefore, the following guideline: "Investigate before you interrogate."

KEY POINTS

- Prior to an interview, and preferably before any contact with the suspect, the investigator should attempt to become thoroughly familiar with all the known facts and circumstances of the offense.
- At the outset of an investigation certain information about the crime should be withheld from the media and all suspects to provide dependent corroboration of any subsequent confession.
- The investigator should first interview those suspects who are least likely to be guilty and work toward the suspect who is most likely to be involved in the offense.
- In cases involving a living victim, such as a robbery or assault, the victim should be the first person interviewed.
- Do not rely upon a physician's estimate of the time of death of the victim or of the time when the fatal wound was inflicted.
- Remember that when circumstantial evidence or especially physical evidence points toward a particular person, that person is usually the one who committed the offense.
- After obtaining information from an investigator, consider the possibility that the investigator may have become so convinced of the suspect's guilt and so anxious to obtain a confession that he may have prematurely confronted the suspect with an accusation or may have indulged in some verbal abuse.
- Consider that an investigator may have worked so many hours or days on a case that, without any malicious intent, he may have withheld relevant information or even supplied unfounded information to the investigator.
- Consider the possibility of rivalry between two or more investigative agencies.
- While listening to a fact-giver's report of the incident in question, jot down notes regarding dates, time, and nicknames of participants or witnesses, and fill in the complete details later rather than interrupt the fact-giver who is giving the report.
- In appropriate situations, encourage the person relating the details of a case to sketch the place of the occurrence and to note on it any relevant points.
- When interviewing a person regarding the facts of a case, ask what he believes may have happened, who he believes to be the chief suspect, and why.
- Regard cautiously the reliability of information submitted by a paid informer.
- View with suspicion any anonymous report implicating a specific person in a criminal offense.
- Ask a child victim of a sex offense involving a stranger to describe the scene of occurrence.
- During an interview with the presumed victim or other reporter of a crime that involves money or property rather than physical offense, a skillful investigator may ascertain that no crime was in fact committed.

KEY TERMS

case facts Information from a variety of sources that is used by an investigator to gain a solid background about a case before conducting an interview or interrogation.

dependent corroboration Information withheld from the suspects and media that is used to verify a guilty person's confession.

fact analysis The ability to identify from factual information the probable motivation for a crime, unique access requirements, window of time during which the crime was committed, and propensity characteristics of the person who committed the crime.

fact-giver Any person who provides information about a case.

investigator The person who actually conducts the interview and possible interrogation of a suspect.

ENDNOTES

1. D. Buckley, "The Validity of Factual Analysis in Detection of Deception," Master's thesis, Reid College of Detection of Deception, 1987. Twenty actual case scenarios involving two suspects were given to 26 college students with no training in fact analysis as well as to 7 investigators specifically trained in this skill. The investigators achieved an accuracy of 91% in correctly classifying the innocent or guilty person, whereas the untrained students' average accuracy was 79%. The difference was statistically significant.
2. In many cases, individuals who display exaggerated traits of community service, helpfulness to others, or adherence to strict laws or religious beliefs are compensating for underlying guilt concerning hidden criminal activity.

EXERCISES

Richard has worked as a teller for a bank for three years. On this particular day he was closing out his cash drawer and discovered a $1000 shortage. He spent about an hour after work trying to identify the cause of the shortage and even took apart his cash drawer to see if money may have gotten caught behind it. The shortage remained unresolved. Working on one side of Richard is Kathy. Kathy has been employed as a teller at the bank for about a year. While she has had some problems balancing her cash drawer on occasion, she has no known financial difficulties. Working on the other side of Richard is a part-time teller named Keith. Keith is 18 years old and has only worked at the bank for a month.

1. Who should be interviewed first during this investigation? Why?

2. What questions should Richard be asked to help resolve this investigation?

3. Which suspect is most likely guilty of the theft? Why?

3

Privacy and the Interview Room

Chapter Objectives

Upon completion of this chapter you will be able to:

- Explain the importance of privacy for a successful interview
- Describe reasons for minimizing reminders of consequences
- Identify the aspects of a properly set up interview room

The Importance of Privacy

The principal psychological factor contributing to a successful interview or interrogation is privacy—being alone with the person during questioning. Investigators seem instinctively to realize this factor in their own private or social affairs, but they generally overlook or ignore its importance during an interview or interrogation.

privacy freedom from distractions; refers to a place where a suspect feels able to confide in an investigator, usually when the investigator is alone with the suspect.

In a social situation, an investigator may carefully avoid asking a personal friend or acquaintance to divulge a secret in the presence of other persons; he instead will seek a time and place when the matter can be discussed in private. Likewise, if an investigator is troubled by a personal problem, he will usually find it easier to confide in one other person. Even a problem that concerns more than one other person is usually discussed with each of the persons on separate occasions. However, during an interview or interrogation, where the same mental processes are in operation (indeed, to an even greater degree by reason of the criminality of the disclosure), investigators generally seem to lose sight of

A suspect or witness is much more apt to reveal any secrets in the privacy of a room occupied only by himself and the investigator than in the presence of an additional person or persons.

the fact that a suspect or witness is much more apt to reveal any secrets in the privacy of a room occupied only by himself and the investigator than in the presence of an additional person or persons. Case 3-1: A Killer's Private Confession, which took place in a small Midwestern town, illustrates this point.

Case 3-1: A Killer's Private Confession

A man was being questioned concerning the killing of his wife, who had been shot on a lonely road not far from a main highway. According to the husband's story, while he and his wife were riding in their automobile, they were held up and robbed. The robber took a ring off the woman's finger and then fired upon her as she called for help. For a number of reasons, the husband's account of the occurrence was viewed with considerable skepticism, and he was suspected of being the actual killer.

For several hours following the shooting, the husband was subjected to considerable questioning—but always in the presence of several persons. Later, at the request of the prosecuting attorney, one of the authors of this text interrogated the suspect. A private room was selected for this purpose, and everyone else was excluded.

From the very moment the suspect entered the room, he displayed every indication of guilt. From the outset, it seemed quite evident that here was a person *who wanted to confess.* As the investigator already knew, the suspect had experienced a very unhappy married life—sexual incompatibility, meddling relatives, and so forth. Now, he actually wanted to unburden himself of these and other troubles generally. He needed some sympathy; he wanted to be told that the shooting of his wife was something that anyone else might have done during weaker moments under similar circumstances. It was essential, however, that he was allowed the opportunity to be alone with the person who would listen to his troubles and offer him the sympathy his mind craved. Until his discussion with this investigator, he had not had the opportunity to do so. When the opportunity presented itself, however, he very readily told how he had killed his wife and why, and he revealed the location where he had discarded the weapon and the ring.

Case 3-1: A Killer's Private Confession was the easiest sort of case. It should have been unnecessary for the local authorities to seek outside assistance. All that was really needed was a little privacy.

The authors of this volume are fully aware of the practical difficulties that may be encountered in arranging for a private interview, even after the investigator is convinced of its desirability. In a case of any importance, each investigator wants to be in on the interrogation, or at least be present when a suspect confesses or when an informer or a witness divulges valuable information. Each investigator wants to improve his efficiency rating or otherwise demonstrate his value to the department or office. In addition, the publicity in the community is considered desirable—to say nothing of the satisfaction to the individual's own ego. All this is perfectly understandable and nothing more than normal human behavior, but it is something that must be controlled in the interest of conducting a productive interview or interrogation.

The person in charge of the investigation, or someone with command rank, should direct that the interrogation be conducted under conditions of privacy. In instances where all investigators are of equal rank, and each one seems to want to participate in the interrogation, they should work out some arrangement among themselves to ensure the element of privacy. It is suggested that the interrogation be conducted by the officer who has demonstrated his skill as an interrogator or, under ideal conditions, by the one who has received special training as a professional interrogator.

Privacy in an interview room can be maintained without denying to any investigator assigned to the case due credit for his efforts. An understanding may be reached among the various investigators to the effect that if a "break" comes when any of them have absented themselves from the interview room for the purpose of ensuring privacy between the interrogating investigator and the suspect or witness, they will all share the credit for whatever results the latter investigator obtains.

In personnel investigations, a security officer or other investigator acting on behalf of the employer may encounter a legal impediment to achieving the condition of privacy. The National Labor Relations Act has been interpreted as giving an employee the right to have, upon request, a union representative or fellow union employee present whenever there is to be questioning about a matter for which there may be disciplinary action.[1] This right has been extended to nonunion employees as well.[2]

Minimize Reminders of Consequences

The motivation for all deception is to avoid the consequences of telling the truth. Suspects lie to escape being prosecuted, being sent to prison, and having to face family and friends with the disgrace of their behavior. As obvious as this seems, there are still investigators who remind suspects of the seriousness of the potential charges against them—how long they will sit in prison if they are convicted, and how their friends and family will abandon them once they find out what they did. After creating these dark and grisly descriptions of what will happen to suspects if they tell the truth, the investigator wonders why suspects are so reluctant to confess! Clearly, during an interview or especially an interrogation, it is psychologically improper to mention any consequences or possible negative effects that a suspect may experience if he decides to tell the truth.

reminders of consequences verbal and visible signs that remind a suspect of the possible negative effects that could result from telling the truth.

Not all **reminders of consequences** are made verbally. As Case 3-2: Facing the Consequences demonstrates, visual reminders of consequences can have the same devastating effect during an interview or interrogation. Police paraphernalia such

Even visual reminders of consequences can have devastating effects during an interview or interrogation.

as handcuffs, mace, or badges should be covered or not worn at all during an interview. For safety reasons, the investigator should not be armed with a gun during an interview or interrogation of a suspect. The walls of the interview room should not contain police memorabilia such as crime scene photographs, a display of agency patches, or certificates indicating attendance at interrogation seminars.

Case 3-2: Facing the Consequences

One of the authors was assisting in the investigation of a half-million-dollar inventory shortage at a warehouse. The loss prevention department had recently installed a specific room for interviewing employees. The private room was custom built, with an observation mirror and a recording device, and adhered to other recommended standards. Yet none of the employees interviewed by the loss prevention investigators revealed any involvement in, or knowledge of, the ongoing thefts. Upon our entering the room, it was very apparent why these interviews had been so unproductive. Taped to the wall directly in front of the person being interviewed was a large poster proclaiming "We Prosecute Shoplifters." Depicted in the poster was a person in handcuffs being escorted by two police officers.

Suggestions for Setting Up the Interview Room

Table 3-1 lists suggestions for setting up an interview room to maximize the possibility of obtaining information. The following sections examine these suggestions in more detail.

Table 3-1 Considerations in Setting Up an Interview Room

Establish a sense of privacy.
Minimize reminders of consequences.
Remove locks and other physical impediments.
Remove all distractions.
Select proper lighting.
Minimize noise.
Arrange chairs properly.
Create an observation room, if at all possible, or equip the room with an electronic recording system.

Privacy

Establish a sense of privacy. The room should be quiet, with none of the usual "police" surroundings and with no distractions within the suspect's view. (If existing facilities permit, a special room or rooms should be set aside for this purpose.) The room should be as free as possible from outside noises and should also be a room into which no one will have occasion to enter or pass through during an interview. This instills a sense of privacy. Also, the less the surroundings suggest a police detention facility, the more likely it is that a suspect or arrestee who is guilty will implicate himself. At the same time, these surroundings will be reassuring to the innocent suspect. Therefore, there should be no bars on the windows. (There should be an alternative means of protection against any attempts to escape.) In a windowless room that has no air conditioning system, a mechanical blower or exhaust system may be installed without much difficulty to improve ventilation and to eliminate, or at least minimize, noises. (The room should have its own thermostatic controls.)

Locks

Remove locks and other physical impediments. For **noncustodial interviews**, there should be no lock on the door of the interviewing room, nor should there be any other physical impediment to an exit by the suspect if he desires to leave the building itself. This will help minimize claims of false "imprisonment." The room should also be devoid of any large objects or drapes that might cause the suspect to believe that a concealed third person can overhear his conversation with the investigator.

noncustodial interview
an interview conducted under circumstances where the subject is free to leave the room.

Distractions

Remove all distractions. Interview rooms should be of plain color, should have smooth walls, and should not contain ornaments, pictures, or other objects that would in any way distract the attention of the person being interviewed. Even small, loose objects, such as paper clips or pencils, should be out of the suspect's reach so that he cannot pick up and fumble with anything during the course of the interview. Tension-relieving activities of this sort can detract from the effectiveness of an interrogation, especially during the critical phase when a guilty person may be trying desperately to suppress an urge to confess. If pictures or ornaments are used at all, they should be only on the wall behind the suspect. If there is a window in the room, it, too, should be to the rear.

Lighting

Lighting fixtures should be arranged in such a way as to provide good, but not excessive or glaring, illumination of the suspect's face. Certainly, any lighting that interferes with the investigator's full view of the suspect's facial features and expressions should be avoided. Also, there should not be any glaring light on the investigator's face. This would not only interfere with the investigator's observations of the suspect, but also may distort the investigator's facial indications of understanding, sympathy, and so forth. Diffused, overhead lighting is more appropriate.

Noise

No telephone should be present in the interview room because, among other disadvantages, its ringing or use constitutes a serious distraction. Also, if the investigator wears a beeper, it should either be put in the vibrator mode or turned off during the interrogation. Any noise emanating from the heating or ventilating system should be minimized to reduce distraction.

Chair Arrangement

The chairs for the investigator and suspect should be separated by about four feet and should directly face each other, without a desk, table, or any other object between them. The chairs should be the type normally used as office equipment and should not have rollers.

Straight-back chairs should be used for the suspect as well as the investigator. Other types of chairs induce slouching or leaning back, and such positions are psychologically undesirable. A suspect who is too relaxed while being questioned may not give his full attention to the investigator, which will create an unnecessary hurdle. Similarly, this is no occasion for the investigator to relax. The investigator's full attention and alertness are highly essential.

Whenever possible, the seating arrangement should be such that both the investigator and the suspect are on the same eye level. Most certainly, to be scrupulously avoided are chairs with lowered front legs or other deviations that place suspects in an "inferior" posture or prevents them from making normal changes in their posture.

observation room a room adjoining the interview room that allows investigating officers to observe and hear the interview while the necessary privacy is maintained.

Observation Room

If available facilities and resources permit, there should be an **observation room** adjoining the interview room. The authors of the text recommend a smaller adjoining room, in the wall of which there is inserted a "one-way mirror"—a panel of glass chemically treated so as to permit someone from within a relatively dark observation room to see into the lighted interview room without being seen. The mirror should be off to one side, away from the suspect (**Figure 3-1**), or at least above eye level if it must be located in front of the suspect. The interview room also should be equipped with a concealed microphone so that the person or persons in the observation room may hear as well as see what occurs in the interview room. (State and local laws should be checked first, however, to ascertain whether there is any legal prohibition against electronic eavesdropping.) Another equally desirable arrangement is to equip the room with a video camera to record interviews and interrogations electronically. It is essential, however, that the camera either be concealed or positioned off to the side, out of the suspect's direct line of vision. It can significantly inhibit the truth-telling process to have a camera or tape recorder visible to the suspect.[3]

An interview/observation room arrangement of the suggested type can be of considerable value in several respects:

1. It affords an opportunity for investigating officers to observe and hear the interview while the necessary privacy is maintained.
2. The suspect's behavior can be evaluated by fellow investigators who have to prepare themselves for later involvement.

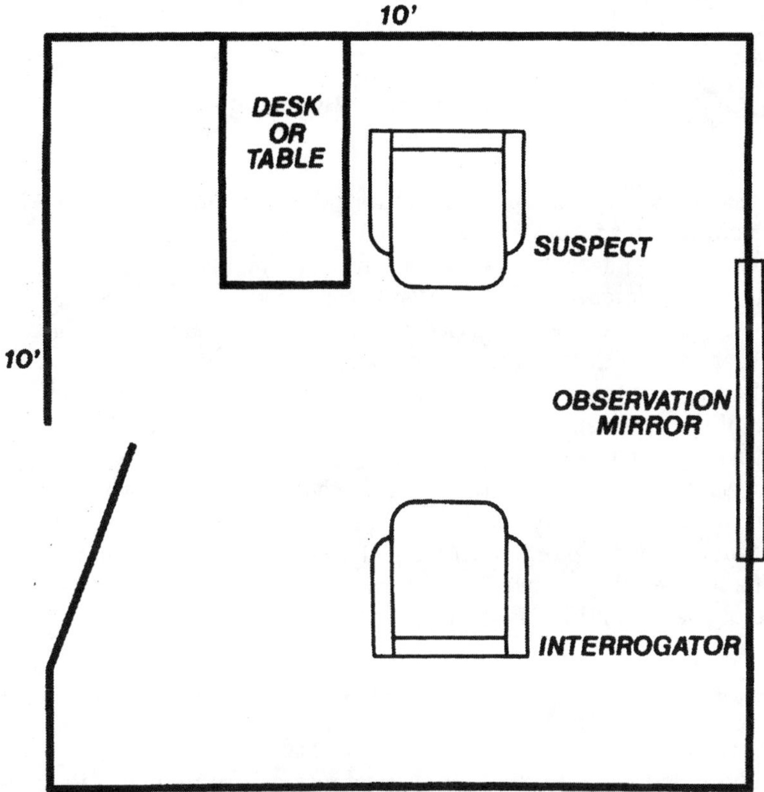

Figure 3-1 Observation room arrangement for suspect in custody.

3. In cases where a female is the suspect, a policewoman or other female may be stationed in the observation room to witness the proceedings as a safeguard against possible false accusations of misconduct on the part of the investigator. The presence of any such witness, whether male or female, is also helpful in other types of situations as a safeguard against false accusations of physical abuse, threats, or promises on the part of the investigator.
4. When a suspect is left alone in the interview room, he can be kept under observation as a precaution against any effort to escape or perhaps even the remote possibility of an attempt at suicide. Moreover, the observation room mirror arrangement may protect the investigator from physical harm by a violence-prone suspect. Although the probability of violence is remote, it is within the realm of possibility, as is evident from the incident described in Case 3-3: The Unseen Advantage.

Another possible usage of an interview room of the type described is illustrated by the following case: Two warehouse employees were suspected of being accomplices in the theft of tires from the company. During their individual interviews, guilt was evidenced by their behavior. However, neither made an incriminating statement, even following an interrogation. It was therefore decided to put them together in the interview room and to observe what occurred. Immediately, one of them placed a finger over his lips, signifying that silence was to prevail. Following the observation of this gesture, the investigator removed the signaling suspect from the room and advised him that his incriminating behavior had been observed from the adjacent room through the mirror.

Case 3-3: The Unseen Advantage

A young, vicious-looking, multiple-rape suspect who was about to be interrogated requested some food, saying he had not eaten anything since his arrest. Food was brought to him and, also pursuant to his request (and inadvisably, as later events established), a bottle of soda. After being permitted to eat and drink alone, the suspect was observed standing next to the interview room door with the bottle in an upraised hand, obviously for the purpose of using it on the investigator's head when he entered. The observer rushed out of the observation room and warned the investigator of the impending danger. After a deliberately prolonged entrance delay by the investigator, the suspect was observed to sit down, whereupon the investigator entered and quickly, but discreetly, removed the bottle without making any comment about the occurrence. The ensuing interrogation resulted in the admission of a number of rapes in addition to the ones for which the suspect had previously been identified as the perpetrator.

He thereupon confessed. When the other suspect was confronted with this development, he, too, confessed his participation in the theft.

As mentioned earlier, in certain situations there may need to be a third person actually present in the interview room either because there is no observation room facility or because of some other factor. In a personnel investigation, for instance, an employee may exercise his right to have a union representative or some other fellow employee present. Also, in such cases, an employer may want to exercise the precaution of requiring that whenever a female suspect is to be interviewed by a male, another female must be present. Some police departments without an observation room facility follow a similar practice, particularly when the female suspect is of an unsavory character and perhaps prone to falsely accuse a police investigator of making sexual overtures. Some state statutes specify that a juvenile suspect can only be interviewed in the presence of a parent or guardian. In all such instances, the third party should be seated in back of and to the side of the suspect, as illustrated in **Figure 3-2**.

Whenever an interpreter is needed to assist in the interview, the interpreter should be seated alongside the investigator, who should be, of course, directly in front of the suspect. **Figure 3-3** illustrates this seating arrangement.

Finally, in view of the foregoing guidelines, it should be obvious that a suspect's own home or office is an inappropriate setting for an interrogation. It is advisable, therefore, to avoid an interrogation in a home or office whenever possible. A noncustodial suspect who refuses to voluntarily come to a police station may be persuaded to meet with the investigator in some neutral location, perhaps a meeting room rented for the purpose of conducting the interview and possible interrogation.

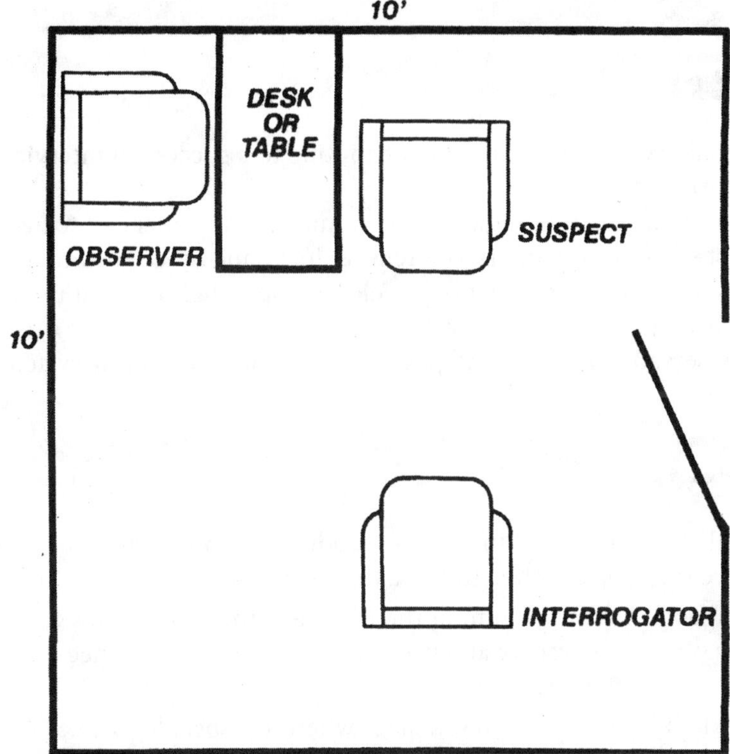

Figure 3-2 Interview room arrangement for suspect with observer present.

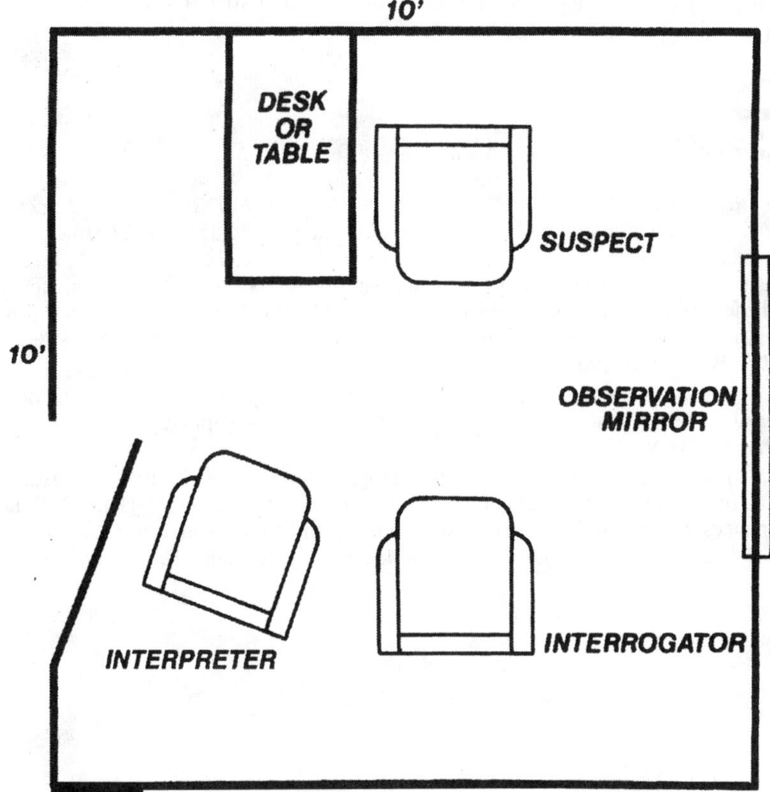

Figure 3-3 Interview room arrangement for suspect with interpreter.

KEY POINTS

- The principal psychological factor contributing to a successful interview or interrogation is privacy.
- When setting up an interview room, minimize reminders of consequences, establish a sense of privacy, remove locks and other physical impediments, remove all distractions, select proper lighting, minimize noise, and arrange chairs properly.
- Set up an observation room if at all possible, or a video monitoring system.

KEY TERMS

noncustodial interview An interview conducted under circumstances where the subject is free to leave the room.

observation room A room adjoining the interview room that allows investigating officers to observe and hear the interview while the necessary privacy is maintained.

privacy Freedom from distractions; a place where a suspect feels able to confide in the investigator, usually when the investigator is alone with the suspect.

reminders of consequences Verbal and visible signs that remind a suspect of the possible negative effects that could result from telling the truth.

ENDNOTES

1. *National Labor Relations Board (N.L.R.B.) v. Weingarten*, 420 U.S. 251 (1975). The issue is uncertain as to the right of a nonunion employee to have someone present. The N.L.R.B. ruled that the right existed, and that decision was upheld in *Dupont v. N.L.R.B*, 724 F. 2d 1061 (3rdCir. 1983). However, the board subsequently announced that it wanted to reconsider its ruling, whereupon the federal court vacated its decision. 733 F. 2d 296 (1984). Since then, the N.L.R.B. has ruled that the right is confined to union employees. Sears, Roebuck & Co., 274 *N.L.R.B 55*, 2/22/85, 53 *Law Week* 2422 (1985).
2. In July 2000, the N.L.R.B. extended this right to have a coworker present during an interview that could result in disciplinary actions to nonunionized workers. (Epilepsy Foundation of Northeast Ohio, in 331 *N.L.R.B. 134* [2000].)
3. A recent study indicated that when the recording device was not visible to a suspect, investigators had a 40% higher confession rate than when the device was always visible. Jayne, B. "Empirical Experiences of Required Electronic Recording of Interviews and Interrogations on Invesitgators' Practices and Case Outcomes," *Law Enforcement Executive Forum,* 4(1), 2004 103–112.

EXERCISES

You must go out of town to conduct a series of interviews on care-givers of a young child who has been sexually abused. There is no suitable office space to use and you do not want to interview these people in their homes. Consequently, you end up renting a meeting room at a local hotel to conduct your interviews. The meeting room has a number of advantages in that it offers privacy and is a neutral setting with respect to reminders of authority. Even though the door does have a lock on it, the door can be opened from the inside. The problem is the size of the room and the existing furniture arrangement. The meeting room is 25 feet by 15 feet with a large conference table in the center of the room surrounded by 12 chairs. How can you rearrange the furniture in this room to make it suitable for interviewing or interrogating?

____

____

____

____

____

____

____

____

____

____

____

____

____

4

Qualifications, Attitude, and General Conduct of the Investigator

Chapter Objectives

Upon completion of this chapter you will be able to:

- Describe traits important in an interviewer
- Discuss the various approaches an interviewer can bring to the interview
- Explain the best interviewer demeanor for a successful interview

Interviewer Traits

Investigators selected for training as professional interviewers and interrogators should fulfill certain general qualifications.

First, special personal attributes should be present. For example, the person should be intelligent and have a good practical understanding of human nature. He should possess suitable personality traits that are evident from a general ability to get along well with others, especially individuals from varying backgrounds or classes. As already mentioned, patience is an indispensable attribute. A high index of suspicion is another important attribute for the successful interviewer. This heightened level of suspicion should not be confused with cynicism. The cynical investigator believes everyone lies; the suspicious investigator actively looks for deceptive behavior or inconsistencies, but recognizes that the majority of people tell the truth.

Second, the specialist should have an intense interest in the field. He should study textbooks and articles regarding behavior analysis, related areas of psychology and psychopathology, and interrogation techniques. He should not only understand how to conduct a proper interrogation, for example, but also be able to explain to a judge or jury the underlying concepts involved at each stage of the interrogation process. The professional interviewer should also attend training seminars conducted by competent, experienced interrogators.

Third, it is essential for the specialist to become aware of the legal rules and regulations that govern interrogation procedures and the taking of confessions from persons upon whom these interrogation tactics and techniques have proved productive.

Interviewer Qualifications

Conducting a proper interview goes beyond just asking questions. Two investigators can question the same suspect, and yet one of those investigators may develop much more meaningful and useful information from the suspect than the other. The personality and demeanor of an interviewer play an important role in his success.

A person is more likely to divulge incriminating or sensitive information to someone who appears *friendly* and *personable*. Most of us have known a teacher or supervisor who approaches everyone as if they were guilty of something. The natural response is to be guarded and defensive toward that person. It is essential that the interviewer be perceived as objective and nonjudgmental. Investigators who are interested in obtaining "just the facts" generally make poor interviewers. Good interviewers have a genuine curiosity and concern about people, guilty or innocent, and sincerely enjoy talking to others. Perhaps most important, the effective interviewer is able to separate the suspect from the crime he may have committed; the interviewer perceives his role as ascertaining the truth, not passing judgment on the suspect's behavior or attitude.

The effective interviewer is able to separate the suspect from the crime he may have committed; the interviewer perceives his role as ascertaining the truth, not passing judgment on the suspect's behavior or attitude.

The successful interviewer must feel comfortable asking questions. An investigator who is uncomfortable asking questions will telegraph that message through nonverbal and paralinguistic behaviors. For example, when interviewing a victim who claims to have been raped, the investigator must be comfortable asking specific questions about the rapist's sexual contact with her. When questioning a person with an elevated status, perhaps a physician or attorney, the investigator must be comfortable asking probing questions. An investigator who is obviously uncomfortable asking questions during an interview creates more nervous tension in the truthful subject, and the deceptive subject may experience greater confidence in his ability to lie. The effective interviewer should have an easygoing confidence that allows the subject to feel comfortable telling the truth but uncomfortable lying.

Initial Interview Procedures

In the early stage of a criminal investigation, the available information is frequently insufficient for an investigator to make even a tentative determination as to whether the suspect is guilty or innocent. In these situations, there are three approaches available to the investigator:

1. Interview the suspect upon the assumption of guilt.
2. Interview the suspect upon the assumption of innocence.
3. Assume a neutral position and refrain from making any statement or implications one way or the other until the suspect has disclosed some information or indication pointing either to guilt or innocence.

The advantages and disadvantages attending each of these three possible approaches are discussed in the following sections.

Assumption of Guilt

This approach possesses the desirable element of surprise. As a result, the guilty lack composure and may disclose the truth about certain pertinent information or perhaps even confess guilt. Another advantage of the approach is that the investigator can observe how the suspect generally reacts when treated as though he were considered guilty. A guilty person will usually display no resentment regarding such treatment, whereas an innocent suspect usually will express resentment to the extent of being very forceful or perhaps even being highly insulting. A guilty suspect is also more likely to react nonverbally to the suggestion of guilt—fiddling with clothing, crossing and uncrossing legs, squirming in the chair, dusting off clothes, or turning his head away as the investigator talks. Noting these differences in reaction can be very helpful in determining whether the suspect is, in all probability, guilty.

There are, however, two disadvantages to this approach when there is very little, if any, evidence to support the **assumption of guilt**. The guilty suspect who does not immediately make some incriminating "slip-up" or confess guilt will be on guard during the remainder of the interview. If the suspect eventually senses the fact that the approach is nothing more than a bluff, he will be more fortified, psychologically, to continue with lying and resistance to telling the truth. On the other hand, the suspect who is innocent may become so disturbed and confused that it will be more difficult for the investigator to ascertain the subject's innocence, or even to obtain possible clues regarding helpful information that might otherwise have been obtainable.

assumption of guilt an interviewing style wherein the investigator approaches each suspect as if the person were guilty of the crime.

Assumption of Innocence

This approach possesses two distinct advantages, but they are offset to some extent by an attending disadvantage. The advantages are as follows:

1. The investigator's statement or implication of a belief in the suspect's innocence will undoubtedly place an innocent party at greater ease and, as a result, the fact of his innocence may become more readily apparent to the investigator. Moreover, under such circumstances, the investigator can more successfully elicit whatever pertinent information or clues the innocent suspect may be in a position to divulge.
2. This approach may cause a guilty suspect to lower his guard and to become less cautious or even careless in answering the investigator. As a result, the individual is more apt to make a remark or contradiction that will not only make the suspect's guilt evident, but which also can be used to advantage during a subsequent interrogation.

assumption of innocence an interviewing style wherein the investigator approaches each suspect as if the person were innocent of the crime.

assumption of a neutral position an interviewing style wherein the investigator approaches each suspect from an emotionally detached perspective with no preconceived expectation of guilt or innocence.

The disadvantage of this approach is that once an investigator has committed himself as a believer in the suspect's innocence, he must more or less confine inquiries to those based upon an **assumption of innocence**, for to do otherwise would tend to destroy the very relationship or rapport that was sought in using this approach. In other words, the investigator is handicapped to the extent that he cannot freely adjust methods and questioning to meet the suspect's changing attitudes or inconsistencies. This is not an insurmountable difficulty, of course, but it is nevertheless a possible disadvantage that the investigator should consider before embarking upon this particular course.

Assumption of a Neutral Position

The **assumption of a neutral position** obviously possesses neither the advantages nor the disadvantages of the other two approaches. For this very reason, therefore, it may be considered the *best* approach to use in the average situation where the investigator's case information and observations have given no encouraging indication that the suspect might be particularly vulnerable to either one of the other two approaches.

Approaching the interview from a neutral, objective perspective has another significant advantage. If the investigator interviews the subject with a preconceived expectancy of guilt or innocence, this bias can influence the questions asked during the interview and possibly the interpretation of a subject's behavioral responses to those questions. In essence, with a predisposed expectancy, investigators may hear and see only those behaviors that fit their expectations.

With a predisposed expectancy, investigators may hear and see only those behaviors that fit their expectations.

The importance of interviewer objectivity is illustrated in Case 4-1: Objectivity Pays Off.

Case 4-1: Objectivity Pays Off

An employee reported various incidents of receiving threatening phone calls, e-mail messages, and even written threats left on her car. The investigators who initially talked to this victim approached the investigation from the expectancy that she must be telling the truth and therefore never asked her if she was making up the story or explored with her possible motives for a false report. The company set up hidden surveillance cameras and took dozens of handwriting samples from co-workers but was unable to identify the harasser. At that stage of the investigation, we were asked to interview possible suspects. After interviewing and clearing about 60 possible suspects, we asked to interview the victim. After conducting an objective interview of the victim, it was apparent that she had made up the story. Following a brief interrogation, she acknowledged making up the story because she wanted the company to transfer her to the same location to which her co-worker boyfriend had been transferred.

Investigator's Demeanor During an Interview

Dress

The investigator should dress in civilian clothes rather than in uniform. Otherwise, the suspect will be reminded constantly of police custody and the possible consequences of an incriminating disclosure. If the uniform cannot be avoided altogether, the coat, badge, gun, and holster should be removed for the duration of contact with the suspect. The investigator should wear conservative clothes (suit, jacket, or dress) and should avoid colorful ties or other conspicuous clothing accessories. Unless weather conditions demand otherwise, a male investigator should wear a coat or jacket throughout his contact with the suspect. An investigator dressed in a short-sleeved shirt with the top button undone does not command the respect the situation requires.

Seating Arrangement

During an interview the investigator should sit approximately four to four-and-a-half feet directly in front of the subject. If the investigator positions his chair off to one side of the subject, this may affect the subject's perceived frontal alignment and direction of breaks of gaze (covered in Chapter 7). The investigator's posture should be relaxed and comfortable, as opposed to forward or rigid. A forward posture by the investigator during an interview is likely to be perceived by the suspect as threatening. **Figure 4-1** portrays the relaxed and comfortable posture of an investigator during an interview.

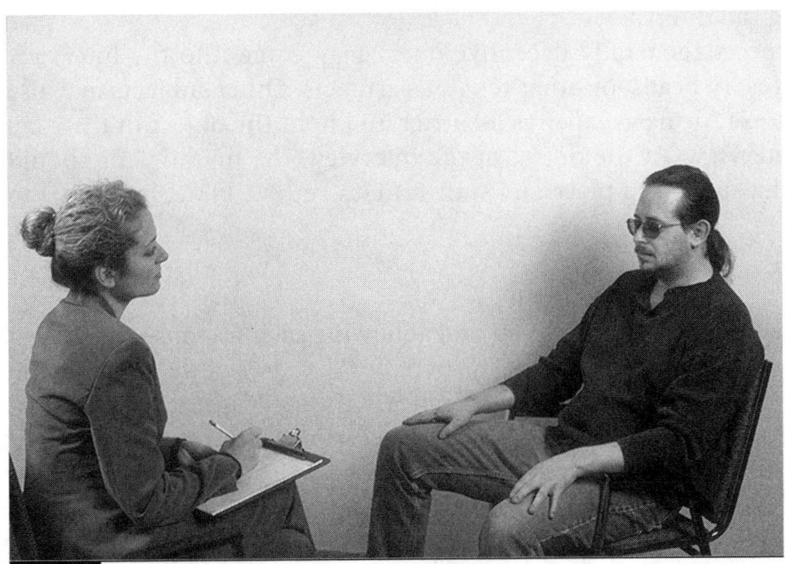

Figure 4-1 Proper posture of an investigator during an interview.

Smoking

Avoid smoking in the suspect's presence. First, if the suspect is a nonsmoker, smoking by the investigator may be offensive. The guilty suspect actively looks for characteristics within the investigator that he can dislike—it is psychologically easier to lie to someone disliked or despised than to a person who is well respected and admired. At no time should the investigator engage in any behavior that would allow a guilty suspect to vent his guilt and apprehension through legitimate feelings of anger or resentment.

Second, if the investigator is not smoking, the suspect who does smoke is less likely to attempt to smoke in an effort to relieve emotional tension or to bolster his resistance to telling the truth. If a request to smoke is made, the investigator may suggest, with justification, that the suspect postpone smoking until he leaves the interview room. Among the rationales for such a request might be that the building is declared nonsmoking or that the investigator suffers from asthma. To facilitate matters with respect to avoidance of smoking by a suspect, it helps if there are no ashtrays present; otherwise, they represent a tacit invitation to smoke.

Question Tone

The investigator's interview questions should be asked in a conversational tone and should always be nonaccusatory. A suspect may perceive a question as being accusatory because of the investigator's tone of voice, the word choices used in asking the question, or the investigator's facial expressions, especially eye contact. It is important for the interviewer to maintain eye contact when asking questions, but he should avoid staring at the subject since this may be interpreted as a threat. With respect to eye contact, the investigator should not wear dark glasses. If the subject is wearing dark glasses, the investigator should ask whether they are prescription lenses. If they are not, the investigator should politely ask the subject if he wouldn't mind removing his glasses during the interview.

Some suspects (generally deceptive ones) may come into the interview with a bible, rosary beads, or other religious artifacts. Other subjects may use a briefcase, purse, or newspaper as a barrier and hold the object in their lap during the interview. At the outset of the interview, the investigator should politely ask the subject to place any such articles (purse, bible, briefcase) to the side.

Notes

The investigator should take a written note following each response the subject offers. It is important to establish this pattern at the outset of the interview so that the subject does not attach any significance to the investigator's note-taking. Conversely, if an investigator only takes notes occasionally during the course of an interview, the suspect will wonder why the investigator decided to write down a particular response and may become guarded and hesitant to offer further information.

The investigator's written notes should not be a verbatim account of the subject's response, but rather capture the key elements of it. In addition to the verbal response, the investigator should write down significant nonverbal behaviors. In this regard, it may be helpful to use abbreviations (**Table 4-1**).

Table 4-1 Examples of Abbreviations for Common Nonverbal Behaviors

. . .	Delayed response (each dot represents a second)
/	Break of gaze
D I-I	Direct eye-to-eye contact
SIC	Shift in chair
X lgs	Cross legs
Rpt Q	Repeats question

Language

Use language that conforms to that used and understood by the suspect. In dealing with an uneducated or unintelligent person, the investigator should use simple words and sentences. When the suspect uses slang or commonplace expressions (for example, in a sex crime case) and gives evidence of being unfamiliar with more acceptable terminology, the investigator should resort to using similar expressions. This can be done in a reserved manner without the loss of the suspect's respect for the position occupied by the investigator. No attempt should be made, however, to imitate the suspect's style of speech, such as making efforts at street slang or other cultural speech styles not regularly used by the investigator.

Finally, after catching a suspect in a lie during an interview, never scold or reprimand him by the use of such expressions as, "Why in the hell did you lie to me?" or "You lied to me once and you'll lie to me again." It is much better to conceal any reaction of resentment, or even of surprise. In fact, the more effective handling of the situation is to merely convey the impression that the investigator knew all along that the suspect was not telling the truth.

KEY POINTS

- Interviewers should have certain special personality traits, such as a good practical understanding of human nature, an ability to get along well with many people, intelligence, patience, and a heightened level of suspicion.
- Interviewers should also have an intense interest in their field and should be aware of the legal rules and regulations that govern interrogation procedures and the taking of confessions from persons upon whom these interrogation tactics and techniques have proved productive.
- The interviewer must be perceived as objective and nonjudgmental by the suspect.
- The interviewer must feel comfortable asking questions.
- A neutral approach to an interview is considered the best one to use in the average situation, where the investigator's case information and observations have given no encouraging indication that the suspect might be particularly vulnerable to either one of the other two approaches (assumption of guilt or assumption of innocence).

Investigator's Demeanor During an Interview

- Dress in civilian clothes rather than in uniform.
- During an interview, sit approximately four to four-and-a-half feet directly in front of the subject.
- Avoid smoking in the suspect's presence.
- Ask interview questions in a conversational tone, and always be nonaccusatory.
- Make a written note following each response the subject offers.
- Use language that conforms to that used and understood by the suspect.
- After catching a suspect in a lie during an interview, never scold or reprimand the suspect.

KEY TERMS

assumption of a neutral position An interviewing style wherein the investigator approaches each suspect from an emotionally detached perspective with no preconceived expectation of guilt or innocence.

assumption of guilt An interviewing style wherein the investigator approaches each suspect as if the person were guilty of the crime.

assumption of innocence An interviewing style wherein the investigator approaches each suspect as if the person were innocent of the crime.

EXERCISES

Identify whether these descriptions of an investigator's behavior during an interview would be considered proper or improper:

1. An investigator starts an interview off with this statement, "Jim, I'm going to question you about a robbery in your neighborhood. I don't like to be lied to, so you better tell me the truth when I ask the questions."

2. At the outset of an interview of a woman who claims she was sexually assaulted, the investigator states, "Mary, I know this is uncomfortable for you and I can't imagine how anyone could do something like this to a nice girl like you but, unfortunately, I do have to ask a few questions just because it's part of my job."

3. A subject has denied ever seeing or handling a bag of cocaine found in his car during a traffic stop: "Bill, if we were to check that bag of cocaine for fingerprints, is there any reason we would find your fingerprints on it?"

4. The subject of an interview is a ten-year-old girl who is claiming that her uncle forced her to engage in oral sex. "Jenny, before we talk about what you told your mom, I just want to go over some words with you just so that when you say something or I say something, we know that we are both talking about the same thing. I'm sure you know that boys and girls are different when they undress, right? What do you call the boy's thing? What do you call the girl's?"

5. An investigator catches a suspect in a lie concerning a question about being at home on a particular date and the investigator responds, "You liar! I know you weren't at home that day because I talked to your neighbors. If you continue to lie to me I'll show you what I do to liars, and you won't like it!"

5

Preparation and Starting the Interview

Chapter Objectives

Upon completion of this chapter you will be able to:

- Explain the differences between formal and informal interviews
- Discuss arranging a formal interview
- Describe preparations for an interview
- Explain establishing rapport at the outset of an interview
- Discuss the use of an introductory statement for suspects
- Discuss the use of an introductory statement for victims

Perspective

As a prelude to the subsequent discussion of interviewing techniques, as well as the one that follows on interrogation, the authors of this text want to make unmistakably clear the sense in which the words *guilt* and *innocence* are used. Legally speaking, of course, a person is "guilty" only after a determination of that fact has been made by a judge or jury. The authors start from the premise of a presumption of innocence and the belief that guilt can only be established by proof beyond a reasonable doubt. An investigator obviously does not have this prerogative. Consequently, the words *guilt* and *innocence* are used here to signify nothing more than the investigator's *opinion* (and sometimes only a tentative one). It simply means that it is his belief that the suspect either committed the crime in question ("guilty") or did not commit it ("innocent"). The terms carry no legal implications whatsoever.

Formal Versus Informal Interviews

formal interview an interview that is conducted in a controlled environment, ideally one that is nonsupportive to the person being interviewed.

custodial suspect a suspect who is in police custody; this type of suspect must be read the *Miranda* warnings and must waive the right to remain silent and the right to have a lawyer present before an interview or interrogation can take place.

Miranda v. Arizona case held before the United States Supreme Court in 1966 resulting in a 5-4 decision mandating that custodial suspects must be informed of certain constitutional rights.

A **formal interview** is conducted in a controlled environment, ideally one that is nonsupportive to the person being interviewed, such as a police station, security office, or a neutral location. During a formal interview the investigator has many luxuries, among the most important being that the interview can be structured to allow for the gathering of the most meaningful information. In addition, under this circumstance, conducting an accusatory interrogation immediately following the interview becomes possible. The procedures outlined in this text primarily relate to the formal interview.

Before a **custodial suspect** may be interviewed, even for the limited purpose of making a tentative determination of the suspect's whereabouts at the time of a crime or other knowledge relating to a crime, he must be given the warnings of constitutional rights that were mandated in the United States Supreme Court's 5-to-4 decision in the 1966 case of ***Miranda v. Arizona***.[1] Also, after the issuance of the warnings, no interview or interrogation of a person in police custody may be conducted unless he has waived the prescribed rights to remain silent and to have a lawyer present. Consequently, the interview procedures discussed in this section may be employed only when (1) the suspect is not in custody or (2) the suspect is in custody and has waived both the right to remain silent and the right to a lawyer. All that follows presupposes a fulfillment of either of these two conditions.

After the issuance of Miranda *warnings, no interview or interrogation of a person in police custody may be conducted unless he or she has waived the prescribed rights to remain silent and to have a lawyer present.*

Many initial contacts a police or security officer has with suspects, witnesses, or victims will occur in an informal environment. Although privacy should always be a primary concern, an informal environment rarely allows for a structured, in-depth interview. Interrogation under these circumstances should only be considered when the person being questioned evidences clear signs of wanting to confess or when the timing and evidence suggest that a confession is likely. For example, a police officer responds to a call from a store owner reporting that a customer shoplifted merchandise. Under this circumstance, it would be appropriate for the officer to place the shopper in a private environment (perhaps the security office or even the back seat of a squad car), advise the suspect of his *Miranda* rights, and conduct an interview and/or an interrogation to learn the truth.

informal interview interview typically conducted at the scene of the crime or during follow-up investigation that is restricted to seeking basic facts about the crime that the interviewee may possess.

Typically, however, during an **informal interview** conducted at the scene of the crime or during follow-up investigation in a suspect's home or place of business, the interview is restricted to seeking basic facts about the crime that the person may possess. Information learned in such an informal setting early in an investigation can be very beneficial later during the investigation, in that contradictions between different versions of events offered by the subject can help identify the guilty party. Similarly, a false alibi offered during an informal interview conducted shortly after the commission of a crime may be easier to detect.

Arranging the Formal Interview

Whenever possible, an interview should be conducted in a noncustodial environment. This condition eliminates the need to advise the suspect of his constitutional rights under *Miranda*. Some investigators experience consistent success when inviting a suspect to voluntarily agree to be interviewed. Others meet with great resistance to any effort to set up a voluntary interview. Clearly, the manner in which the suspect is approached will influence the investigator's success. In this regard, the following suggestions should be kept in mind.

1. **Do not tell a suspect that he is the prime suspect in the case.** A guilty suspect is much more likely to agree to meet with an investigator if he believes the investigator has not already established a strong case against him. In this regard, the investigator should avoid mentioning specific evidence against the suspect or contradictions in the suspect's earlier statement during the initial contact. The pretense for the interview should be fairly vague, such as, "I would like to clarify some information you reported earlier. Would it be convenient to stop by the station tomorrow morning?" When inviting the suspect to be interviewed, the investigator should not withhold the actual purpose for the interview. The suspect needs to be truthfully informed about the issue under investigation so that he can make a knowledgeable decision whether or not to cooperate with the investigators. What is being suggested is that if a suspect is approached in a challenging and authoritative manner, he is unlikely to voluntarily submit to a subsequent interview.

The investigator should avoid mentioning specific evidence against the suspect or contradictions in the suspect's earlier statement during the initial contact.

2. **Bring up the interview in a casual manner that appears beneficial to the suspect.** As an example, the investigator might state the following: "Tony, I am just completing our investigation into those cars that were taken from the dealership where you work. I've had a chance to meet with a lot of the employees there and I'm hoping you could stop by this afternoon after work to help fill in a few details. Would you be able to make it here by 4:30?" Another approach to consider is as follows: "Pat, I've been able to eliminate a number of people in this case by having them come in to talk to me. I'd like to arrange a time to meet with you as well. Could you stop by and see me tomorrow morning around 9:00?"
3. **Imply that other people involved in the investigation have agreed to meet with you, or have already been interviewed.** This places the guilty suspect in a dilemma, in that if he does not agree to be interviewed it may be perceived as evidence of his guilt. This approach will also be beneficial during the interview of an innocent suspect, who may not otherwise cooperate because of a belief that he is being singled out as the guilty person.

When a suspect does voluntarily submit to an interview, it is our recommendation to **advise the suspect that he is not in custody** and is free to leave at any time. Although such a statement is not legally required, it can prove very beneficial in court if a defense attorney attempts to argue that the interview was custodial and therefore *Miranda* rights should have been issued and waived.

During a voluntary interview that leads to an interrogation, the investigator must respect the suspect's right to leave or terminate the interrogation at any time. **Statements that threaten or insinuate possible arrest will nullify the voluntary nature of the interrogation.** For example, an investigator who states, "Listen, we can get this clarified right here and now or you can spend the night in jail and think about things" must now advise the suspect of his rights under *Miranda*. In a private security situation, the investigator should avoid any similar threats, such as, "You're not leaving this room until you tell the truth!" Such a statement could be used as evidence against the investigator in an attempt to establish false imprisonment.

Because arguments surrounding *Miranda* issues are so frequently encountered during suppression hearings, especially as related to the suspect's perceptions at the time of an interrogation, it is our recommendation that investigators remind the suspect who is voluntarily being interrogated of his right to terminate the interrogation. Such a statement should be made around Step 6 of the interrogation process (discussed later in this text). To remind a suspect earlier during the interrogation process that he is free to go will only serve as an invitation for the guilty suspect to leave the accusatory environment. On the other hand, if the reminder of the voluntary nature of the interrogation is made *after* the suspect has confessed, it leaves open the question of the suspect's perceived ability to terminate the interrogation prior to his confession. Our recommendation, therefore, is that once the suspect exhibits behavioral signs of wanting to tell the truth, the investigator should make a statement similar to the following:

> *Jim, you came here today by yourself. No one forced you to talk to me, and you know that door is unlocked and you can walk out any time you choose. But the fact that you came in here voluntarily tells me you are basically an honest person who made a mistake and wants to clarify matters.*

Such a statement made before the suspect confesses holds great weight in court, establishing the voluntary nature of the interrogation.

Preparing for the Interview

Prior to meeting the suspect for the interview, the investigator should spend time familiarizing himself with dates, locations, people's names, and the suspect's background. These should be summarized on a *cover sheet* within the case file that the investigator can readily access. The investigator who spends time during an interview flipping through unorganized police reports or other documents in an effort to locate a person's name or particular date leaves the suspect with the impression that the investigator is not prepared, and therefore is an easier target to lie to.

Key topics of the interview should be outlined on an interview form as a reminder to the investigator of what needs to be covered with the suspect. This procedure allows the investigator to mentally prepare for the interview before meeting the suspect and also serves as a road map during the interview to keep the investigator's questions on track. The interview notes, however, should not be refined to the extent that the investigator literally writes out each question he anticipates asking. To do so restricts the natural flow of information gathering as well as spontaneous interaction with the suspect, such as asking appropriate follow-up questions.

Establishing Rapport

rapport a relationship marked by conformity.

Before asking questions directly relating to the issue under investigation, the investigator should establish a rapport with the suspect (**Table 5-1**). Rapport has different meanings under different circumstances. It can mean establishing a level of comfort or trust, or it may connote a common ground or similarity between two people. During the interview of a person suspected of committing a crime, the definition of rapport that most accurately fits is "a relationship marked by conformity."

Table 5-1 Goals of Establishing Rapport at the Outset of an Interview

1. The suspect is given an opportunity to evaluate the investigator. Hopefully, the suspect will conclude that the investigator is professional, nonjudgmental, and knowledgeable.
2. The investigator can make an initial assessment of the suspect. This includes such observations as the suspect's communication skills, general nervous tension, normal level of eye contact, and a behavioral baseline.
3. The investigator should establish a question-and-answer pattern for the interview.

Some investigators are skilled at small talk—they can discuss sports, news events, or hobbies with almost anyone. For some suspects, this can be an effective approach to establishing rapport. A caution, however, should be kept in mind. If the suspect believes that the investigator is purposefully attempting to establish common ground, this technique can backfire and actually make the suspect more suspicious of the investigator's motives.

Efforts to establish rapport should appear natural and unassuming. One of the easiest ways to do this is to **begin the interview by establishing background information about the suspect**, starting with the spelling of his last name. Further clerical information can be developed, such as the suspect's address, Social Security number, and phone number. The investigator may then ask about the suspect's present or past employment or, if the suspect is a student, ask questions about classes or school activities. When obtaining background information from the suspect, the investigator should make a written note following each response. This will establish a pattern for the remainder of the interview.

The Use of an Introductory Statement

Before agreeing to be interviewed, the subject knows whether or not he is involved in the offense, has complicity in the offense, or possesses guilty knowledge. The guilty suspect has also made a tentative decision as to what he will admit and what lies he will tell. Once rapport has been established during a formal interview, the investigator should generally make an **introductory statement**. There are several purposes for offering such a statement: (1) to clearly identify the issue under investigation, (2) to establish the investigator's objectivity concerning the suspect's truthfulness or deception, and (3) to persuade the suspect that if he lies, his deception will be detected.

introductory statement
a statement made (1) to clearly identify the issue under investigation, (2) to establish the investigator's objectivity concerning the suspect's truthfulness or deception, and (3) to persuade the suspect that if he lies, his deception will be detected.

Our experience has shown that making such an introductory statement greatly increases behavior symptoms displayed by both truthful and deceptive persons. It is also beneficial in situations where the investigator conducts an interrogation following the interview because (1) the investigator has established his objectivity at the outset of the interview, and (2) the investigator has established his confidence in detecting deception.

Statements for Suspects

A suspect should be reassured that if he is innocent, the investigation will indicate that and, conversely, that if he committed the crime his involvement will also be identified. One of the greatest fears of an innocent suspect is that his denials of involvement will not be believed. Innocent suspects experience relief when they are convinced of the investigator's objectivity. A guilty suspect who has entered the interview with a mind-set of "beating" the investigator experiences a greater fear of detection when the investigator convincingly states that the investigation will clearly indicate the suspect's involvement. The following is an example of an introductory statement suitable for any suspect:

> *Joe, during our interview we will be discussing [issue]. Some of the questions I'll be asking you I already know the answers to. The important thing is that you be completely truthful with me today before you leave. If you had nothing to do with [issue], our investigation will indicate that. But if you did [issue], our investigation will clearly indicate that as well.*

In most cases, the investigator should state, or intimate, that there are independent means to detect any lies told. In the previous example, the investigator's statement that he already knows the answers to some of the questions he will be asking increases the deceptive suspect's fear of detection, in that he is not certain in which areas the investigator has already established the truth. Another effective statement that accomplishes this same goal is to make reference to physical evidence that will shortly be available. For instance, "This morning we will be getting the results back from the crime lab on hair and fiber analysis found at the scene. At that point we will have definite information as to who caused her death."

When interviewing a suspect who, in all probability, is guilty of the offense, the investigator should emphasize his objective role in the investigation.

Setting the Stage for Truth Telling

This introductory statement may be appropriate for a suspect being interviewed concerning child sexual abuse, where the victim's statements appear to be truthful:

> *George, during this interview we'll be discussing the allegations made against you. I want to make certain that you understand what my role is in this whole thing. My only concern today is establishing the truth—what did or*

did not happen. When I interview someone, it really makes no difference to me one way or another what they did, as long as they tell the truth about it. What sometimes happens is that a person might be afraid to acknowledge certain statements or actions because, in their mind, they're afraid of how other people might view that. The problem, of course, is that if it can be proven that a person didn't tell the truth about small things, there is a natural tendency to think that he might also be lying about major issues. So again, the important thing for you is to tell the complete truth here today.

Statements for Victims and Witnesses

Exhibit concern and understanding toward sex crime victims, who generally are very reluctant to reveal the details of the offense. Such victims often have difficulty in relating precisely what the offender did and said. The investigator can ease this burden by suggesting, during the introductory statement, that the victim consider the investigator very much in the same light as a doctor whom they might consult regarding a sensitive problem. This tends to relieve the victim's embarrassment. For the same reason, the investigator should be the first person to use sexual terminology during such an interview. An example of such a statement follows:

> *Because of the nature of this incident we'll be talking about sexual terms like "penis" and "vagina." I talk to women on a regular basis in these types of circumstances about this sort of thing, so I'm not uncomfortable discussing sexual matters, but I realize that it can be difficult to discuss personal matters with a stranger. It might be helpful to think of me as a doctor who you wanted to talk to about a sensitive matter.*

Allow the adult victim to tell her story without interruption, and then delicately ask specific questions concerning aspects of the occurrence that were unclear or incomplete. Care must be taken, however, not to sympathize to the point where the investigator, in an effort to avoid upsetting the victim, asks leading questions such as, "I'm sure you went along with him because you were intimidated by this man's size, is that right?" It is also improper to offer statements of sympathy to the victim such as, "Oh, you must feel just terrible" or "I can't believe this guy did that to you!" Such statements send a clear message that the investigator accepts everything the victim says as true and can greatly increase the fabricating victim's confidence in telling her lies. Similarly, the investigator should avoid nodding his head in agreement with the victim's statements. This, too, sends the message that the victim's statements are being accepted at face value. The investigator should remain sensitive yet objective, with the goal of ascertaining the truth.

Consider asking the victim, while being left alone, to write out the details of what the offender did and said. Resorting to a written account of a reported offense or accusation may also be of value in those instances where doubt prevails as to the validity of the alleged victim's assertions. This technique assumes, of course, that the victim is able to do the necessary writing. The victim may be requested to write a detailed account of his whereabouts, activities, and observations over a reasonable span of time before and after, as well as during, the alleged event. For example, if a man claims to have been robbed, the investigator should ask him to write (if he can) everything about what happened to him. If such a written statement is obtained, it can not only be used as the basis for subsequent interview questions, but can also be analyzed for truthfulness, as will be discussed in the next chapter.

The investigator should not refer to the victim's account as a *statement* or *story;* the former terminology has legal connotations, and the latter intimates that the victim's report is made up. An introductory statement appropriate for the robbery example is as follows:

> *Mike, in situations like this I've found that people sometimes feel more comfortable writing out what happened so they don't feel pressured into answering a whole bunch of questions. If it's all right with you, what I'd like you to do is write out everything that happened to you last Saturday night. I will step out of the room for a couple of minutes so that you can concentrate on including everything in your account.*

During the introductory statement to a child victim of a sex offense, the investigator should clearly identify himself and the purpose of the interview. The interviewer should exhibit a calm, patient, and casual manner. It is usually advantageous to initiate the interview with a general discussion of the child's interests, daily activities, names of brothers and sisters, and so forth. Once a rapport has been developed and the interviewer has established some basic understanding of the child's level of speech and use of words, the child should be encouraged to relate in his or her own words the event in question.

A very important question to ask initially of a child victim is, "Who have you already talked to about this?" When the answer involves someone who is not professionally trained in interviewing children (a parent, teacher, or close friend) the investigator should make a statement similar to the following:

> *Julie, my job is to talk to people. Some of the people I talk to have done things wrong. Other people I talk to have been hurt or frightened by someone else. For me to do my job, it is important that the person I talk to tells me the complete truth. Part of my training is to recognize when someone doesn't tell the complete truth. You know what a lie is, right? And you know what telling the truth is? During our conversation today it is important that you only tell me the truth. Why do you think that is important?*
>
> *I know that you have already talked to other people about what happened, and that's fine. What I sometimes find is that someone might tell their mother or best friend about something and, because*

of the person's reaction, they change a little bit of what really happened. That's okay with someone else, but with me right now it's real important that you tell me only things that actually happened. Does that make sense to you?

Contrary to eliciting an open account from an adult victim, with a child it is essential to develop the information "bit by bit" rather than to seek it in a full recitation. It is critical, however, not to suggest, within the investigator's question, that the child was victimized. Therefore, the following question would be *improper*: "Anne, where did this man touch you?" Rather, the *proper* question would be, "Anne, did this man do anything that made you feel uncomfortable?"

When discussing parts of the body, it may be helpful to have a doll or a book of illustrations available for reference. Extreme caution must be exercised, however, to avoid suggesting what was allegedly done to or with those parts of the body, and to avoid overquestioning a child, especially by several persons on different occasions, because the child may ultimately feel obligated to supply information the questioner seems to want.

During an introductory statement for a witness, address the witness's fears openly and offer appropriate reassurances. A truthful witness may withhold information for a number of reasons. Primarily, these are the fear of having to testify; the fear of retaliation by the person being named, or by his or her associates; and a reluctance to get somebody else in trouble. A key point to keep in mind during the interview of a witness is that there is safety in numbers. That is, if the witness is led to believe that others have also come forward with information similar to the witness's own, he will feel more comfortable "going along with the crowd," and the related fears of being a witness will be greatly reduced.

The introductory statement that follows may be appropriate for a witness in a drive-by shooting involving gang members:

Mary, I really appreciate your willingness to talk to me about what you saw that day. A number of people have already talked to me or other investigators about their observations, so you may not have much more to offer than what we already know, but I like to be thorough and cover all bases. We have some great leads on this guy, and between our efforts and cooperation from good citizens like you, I'm sure this case will be closed soon.

As this introductory statement illustrates, the investigator should not only imply that other witnesses have come forward, but also emphasize the witness's civic duty to help the police. Expressing optimism that the offender is already on the verge of being arrested is also very reassuring for the reluctant witness. The issue of possible future testimony should never be brought up until *after* the witness has revealed verbally all that he or she knows. With respect to specific questions asked about possible retaliation, the investigator should respond truthfully based on the known circumstances of the case. Movies and television portrayals greatly exaggerate the incidence of offender retaliation against a witness, but it does occasionally occur and should be addressed truthfully, based on the investigator's judgment.

KEY POINTS

- When conducting a formal interview of a suspect, witness, or victim, the investigator should spend time beforehand preparing and planning out the interview.
- It is helpful to prepare an interview sheet that lists specific questions or topical areas, in abbreviated form, to be covered during the interview. This interview sheet should allow sufficient space for the investigator to document, in writing, the essence of the subject's response to each question and allow enough space to add additional questions asked.
- The first several minutes of an interview are critical, in that the subject forms first impressions of the investigator's objectivity, confidence, and general personality.
- Several minutes should be spent developing a rapport with the subject before the principal issue under investigation is introduced.
- When introducing the principal issue under investigation, it is often beneficial to use an introductory statement to get the subject in the proper mind-set for the interview.
- Introductory statements will vary depending on circumstances, but in essence, they should offer reassurance to the innocent person while at the same time increasing the apprehension of the guilty.

KEY TERMS

custodial suspect Suspect who is in police custody; this type of suspect must be read the *Miranda* warnings and must waive the right to remain silent and the right to have a lawyer present before an interview or interrogation can take place.

formal interview An interview that is conducted in a controlled environment, ideally one that is nonsupportive to the person being interviewed.

informal interview Interview typically conducted at the scene of the crime or during follow-up investigation that is restricted to seeking basic facts about the crime that the interviewee may possess.

introductory statement A statement made (1) to clearly identify the issue under investigation, (2) to establish the investigator's objectivity concerning the suspect's truthfulness or deception, and (3) to persuade the suspect that if he lies, his deception will be detected.

Miranda v. Arizona Case held before the United States Supreme Court in 1966 resulting in a 5-4 decision mandating that custodial suspects must be informed of certain constitutional rights.

rapport A relationship marked by conformity.

ENDNOTES

1. 394 U.S. 436 (1966)

EXERCISES

1. Last Friday someone entered a manager's office on the sixth floor of an office building and stole $80 in cash from a petty cash fund, as well as an MP3 player from a desk drawer. Surveillance video indicates that a custodian by the name of Fred was on the sixth floor around 9:00 P.M. Friday, even though he was not assigned to clean that floor. In addition, the next day Fred was seen with an MP3 player that matches the description of the one stolen from the manager's office. What would be an effective technique to invite Fred to be interviewed concerning the theft?

2. What questions could you ask Fred to establish rapport?

3. What would be an appropriate introductory statement to use during Fred's interview?

____

____

____

____

____

____

____

____

____

____

Formulation of Interview Questions

6

Chapter Objectives

Upon completion of this chapter you will be able to:

- Define an initial open question
- Explain why asking an initial open question is important
- Describe proper phrasing of open questions
- Discuss eliciting a full response
- Evaluate the response to an open question for truthfulness
- Clarify the open account
- Ask direct questions
- Describe the process of asking follow-up questions
- Manage evasive responses, qualified responses, and omissions

Perspective

The manner in which questions are phrased during an interview can increase or decrease the value of the subject's response to the question. Some questions actually invite deception and are obviously undesirable, while others create much greater anxiety within the deceptive subject if he chooses to lie to them, and are therefore more productive to ask during an interview. For example, given the following two questions, the second one is more likely to result in meaningful information:

Q1: "In the last 10 years, have you cheated on your tax returns?"

Q2: "In the last 10 years, what tax deduction have you taken that you are most concerned about?"

It is of interest to note that social learning teaches to ask questions in a delicate and sensitive manner, with the underlying assumption that the person responding will answer truthfully and volunteer the needed information. For example, two close friends may be sharing a drink and one of them asks, "How are things between you and Gloria [the friend's wife]?" Introducing the sensitive topic of known past marital problems with this nonintrusive question is ideal between friends. In all probability the question will stimulate significant information and further discussion. However, the witnesses, victims, and suspects who an investigator interviews are not personal friends, nor do they generally experience an overwhelming desire to incriminate themselves or others. Because of this, an investigator must learn different questioning skills than those customarily used between friends and family, and must give careful thought to exactly how inquiries are formulated during the course of an investigative interview.

Asking an Initial Open Question

When attempting to determine what happened to a victim, a suspect's alibi, or what a witness saw or heard, the investigator should elicit this information by asking an initial open question early during the interview (see **Table 6-1**). An open question is one that calls for a narrative response.

open question a question that calls for a narrative response.

Examples of Open Questions

- "Please tell me everything you know about the fire at your warehouse."
- "Please tell me everything that happened to you after school last Friday night." (claim of rape, battery, or robbery)
- "Please tell me everything about the accident you witnessed."
- "Tell me everything you did from noon on Saturday until you went to bed." (evaluate an alibi)

Too often, investigators elicit this type of information by asking closed questions. For example, in a case involving a robbery that occurred at 7:45 p.m., the investigator might ask a suspect, "Where were you last Friday at 7:45?" The guilty suspect is likely to lie to this highly focused question by providing a fabricated statement, and the investigator is left with the difficult task of detecting deception based on a single observation of behavior.

Consider the following response to an open question concerning a subject's alibi where the issue under investigation is a drive-by shooting that occurred at 6:45 p.m. The open question asked of the suspect was, "Please tell me everything you did last Saturday between noon and the time you went to bed."

> *Over the noon hour I was shooting buckets with some friends and we decided to go to the McDonald's on Sunset for lunch. We hung*

Table 6-1 Benefits of Asking an Initial Open Question Early During an Interview

1. Because the subject is free to include or exclude whatever he wants to within his response (except in the case of a fabricated victim's account), the subject is unlikely to include false information. Open questions do not invite fabrication. Information volunteered during a response to an open question—for example, a subject's alibi—will probably all be truthful, although perhaps incomplete.
2. The subject's response to an initial open question can be evaluated for editing, to determine where the subject intentionally excluded specific information within the account.
3. Responses to open questions generally do not commit the deceptive subject to a position of denial, whereas a series of closed questions may cause the subject to stick to a lie he told early during the interview process.

around McDonald's for a while and went over to a friend's house to see who was there. We were at her home for a while, sitting and talking. After that we wanted to see a movie. The movie ended at about 7:00. Eventually, we went over to Paul's house, talked and stuff, and I walked home from Paul's house around 9:00. I spent the rest of the night on the phone and listening to CDs in my room. I probably fell asleep around 11:00 or so.

This alibi does not include any false information, even though the subject was involved in the shooting incident. (Notice that the subject never stated that he went to the movie.) As will be described shortly, this alibi can be analyzed for editing and, by asking clarifying questions, the investigator may be able to establish that the suspect, in fact, had no alibi at the time of the crime. On the other hand, had the investigator elicited the alibi by asking a direct question (i.e., "Where were you at 6:45 last Saturday night?"), the subject would likely lie and then be committed to the position that he was at a movie when the drive-by shooting occurred, as illustrated by the following dialogue:

Q: "Where were you at about 6:45 last Saturday night?"

R: "I was with Paul and Greg at a movie."

Q: "What movie was that?"

R: "*The Rock*."

Q: "When did you leave the movie theater?"

R: "The movie ended around 7:00, so it would have been about 7:10 or 7:15."

Q: "And then what did you do?"

R: "We were in Paul's car and he drove to his house, where we talked for a while and I walked home at 9:00."

Eliciting an alibi in this manner actually forces a guilty suspect to lie to the investigator's questions. It is an obvious principle of interviewing, but one worth mentioning: **It is always more advantageous to have a subject omit part of the truth than to fabricate information through a lie.** Developing truthful information that was omitted from a response is much easier than learning the truth from a subject who is committed to a lie already told (which generally requires interrogation). Open questions do not invite a guilty subject to lie to the investigator's question.

Phrasing Open Questions

Our social instincts teach us to ask open questions in a noninvasive manner. For example, "How was your day at work?" or "What happened at school today?" These questions are certainly adequate to allow a person willing to disclose problems at work or school to reveal that information. However, they clearly are ineffective for the person motivated to deceive.

During the interview of a person suspected of involvement in a crime or of fabricating an event, **the initial open question should be phrased in the broadest sense possible**, for example, "Tell me *everything* you did. . . ." The investigator should not place any parameters in the question that might limit the subject's response. Therefore, when questioning a wife concerning domestic violence, question 1 is improperly asked, whereas question 2 is properly asked:

> Q1: "Why don't you start off by telling me what your husband did to you?"
>
> Q2: "Please tell me everything that happened here this evening."

The first question is improper because it assumes that the husband in some way injured the wife and limits the wife's response to her husband's physical actions. The second question offers no direction to the wife, and she can report whatever she chooses.

Typically, truthful accounts will start off at some point in time prior to the main event. Before responding to an open question, however, a deceptive subject may ask the investigator, "Where would you like me to begin?" or "What would you like to know?" The investigator should respond, "Wherever you want to begin" or "Everything that happened."

Eliciting a Full Response

Once the subject starts responding to the initial open question, the investigator should allow him to continue with his response without asking any questions. If the investigator were to interrupt the account by asking a question, the truthful subject might edit the account to provide what he believes the investigator wants to know. Also, interruptions as a result of questions break the subject's flow of ideas and the continuity of the account, which restricts the investigator's ability to evaluate the account for edited information.

forced silence a technique used by investigators to encourage a full response to the initial open question.

To encourage a full response to the initial open question, the investigator may use a technique called forced silence. After the subject pauses, the investigator might say something like "All right" or "Okay," followed by silence. Inevitably, the subject will break the silence and continue with his response. When the response is complete, the subject will generally let the investigator know this with a statement such as, "And that's everything I did."

Evaluating Responses to Open Questions

When relating an incident such as being the victim of a robbery or sexual assault, **the truthful account almost always contains three parts** (**Table 6-2**).[1] The account will start off with an introduction, which sets the stage for the main incident. The second portion will be the incident itself, and the final stage will be an epilogue in which the subject explains what he did after the incident or how the incident affected him emotionally. In a truthful account, the subject's actions, thoughts, and behaviors resulting from the incident become just as significant as the behavioral components.

Table 6-2 Three Parts of a Truthful Account

1. Introduction: Sets stage for main account
2. Main event
3. Epilogue: Results of the event

The following account of a car-jacking is typical of a truthful account:

> *Well, I was on my way to pick up my two children, Dave and Laura, from pre-school. I got off work at about 6:15 and I had to pick them up over on Lake Avenue before 7:00. Rush hour traffic was pretty bad and I was afraid I might be late. I was late picking the kids up last Tuesday and the teacher gave me a hard time about it so I decided to take a short cut through the neighborhood off of Lombard. [Introduction]*
>
> *I was distracted by the time and wasn't really thinking too much about where I was. At any rate, I was stopped at a red light on Lombard and St. Paul, and the car behind me bumped me. I was sort of startled but it was just a bump and I didn't think there would be any damage. When I turned around I saw this guy approach my window so I opened the door to talk with him. He told me there was damage to the back of my car, so I got out of my car to see the damage. He grabbed me over here by the shoulder and said, "Take a hike," and pushed me away. He got into my car and did a U-turn going down St. Paul Drive in the other direction. He squealed the tires and I had to jump out of the way. The car that bumped me then did the same thing. [Main event]*
>
> *This whole thing happened in just a matter of seconds. I feel like such a fool because I've read about car-jackings but I didn't think it would ever happen to me, you know. I wasn't physically hurt but*

> *was sort of in a daze, and here I was in the middle of an unfamiliar neighborhood. I wasn't sure what to do. I walked to a Walgreens down the block and they had a pay phone where I called the police and then the day care center. The teacher agreed to wait for me and after I talked to the police I called a taxi and went and picked them up. And that's everything. [Epilogue].*

On the other hand, a fabricated account often does not contain these three segments. The deceptive subject, who does not want to lie unnecessarily, may provide an introduction and a main event but offer a very sketchy epilogue or skip the epilogue altogether. It is also suspicious when the amount of detail varies from one segment to the next. For example, if a victim spends 90% of the response offering a very detailed introduction and then glosses over the main event, this would be suspicious. Contrast the earlier truthful response to this fabricated statement:

> *Well, I was on my way to pick up my children from day care and decided to take a short cut off of Lombard down to St. Paul. As you know, that's a pretty bad neighborhood, and when I was stopped at a light I thought I felt a jolt like someone hit me from behind, and this guy comes out and grabs me and pulls me out of the car and jumps in and drives away. It all happened so fast I didn't get a good look at him. That's pretty much everything.*

The following sections examine more elements that investigators should listen for in a subject's response to an initial open question.

Indications of Truthfulness

Similar Detail Throughout the Account

Depending on the significance and recentness of the event being related, along with a person's background, education, and communication skills, different individuals will include different amounts of details within an account. However, if the account is factual, there should be a similar amount of detail throughout one individual's account.

Out-of-Sequence Information

Memories are not stored in real time, the way a video camera records images. Rather, people have primary memories, which may then stimulate secondary memories. These less important memories may occur to the subject out of sequence within the account. The fact that the subject includes out-of-sequence information offers support for the statement being derived from factual recall.

In the first account of the car-jacking incident given earlier, the statement about being late picking the kids up last Tuesday is out of sequence. The subject decided to include the information in his account because it was factual; guilty suspects typically do not lie unnecessarily during a response to the investigator's question.

Expressions of Thoughts and Emotions

When relating a traumatic incident, it is very suspicious if the suspect does not include thoughts or emotional states because, psychologically, they are linked so closely with behaviors. The truthful account of the car-jacking incident includes a number of such thoughts, including "I didn't think there would be any damage," "I felt like a fool," and "I was sort of in a daze."

Indications of Deception

Varying Levels of Detail

The investigator should be suspicious that an account may be deceptive if it contains a great deal of detail leading up to the main incident, but the description of the main incident lacks an equivalent level of detail. Similarly, if the introduction and epilogue are very sketchy but the subject offers a very detailed main event, this should be viewed suspiciously as well.

Perfect Chronology Within the Account

An account that goes from A to Z without ever skipping back in time is somewhat suspicious. This may be an indication that the account is rehearsed or is being generated spontaneously as the subject is telling the story. The absence of out-of-sequence information suggests that the subject is not relying on normal patterns of recall. A truthful account that has been retold many times, however, may be chronological.

The Absence of Thoughts or Emotions

Deceptive accounts are frequently focused entirely on behaviors: what happened, when it happened, how it happened, what was said, and so forth. Because the account is fabricated, these reported behaviors occur in isolation from the normal process of experiencing thoughts or emotions.

In a case involving a fabricated robbery, the subject was asked, "What was your reaction when you saw the man approach your vehicle?" His response was that he moved the money bags to one side. The investigator again attempted to elicit the subject's thoughts or emotions by asking, "What were your thoughts when he approached you?" to which the subject responded, "I just stepped on the brake and moved the bags." At no time did the subject state that he was afraid or had thoughts of being hurt or killed. During an interrogation following this interview, the subject admitted stealing the money himself and making up the story about being robbed.

Phrases Indicating a Time Gap

There are key phrases to listen for during an open account that indicate that the subject has consciously edited information from the account. Examples of these phrases include the following:

"The next thing I remember . . ."

"Before I knew it . . ."

"Eventually . . . "

The following are two actual victim statements, both containing time-gap phrases. In both examples, clearly the "victim" has edited information leading up to the main event.

I got up from my chair and went into his house. When I came back outside he had spread a blanket on the ground, and he asked me to join him. I sat down on a corner of the blanket and the next thing I recall is being on my back with my clothes up around my neck and him fondling me.

I asked the officer why we were stopped and he told me that if I say one more word he was going to kick my [expletive]. I said I was sorry and I was just asking. The next thing I knew, I was on the ground getting kicked.

In both of these accounts, common sense reveals that the precipitators for these attacks were omitted from the narrative. This does not necessarily mean that these are fabricated accounts, but rather that the victim chose not to include the events immediately leading up to the alleged sexual assault or police beating. This omission might have been because of embarrassment or shame, which may indicate possible truthfulness, or perhaps because the victim was responsible for the action, which may negate the claim. The point is, **time-gap phrases** help direct the investigator's attention to a portion of an account that requires clarification.

time-gap phrase phrases that indicate omissions in the account of an event (e.g., "Before I knew it . . ." and "The next thing I remember . . .") and help direct the investigator's attention to a portion of an account that requires clarification.

implied-action phrase phrases that require the listener to make assumptions about what probably happened (e.g., "He began . . ." and "I wanted to . . .").

Implied-Action Phrases

Deceptive subjects rely extensively on the investigator making assumptions about what probably happened. A good rule to follow is that **if the subject did not specifically state that something happened, the investigator should not assume that it did.** Typical **implied-action phrases** include the following:

"I thought about . . ."

"He started to . . ."

"He began . . ."

"I wanted to . . ."

In one case our office investigated, a 17-year-old student claimed she was raped in a bathroom stall at her high school. When responding to the initial open question, she stated, "And he starts to threaten me and tells me that if I scream or didn't cooperate he will hurt or kill me." Later during her response she stated, "And he starts pushing me up against the back of the stall so I was, kind of, you know, pinned in." Of significance is that the student never said that the man actually made these statements, or pushed her up against the back of the stall. Rather, she said that he "starts" to engage in these behaviors.[2] Following an interrogation, this subject confessed to making up the rape story to explain her absence from class.

Clarifying the Open Account

Once the subject has completed his response to the initial open question, the investigator should go back and ask clarifying questions. **Table 6-3** lists areas of an account that might require further clarification.

Clarifying questions are open-ended questions that can be divided into three categories (**Table 6-4**). In the first category are questions designed to **elicit further information within a section of the account**. The following are examples of this type of question:

"Please tell me more about the man who approached your car."

"Please describe the vehicle that hit you."

"What did you do after they drove away?"

"Tell me more about the movie."

Table 6-3 Guidelines for Areas Requiring Clarification

Guidelines for Areas Requiring Clarification
Sketchy details
Illogical or unexplained behavior
Time-gap phrases (e.g., "The next thing I knew")
Implied-action phrases (e.g., "I wanted to go shopping")
People who are not identified (e.g., "We went to the mall")
Conversations (e.g., "I was on the phone for a while")
Qualifying phrases (e.g., "I believe," "I think," "As I recall")

Table 6-4 Types of Clarifying Questions

Types of Clarifying Questions
Questions designed to elicit further information within a section of an account
Questions seeking an explanation for events
Questions designed to develop information about the subject's feelings or thoughts

The second category of clarifying questions seeks an **explanation for events.** The following list illustrates these types of questions:

"Could you explain more fully why you were in that neighborhood?"

"Why did you initially get out of the car?"

"Why did you decide to go to that movie?"

"Why did you wait for three days to report this?"

The final category of clarifying questions develops **information about the subject's feelings or thoughts.** Some examples of these questions are as follows:

"What was your first reaction when you saw the man approach you?"

"How do you feel toward the man who stole your car?"

"Who have you discussed this incident with?"

After the investigator has asked a series of clarifying questions, the subject has volunteered all of the information that he is going to. At this point, the investigator should ask direct questions to develop details of the event or situation that were not included in the subject's response to open questions.

clarifying questions open-ended questions that (1) are designed to elicit further information within a section of the account, (2) seek an explanation for events, or (3) develop information about the subject's feelings or thoughts.

direct questions usually closed questions asked to elicit a specific position or answer from the subject.

Asking Direct Questions

As the name implies, direct questions are usually closed questions asked to elicit a specific position or answer from the subject. Although direct questions are an efficient way to learn information, a deceptive subject is also more likely to lie to these questions. Essentially, direct questions force a deceptive suspect to either offer incriminating evidence or to lie. Therefore, in addition to asking direct questions properly, the investigator must carefully monitor the subject's behavior when responding to them. The specific behavior symptoms to observe will be presented in the next chapter.

Whenever practical, ask an open question rather than a direct question. As previously stated, much more information can be learned by asking an open question than a closed one, as illustrated through the following two examples:

Q1: "What is your understanding of the purpose of the interview with me here today?" [Open]

Q2: "Do you know why I've asked to talk to you?" [Closed]

When seeking a possible admission, use nondescriptive language. Subjects will instinctively take a position of denial when the investigator's question contains descriptive or legal terminology such as "steal," "rape," "murder," or "rob." Therefore, the first of the following questions is unlikely to elicit meaningful information, whereas the second one may:

Q1: "Who do you think was involved in this robbery?" [Improper]

Q2: "Who do you think may have been involved in taking the money from the gas station?" [Proper]

Do not predicate a question on information the subject provided at some earlier point in time. Even though the investigator may have substantial knowledge of what the subject told another investigator or wrote in a statement, the investigator should ask each question as if he does not know the answer to it. By predicating a question on earlier information, the investigator not only reminds the subject of what his previous response was but also makes it difficult for the subject to change the earlier statement, thereby possibly committing a guilty subject to further denial.

For example, if an assault victim is asked the question, "I see here in your statement that the man who attacked you was six feet tall. Can you give me a more complete description of what he looked like?" she is unlikely to respond, "Well after thinking about things I think his height was closer to five feet six inches." If the question is phrased as "Please describe everything about the man who attacked you," however, the victim is more likely to change her original description of his height if, in retrospect, she believes he was shorter than six feet. Here is another example of improper and proper question phraseology:

Q1: "You told the other investigator that you left the movie theater at about 7:10 that evening. Is it possible that it could have been closer to 6:30?" [Improper]

Q2: "What time did you leave the movie theater?" [Proper]

Also, if the investigator has specific information about the suspect's past (e.g., a prior arrest or specific information that links the suspect to the crime scene, such as an eyewitness who saw the suspect leave the scene of a fire), this information should not be revealed until the suspect is asked a question about it. A suspect who lies about such matters (e.g., denies any previous arrests or denies being in the area of the crime) is much more likely to be involved in the incident under investigation.

Do not combine two issues within the same question. Consider the compound question, "Did you see Jim at all that night or talk to him that night?" If a subject answers "No" to this question, the investigator has no idea if the subject is denying both actions or just one of them. To complicate detecting deception, a guilty subject who talked to Jim over the phone but did not meet with him personally will psychologically focus on that portion of the investigator's question to which he is telling the truth (talking to Jim that day). As a consequence, his behavior will appear truthful. The following dialogue illustrates the benefit of separating these two issues by addressing them in different questions:

Q: "Did you see Jim at all that night?"

A: "No, not at all."

Q: "Did you talk to Jim at all that night?"

A: "Um . . . not in person."

Direct questions should be short and succinct. An investigator may start off by asking a direct question that is short and to the point. However, as part of our social learning, if the investigator detects hesitancy on the part of the suspect, he may continue talking in an effort to ease the suspect's anxiety. The resulting question is often much more specific than the original one asked by the investigator. This is called tagging a direct question. Consider the following dialogue:

Q: "Did Andrea ever see your bare penis?"

A: "Um . . ."

Q: "You know, kids that age are naturally curious and sometimes they might walk in when you're taking a shower, or when you're getting ready for bed, and see you naked under that circumstance. Has that happened at all?"

A: "No, not at all."

In this case the subject walked into the victim's bedroom and exposed his bare penis to her. The investigator's first question was proper and addressed that possibility. However, once the investigator **tagged** the question with specific examples (being seen in the shower or getting ready for bed) the question became so specific that the subject was able to answer it truthfully without incriminating himself.

tagging a questioning error that involves the investigator asking a direct question and then continuing to talk, perhaps by suggesting possible responses to the question or clarifying the question.

Do not include memory qualifiers within your question. Deceptive subjects will use memory qualifiers within their answer to a question to reduce personal responsibility within the response. An example of this is, "Not that I can recall." However, if the investigator's question contains a memory qualifier, the deceptive subject feels much more confident in his denial, as the following example illustrates:

Q1: "Do you remember if you had an argument with James that night?" [Improper]

A1: "No."

Q2: "Did you have an argument with James that night?" [Proper]

A2: "Not that I recall."

By removing the **memory qualifier** in the second question, the subject's response changes substantially. In effect, he now acknowledges the *possibility* of having had an argument with the victim on the night of the crime.

memory qualifier word(s) that express uncertainty when a person is recalling past events.

negative question a question that expects agreement with an implication contained within the question.

Do not ask negative questions. A **negative question** is one that expects agreement with an implication contained within the question. These are the easiest questions to lie to, and yet are frequently asked during interviews. The following are examples of negative questions:

"You don't know who did this, do you?"

"So you've never discussed sexual matters with your stepdaughter?"

"You weren't using any drugs that night, were you?"

Often, negative questions are asked as an improper follow-up to an evasive response offered by the subject. The investigator recognizes that the subject's initial response was less than complete but incorrectly summarizes the subject's position by asking a negative question, as the following dialogue illustrates:

Q: "This lady lives right downstairs from you. Have you ever been inside her apartment for any reason?"

A: "I'm sure I would remember being inside her apartment."

Q: "So you've never been inside her apartment?"

A: "That's right."

Do not ask challenging questions. The interviewing process should be nonaccusatory. With some subjects this is a difficult guideline to follow. However, the investigator must remember that once questions are asked in a challenging or accusatory manner, the subject will offer less and less information. Furthermore, questions asked in a threatening or offensive tone may produce misleading behavior from the suspect.[3] The following is an example of *improper* questioning:

Q: "That evening were you in a car on 5th Street at any time?"

A: "I told you, when this thing went down I was at a movie."

Q: "That's not what I asked you. Listen to my question! Were you in a car on 5th Street?"

A: "I already told you where I was. If you have any more questions you can talk to my attorney!"

A much better approach to this evasive response would be, "I understand, but what I was wondering is whether, at any time, you were in a car on 5th Street that evening?" Another way to keep interview questions nonchallenging is for the investigator to assume the blame for not understanding the subject's answer. The investigator may say, "I'm somewhat confused about something" or "I may have misunderstood your earlier statement."

Asking Follow-up Questions

Asking proper direct questions is certainly no guarantee that a deceptive subject will tell the truth to the question. Rather, proper formulation of interview questions makes deception more apparent within the subject's response. While the specific behavioral cues of deception will be covered in Chapter 7, it is important to appreciate that there are two distinct reasons for evaluating a subject's behavioral response to interview questions. The first is to form an opinion of the suspect's probable truthfulness. Second, the investigator should use behavior symptoms to help direct the selection of follow-up questions to ask. It is in this regard that the following suggestions are offered.

follow-up question a question that is specifically directed at some aspect of the subject's original response and is instrumental in clarifying a subject's behavior.

Because **follow-up questions** are specifically directed at some aspect of the subject's original response, they are instrumental in clarifying a subject's behavior. Therefore, a subject's responses to follow-up questions are often much more useful in identifying truth or deception than the initial response to the original question. The following example illustrates this concept, where the response to the follow-up question from the first subject is more typical of truthfulness. Conversely, the second subject offers a response to the follow-up question more indicative of deception:

> *A subject's responses to follow-up questions are often much more useful in identifying truth or deception than the initial response to the original question.*

I: "What do you think should happen to the person who stole this $2000?"

S: "Well, that's not really my decision to make."

I (Follow-up): "I understand, but if you could make the decision, what do you think should happen to the person who did this?"

S1: "Well, because this theft is hurting my share of the profits, I would like to get my hands on him first. I think jail would probably be the best solution."

S2: "I think you have to look at a person's record and stuff. You know, find out why he did it and consider all the circumstances."

Handling Evasive Responses

evasive response a response that does not offer a definitive answer to a direct question.

An <u>evasive response</u> is one that does not offer a definitive answer to a direct question. Often evasion is a symptom of deception, but some truthful subjects will evade a direct answer to the investigator's initial question for a number of reasons. In the case of an evasive response, the investigator should simply rephrase the same question, as the following dialogue illustrates:

I: "When is the last time you saw Sally?"

S: "Like I said, I drove her home and dropped her off around 7:30 or so."

I: "I understand that you drove her home around 7:30, but when is the last time you actually saw her?"

S: "Well, she invited me in for a drink and I accepted, but didn't stay that long. I would have to say that the last time I saw her would have been around 8:00 or 8:30—something like that."

Responding to Qualified Responses

qualified response a response that contains words or phrases that decrease the level of personal commitment or confidence within the subject's response.

hypothetical follow-up question a question asked by the investigator to clarify the subject's position when qualifiers are used by the subject in a response. Hypothetical questions often start with the phrase "Is it possible" or "Do you think that perhaps."

A <u>qualified response</u> contains words or phrases that decrease the level of personal commitment or confidence within the subject's response. When such qualifiers are used, the investigator should consider asking a <u>hypothetical follow-up question</u> to clarify the subject's position. Hypothetical questions often start with the phrase "Is it possible" or "Do you think that perhaps." The following dialogue illustrates this technique:

I: "At any time were you given the combination to the safe?"

S: "To the best of my knowledge I never had the combination."

I: "Is it possible that you were given the combination at some point in time?"

S: "Well, now that you mention it, there was an incident where Jim called in sick and I talked to him on the phone because I had to open that morning. I believe he did give me the combination to the safe when I talked to him."

Responding to Possible Omission

During the course of an interview, a guilty subject may avoid lying to the investigator's question through omission. What the suspect offers within his response is the truth, but it represents only part of the truth. The investigator should always listen for possible omission when questioning a subject about frequencies of behavior or dates. In the following example, the first suspect is telling the complete truth, whereas the second one has omitted important information:

I: "Has your driver's license ever been suspended?"

S1: "The only time that happened was back when I was 19. I didn't have enough money to pay a couple of parking tickets and my license was suspended for three months until I paid them."

S2: "Yes it was. Back when I was 19, it was suspended for a few months for unpaid parking tickets."

Although the second subject has not lied during his response, he also has not told the complete truth. In fact, his license had been suspended on three occasions.

Whenever a subject acknowledges that something happened, the investigator should ask, as an automatic follow-up question, "Besides that time, what other time?" The following dialogue is from an actual case in which the suspect was being questioned concerning involvement in a robbery/homicide in which the store owner was killed with a 9-mm handgun:

I: "When is the last time you fired a handgun?"

S: "A couple of years ago I went target shooting with a buddy and I used his gun—it was a .22 or something, but that goes back a long way."

I: "Besides target shooting with that .22, what other handguns have you fired in the last couple of years?"

S: "Well, I take that back, there was another time I fired a .38 revolver with a friend, just in an alley fooling around. That had to be last year. It was the summer, I don't know—July or something."

I: "Besides those two handguns, what other handguns have you fired recently?"

S: "I didn't actually fire it, but back in November a friend had a 9 mm, and I sort of dry fired it. It was nothing."

This line of questioning was very important in solving the case in that it established the suspect's access to the same-caliber weapon as was used in the commission of the crime. Once the suspect gave the investigator the name of the "friend," it was determined that the suspect bought the 9-mm handgun from this person. Subsequent developments disclosed this 9-mm handgun to be the one the subject used during the murder of the robbery victim.

KEY POINTS

- An investigator's ability to develop meaningful information from a suspect, witness, or victim relates directly to his skill in formulating questions properly and asking appropriate follow-up questions when they are needed.
- Early during the interview, ask the subject an initial open-ended question to elicit his version of events concerning the issue under investigation. Allow the subject to completely respond to that question, without interruptions, while making written notes of key information.
- Ask clarifying questions that relate back to the subject's response to the initial open-ended question. These should be open questions that allow the subject to expand on information already provided to the investigator.
- Ask direct questions to elicit a definitive position from the subject in areas that remain unclear or to develop information that was not yet discussed.
- If a response to a direct question contains symptoms of possible deception, the investigator should ask appropriate follow-up questions to further develop information or draw out behavior.

Indications of Truthfulness

- Similar amount of detail throughout the account
- Out-of-sequence information
- Expressions of thoughts and emotions

Indications of Deception

- Varying levels of detail
- Perfect chronology within the account
- Absence of thoughts or emotions
- Phrases indicating a time gap
- Implied-action phrases

Three Types of Clarifying Questions

- Questions designed to elicit further information within a section of an account
- Questions seeking an explanation for events
- Questions designed to develop information about the subject's feelings or thoughts

KEY TERMS

clarifying question Open-ended questions that (1) are designed to elicit further information within a section of the account, (2) seek an explanation for events, or (3) develop information about the subject's feelings or thoughts.

direct question Usually closed questions asked to elicit a specific position or answer from the subject.

evasive response A response that does not offer a definitive answer to a direct question.

follow-up question A question that is specifically directed at some aspect of the subject's original response and is instrumental in clarifying a subject's behavior.

forced silence A technique used by investigators to encourage a full response to the initial open question.

hypothetical follow-up question A question asked by the investigator to clarify the subject's position when qualifiers are used by the subject in a response. Hypothetical questions often start with the phrase "Is it possible" or "Do you think that perhaps."

implied-action phrase Phases that require the listener to make assumptions about what probably happened (e.g., "He began . . ." and "I wanted to . . .").

memory qualifier Word(s) that express uncertainty when a person is recalling past events.

negative question A question that expects agreement with an implication contained within the question.

open question A question that calls for a narrative response.

qualified response A response that contains words or phrases that decrease the level of personal commitment or confidence within the subject's response.

tagging A questioning error that involves the investigator asking a direct question and then continuing to talk, perhaps by suggesting possible responses to the question or clarifying the question.

time-gap phrase Phrases that indicate omissions in the account of an event (e.g., "Before I knew it . . ." and "The next thing I remember . . .") and help direct the investigator's attention to a portion of an account that requires clarification.

ENDNOTES

1. Some of the guidelines suggested for evaluating an open account incorporate concepts from "Content Analysis," a technique for evaluating a statement written by a victim, witness or suspect. Our empirical experience in applying these guidelines to verbal accounts support their usefulness in that situation as well.
2. Also of significance in this account is that the victim is using present tense nouns yet talking about something that should have occurred in the past. For a more in depth discussion of semantics and evaluation of an open account, see Rudacille, W., *Identifying Lies in Disguise,* Dubuque: Kendall/Hunt, 1994; Rabon, D., *Investigative Discourse Analysis,* Durham: Carolina Academic Press, 1994.
3. A good example of the misleading nature of behavior produced by accusatory questioning is a laboratory study in which college students were "interviewed" concerning their alibi during a mock crime. See Kassin, S. & Fong, C., "I'm Innocent!: Effects of Training on Judgments of Truth and Deception in the Interrogation Room," *Law and Human Behavior,* 1999, Vol 23 No 5.

EXERCISES

1. Re-phrase each of the following interview questions so they are asked properly.

A. "Where were you last Saturday at 3:15 in the afternoon?"

B. "Did you sell any marijuana at the ball game or did anyone approach you asking to buy drugs?"

C. "Do you recall leaving the bar with anyone last night?"

2. Ask an appropriate follow-up question for the following dialogues.

Q: "Did you return to work last Friday night?"

A: "My wife had the car."

Follow up:

Q: "Did you handle a gun over the weekend?"

A: "To the best of my knowledge I didn't."

Follow up:

Q: "Have you ever been questioned before concerning sexual contact with a minor?"

A: "When I in high school there was an incident involving this girl I was dating. She was 16 and I was 18."

Follow up:

7 Behavior Symptom Analysis

Chapter Objectives

Upon completion of this chapter you will be able to:

- Explain the underlying principles of behavior analysis
- Discuss the evaluation of a subject's attitudes
- Discuss evaluation of verbal behavior
- Discuss evaluation of nonverbal behavior

There is a kind of confession in your looks, which your modesties have not craft enough to color.

—Hamlet to Rosencrantz and Guildenstern, in Shakespeare's *Hamlet,* Act 2, Scene 2

Overview of Research on Related Behavior Analysis

Physicians, psychiatrists, psychologists, and many other professionals have long recognized the value of evaluating a person's behavior in order to arrive at a diagnosis. This attitude has been based on the principle that there are several levels of communication and that the true meaning of the spoken word is amplified or modified by other channels, including speech hesitancy, body posture, hand gestures, facial expressions, and other body activities. In other words, a person can say one thing while his body movements, facial expressions, or tone of voice may reveal something entirely different.

Pioneers in the field of criminal interrogation, as it is known today, gave little consideration to behavior symptoms. Overlooking the professional importance and potential value of such individual characteristics, the early investigators relied almost completely upon the content of what the suspect said. Some had nothing more than a "gut feeling" that the suspect was guilty or innocent. Evidence of behavioral differences between truthful suspects and lying suspects was thought to be of questionable merit and generally was not given conscious consideration. Most certainly, however, some investigators had developed a skill for assessing behavior, but few disclosed it, or perhaps lacked the ability to articulate or record their observations. Furthermore, it was not unusual for some of them to believe that they were endowed with a "sixth sense" when, in fact, their skill was derived from a special application of their natural five senses, developed through practice, and from reliance upon a very good memory bank.

Beginning in 1942, John Reid, the coauthor of the first three editions of *Criminal Interrogation and Confessions,* systematically recorded the behavior symptoms of all suspects who were given polygraph examinations at the Chicago Police Scientific Crime Detection Laboratory. In this research, he compared behavior symptoms and polygraph test results. It was reasoned that since the polygraph records physiological changes during the time questions are asked, and since behavior symptoms are signs accompanying physiological changes, there might be a correlation between polygraph test results and the verbal and nonverbal responses of a suspect. Responses of the subjects were noted during the interview prior to taking the test, while taking the test, and during an interrogation that followed. Observations were also made by someone who looked through a transparent wall mirror at each subject during the entire time the subject was in the polygraph examination room, either alone or with the examiner. When the polygraph test results were confirmed by evidence of guilt (e.g., a confession or the finding of substantiating facts) or of innocence (e.g., the investigator's definite diagnosis to that effect or the establishment of another person's guilt), a comparison was made between those results and the observed behavior symptoms of the suspects.

After a compilation of verified cases and a statistical analysis of the behavior symptoms exhibited by polygraph test subjects, it was encouraging to find that the majority of the verified truthful individuals had been tentatively identified as such by the polygraph examiner during the pretest interview, and a considerable number of the verified lying subjects had been tentatively identified as liars even before the polygraph tests had begun. It was established, however, that truthful suspects were easier to recognize from behavior symptoms alone and that lying suspects were more difficult to identify in this manner.[1]

While this initial research offered promising results, a number of variables could have influenced the findings. Specifically, behavior symptoms may be more apparent during a polygraph environment than outside of one. Further, the behavioral assessments may have been biased because the examiner had investigative and background information about each subject. In the 1990s, John E. Reid and Associates was awarded two federal contracts to specifically investigate behavioral differences between truthful and deceptive suspects outside of the polygraph environment.[2] In these two studies, a total of 80 videotaped interviews of actual suspects were prepared under different conditions that permitted trained evaluators to evaluate the subjects' verbal, paralinguistic, and nonverbal behaviors separately and together. In the second study, when evaluators were exposed to all three channels of communication, their average accuracy, excluding inconclusive opinions, was 86% for truthful suspects and 83% for deceptive subjects.[3] It should be pointed out that this finding was based on the evaluation of only 15 behavior-provoking questions asked during each interview, and that evaluators were not provided with any case information or background about the subjects.

The previously mentioned studies all utilized investigators with many years of experience in observing behavior symptoms. An important issue to address is whether persons without such experience can be trained to make behavioral assessments of criminal suspects. To investigate this question, a total of 53 college students with no previous training or experience in behavior symptom analysis were asked to evaluate ten videotaped interviews of verified deceptive or truthful suspects. Twenty-seven of these students then received six hours of training in behavior symptom analysis. These students, along with the 26 others who received no such training, then evaluated the ten videotaped interviews a second time. The students who did not receive any training in behavior symptom analysis did not improve their ability to identify truthful or deceptive subjects. However, those who received training significantly increased their accuracy in identifying truthful and deceptive suspects, with an average accuracy of 82%.[4]

Not all research conducted in the area of behavior symptom analysis has produced such favorable results. One such study was reported by Kraut and Poe.[5] Videotaped interviews of 62 volunteer suspects were evaluated by 49 laypeople and 39 customs inspectors. Half of the "suspects" were instructed to lie about possessing contraband, and the other half were instructed to tell the truth. Neither lay judges nor the customs inspectors were able to identify truth-tellers from liars above chance levels.

In a similar study, Kohnken had 80 police officers review videotaped interviews of college students who were instructed to either tell the truth or lie about a crime scene they witnessed.[6] Even after receiving specific training in behavior symptom analysis, the police officers were not able to identify which college students were telling the truth and which were lying.

In a third laboratory-based study, Ekman and O'Sullivan selected ten 1-minute videotapes of women who were instructed to either lie or tell the truth about their feelings concerning a viewing of a traumatic event.[7] The videotapes were evaluated by members of various groups who have a professional interest in detecting deception, including the U.S. Secret Service, federal polygraph examiners, police officers, judges, and psychiatrists. Only the Secret Service agents were able to identify truth and deception above chance levels (64%).

The laboratory research findings, which fail to demonstrate any statistical significance of detecting truth or deception, have two important distinctions from the previously mentioned field studies: (1) "Suspects" were given the task of playing the role of an innocent or guilty person, and (2) there was no effort to duplicate questioning techniques used in studies investigating actual criminal suspects.

In general, research based on artificially motivating subjects to lie or tell the truth has not demonstrated significant accuracies for behavior-based assessments.

It would appear that a suspect's motivation to avoid real consequences of having deception detected, or the failure to have their truthfulness revealed, plays an instrumental role in behavior analysis. In addition, laboratory-based studies do not utilize a structured interview approach, as was used in all of the previously mentioned field research involving actual criminal suspects. The effectiveness of a structured, clinical approach to the interview process was apparent in the previously mentioned field study involving 53 college students. During their initial evaluation of the ten behavior analysis interviews, the students' average accuracy was above chance levels.

Underlying Principles of Behavior Analysis

verbal channel word choice and arrangement of words to send a message.

paralinguistic channel characteristics of speech falling outside of the spoken word.

nonverbal channel posture; arm and leg movements; eye contact; and facial expressions.

To appreciate the role that observing behavior symptoms plays in detecting deception, it must be realized that there are three distinctly different channels in which we communicate:

- Verbal channel: Word choice and arrangement of words to send a message
- Paralinguistic channel: Characteristics of speech falling outside of the spoken word
- Nonverbal channel: Posture, arm and leg movements, eye contact, and facial expressions

These channels can work together to send the same message, or conversely, to send conflicting messages. Behavior analysis involves the study of inferences made from these behavioral observations.

A number of basic principles are involved in behavior analysis.

1. **There are no unique behaviors associated with truthfulness or deception.** The behavioral observations an investigator makes of a suspect do not specifically correlate to truth or deception. Rather, they reflect the subject's internal emotional state during a response. These emotions can range from anger, confidence, and certainty to fear, guilt, apprehension, or embarrassment. Clearly, some of these emotions are more closely associated with truthfulness (confidence, certainty, conviction) and others with deception (fear, guilt, apprehension, conflict). Behavior analysis, therefore, involves making inferences about a subject's truthfulness based on behavioral observations, none of which is unique to truth-telling or lying.
2. **Evaluate all three channels of communication simultaneously.** When the three channels of communication each send the same message, the investigator can have high confidence in believing the subject's verbal message. However, when inconsistencies exist between the three channels, the investigator needs to evaluate possible causes for this inconsistency.

   The two subjects illustrated in **Figures 7-1** and **7-2** were both asked, "How do you think our investigation will come out on you?" to which they both responded, "I'm sure it will show my innocence." The subject pictured in Figure 7-1 is communicating high confidence nonverbally. However, the nonverbal behavior of the subject in Figure 7-2 reflects uncertainty. This subject is sending inconsistent messages.
3. **Evaluate paralinguistic and nonverbal behaviors in context with the subject's verbal message.** To assess the probable meaning of a subject's emotional state,

Figure 7-1 Nonverbal behavior supportive of a verbal response.

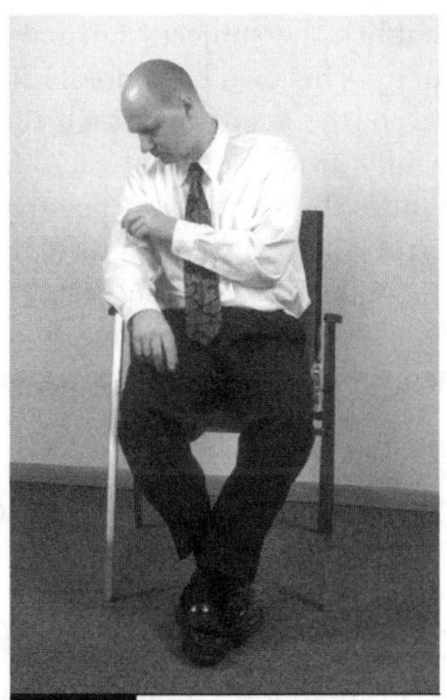

Figure 7-2 Nonverbal behavior contradicting a verbal response.

a subject's paralinguistic and nonverbal behaviors must always be considered along with the verbal message. Consider the following two examples:

Q1: "Mike, have you ever been questioned before concerning theft from an employer?"

A1: "Well, um, two years ago I worked at a hardware store and they had an inventory shortage, so all of the employees were questioned, and, in fact, I did take some things from there." [Subject crosses his legs, looks down at the floor and dusts his shirt sleeve.]

Q2: "Joe, did you steal that missing $2,500?"

A2: "No, I did not." [Subject crosses his legs, looks down at the floor and dusts his shirt sleeve.]

These two subjects are displaying identical nonverbal behaviors during their responses. However, the interpretation of the behaviors is completely different. In the first example, the subject is telling the truth, but feels embarrassed and possibly even threatened by revealing his prior theft. In the second example, the verbal content of the subject's response does not explain the accompanying nonverbal behaviors, so the investigator should consider these behaviors as reflecting possible fear or conflict: emotional states that would not be considered appropriate for a truthful subject, given the content of the verbal response.

4. **Evaluate the preponderance of behaviors occurring throughout the interview.** One of the findings of the previously mentioned research is the importance of rendering opinions based on an evaluation of the subject's behavior throughout the course of an entire interview. When evaluators were exposed only to individual questions within the interview, their accuracy was considerably less than when they evaluated the subject's responses to all 15 questions. Similarly, the likelihood of correctly assessing behavior over a 5-minute interview will be considerably less than if the behavioral assessments are made over a 30- or 40-minute interview.

5. **Establish the subject's normal behavioral patterns.** Each person interviewed will have his own behavioral idiosyncrasies: the way they gesture, their style of speech, the degree to which they establish eye contact, and so forth. Consequently, at the outset of each interview the investigator should spend several minutes discussing nonthreatening information (perhaps in casual conversation or collecting biographical information) so as to establish a behavioral baseline for the particular subject. Then, as the interview progresses and the subject exhibits behavioral changes when the issue under investigation is discussed, these changes may take on added significance.

Evaluating the Subject's Attitudes

attitude a predisposed expectation toward a situation or event; during an interview with a criminal investigator, it is based on the subject's knowledge of his guilt or innocence with respect to the issue under investigation.

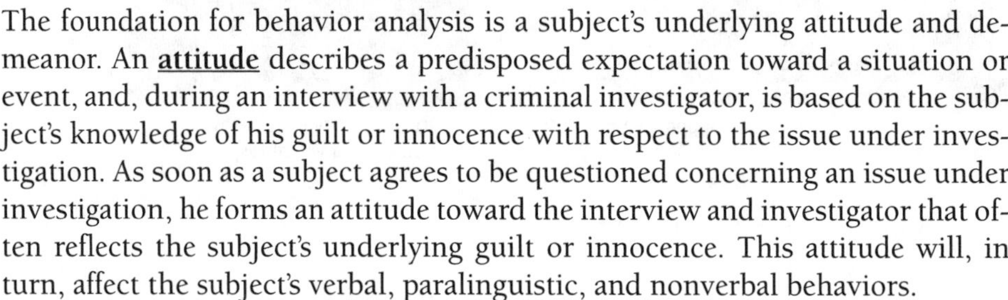

The foundation for behavior analysis is a subject's underlying attitude and demeanor. An attitude describes a predisposed expectation toward a situation or event, and, during an interview with a criminal investigator, is based on the subject's knowledge of his guilt or innocence with respect to the issue under investigation. As soon as a subject agrees to be questioned concerning an issue under investigation, he forms an attitude toward the interview and investigator that often reflects the subject's underlying guilt or innocence. This attitude will, in turn, affect the subject's verbal, paralinguistic, and nonverbal behaviors.

To illustrate the relationship between attitudes and behavior, consider two people sitting in the front lobby of a dentist's office. One person is a patient scheduled for dental surgery, and the other is a mother waiting for her child who is getting his teeth cleaned. These two people have different attitudes concerning their presence in the waiting room and, because of that, will predictably engage in different behaviors. The mother may chat at ease with the receptionist or become engaged in a magazine article while she sits in a relaxed posture in the chair. The patient, on the other hand, may pace the floor, pick up a magazine, and absentmindedly flip through the pages without reading any particular article. At the sound of a door opening, the patient may show a startle reaction, looking toward the doctor's suite while frequently checking his watch.

personality fairly rigid and inflexible traits that are not condition specific.

An attitude, as we are using the term, psychologically influences an individual's attention, perceptions, thoughts, and ideas, which, in turn, are reflected in the person's behavior and emotions. This term should not be confused with personality, which consists of fairly rigid and inflexible traits and is not condition specific. An attitude is developed around an individual's expectations of a specific situation or event.

Based on our years of observation, as well as specific research findings, we can offer the following guidelines regarding attitudes.

Attitudes Most Commonly Seen in Truthful Versus Deceptive Subjects During an Interview

Spontaneous vs. Guarded

The truthful subject offers longer responses during an interview, volunteers information, and gives responses that are free-flowing. The deceptive subject, on the other hand, may offer very short responses containing only minimal information. This guarded attitude may represent the deceptive suspect's caution so as not to be caught in a contradictory statement or may merely be an anxiety-relieving effort to avoid telling unnecessary lies in response to a question.

Sincere vs. Insincere

The truthful subject openly expresses appropriate emotional states. If the subject is upset, anxious, or concerned, these emotions will be communicated on all three channels. Some deceptive subjects, on the other hand, will come across as phony during an interview, often being overly friendly and polite to the investigator. They may start the interview with a handshake and flatter the investigator in some manner, perhaps by complimenting the investigator's suit or mentioning the name of a fellow police officer. The insincere subject sells his innocence as if it were a product, while the sincere subject states his innocence as an irrefutable fact.

The insincere subject sells his innocence as if it were a product, while the sincere subject states his innocence as an irrefutable fact.

Helpful vs. Unhelpful

The truthful subject is as anxious as the investigator is to catch the guilty person. Consequently, he will openly discuss possible suspects and motives and speculate about how the crime may have been committed. These assessments will be realistic and well founded. The last thing a deceptive suspect wants to do is to help the investigation. Therefore, deceptive suspects are reluctant to talk about possible suspects or people who could be eliminated from suspicion. The deceptive suspect may even take the position that no crime was committed (e.g., the disappearance of money was a paperwork error, a fire was caused by electrical problems, etc.) and offer unrealistic explanations to explain away obvious facts.

Concerned vs. Unconcerned

The truthful suspect comes across as very concerned during an interview. He approaches the interview in a serious manner and pays close attention to the interviewer's questions—after all, his reputation, possible livelihood, and freedom are at stake. The deceptive suspect, however, may approach the interview quite nonchalantly and downplay the significance of being a suspect in the investigation. The deceptive suspect may engage in levity or answer questions inappropriately because he is not paying close attention to the interviewer's questions.

A telling difference between the truthful suspect and the deceptive suspect is that the truthful suspect will have given much thought about the guilty person—who that person might be, why and how he committed the crime—and will express harsh judgments toward the person guilty of committing the crime. The deceptive suspect, of course, has not gone through that same thought process. When asked to speculate about the person who committed the crime, the deceptive suspect may simply state that he has not given that issue much thought; he feels uncomfortable providing insight regarding the crime he committed. For much the same reason, he is unlikely to express harsh judgments against the guilty person.

Cooperative vs. Uncooperative

A truthful suspect perceives the interview as an opportunity to be exonerated, either by answering the investigator's questions truthfully or by providing information that may be helpful in catching the guilty person. Consequently, truthful suspects generally agree to be interviewed, will keep their interview appointment, and will provide reasonable documentation such as phone bills, parking stubs, or a bank statement to support their statements. During the interview they openly respond to the investigator's inquires and make no attempt to rush the process. The deceptive suspect, on the other hand, may offer weak excuses as to why he is unavailable to be interviewed or may fail to show up for scheduled interviews. During the interview itself, the deceptive suspect may present a variety of complaints, ranging from the length of the interview to the room temperature being too warm or cold. The deceptive suspect is unlikely to follow through with promised documentation requested by the investigator.

Evaluation of Verbal Behavior

A subject who is properly socialized and mentally healthy will experience anxiety when he lies. This anxiety may result from internal conflict, from knowing that his response is not the truth, or from fear of the lie being detected. Whatever the source, during an interview, lies result in anxiety, and many of the behavior symptoms revealed by a deceptive suspect represent conscious or preconscious efforts to reduce this internal anxiety. This fundamental concept forms the basis for evaluating a subject's verbal, paralinguistic, and nonverbal behaviors. In essence, the mind and the body work together to relieve the anxiety associated with a lie.

We can all relate to the common experience of having to lie to someone over the phone. For example, a boss may instruct a secretary that if a particular person calls to not put the call through. When the person does call, the secretary certainly does not want to tell the person the complete truth, "Mr. Buckley doesn't want to talk to you," so she must lie. She could tell any number of lies, such as, "He was hospitalized this morning," "He's no longer with this firm," or "He's out of town." But these are "big" lies that unnecessarily generate a great deal of anxiety, especially if detailed follow-up information is requested. Most likely, she will choose a verbal response that causes the least amount of internal anxiety, such as, "I'm sorry, he's on the other line" or, better yet, "He's not available right now." Even the slight anxiety these responses cause may result in tell-tale paralinguistic behaviors, such as a delay before responding, or nonverbal behaviors, such as a change in posture or a hand coming in contact with the face. Each of these behaviors, in their own way, helps reduce the secretary's internal anxiety experienced because of lying.

As the response moves farther from the truth, a subject will experience more and more internal anxiety as a result of the deception.

When a deceptive subject is asked a direct question during an interview, he has essentially four verbal response options from which to choose. **Table 7-1** illustrates these options, along with the important role internal anxiety plays in selecting a verbal response.

truthful response a statement that reflects the truth and, therefore, does not cause any internal anxiety as a result of deception.

A <u>**truthful response**</u>, which may be a statement such as "Yes, I did" or "No, I didn't," does not cause internal anxiety as a result of deception. However, as the response moves further from the truth, the subject experiences more and more internal anxiety as a result of his deception.

Table 7-1 Verbal Response Options

"Did you [do issue]?"		
A	↑	Deception: "No, I did not."
N		
X		Evasion: "Why would I do something like that?"
I		
E		Omission: Shakes head "no."
T		
Y		Truth: "Yes, I did."

An **omissive response** may consist of a nonverbal response alone or a verbal answer that accepts physical responsibility for the act but denies criminal intentions ("I may have done it accidentally"). A suspect guilty of child molestation may acknowledge touching the child's private parts for hygienic purposes or inadvertently. Because this is an omissive position, the subject does not experience much internal anxiety associated with his response.

omissive response a response that may consist of a nonverbal response alone or a verbal answer that accepts physical responsibility for an act but denies criminal intentions.

evasive response a response that implies innocence without stating it.

deceptive response a response that is associated with the greatest level of internal anxiety.

The next level, an **evasive response**, implies innocence without stating it. The suspect is not lying, but is also not accepting any physical responsibility within his response. Therefore, the subject experiences more internal anxiety through evasion than omission. Finally, the subject may choose to lie to the question outright. A **deceptive response** is associated with the greatest level of internal anxiety.

It is a tenet of human behavior that anxiety is unwelcome and undesirable. Therefore, whenever possible during an interview, a suspect will engage in behaviors that reduce the level of internal anxiety experienced. With respect to verbal response options, if given a choice, the guilty subject would much rather engage in evasion or omission than outright deception. The truthful suspect, who experiences no conflict or fear from his response, expresses his responses in a definitive and emphatic manner.

Guidelines for Evaluating a Suspect's Verbal Response to an Interview Question

Truthful Subjects Respond to Questions Directly; Deceptive Subjects May Answer Evasively

Consider the following two responses to this question posed to a homicide suspect: "When is the last time that you saw Tom Smith?"

> R1: "It was Friday at about 5:30. I drove Tom home from work because we car pool and that was my night to drive. I dropped him off at his house right around 5:30. That's the last time I saw him alive."
>
> R2: "Tom and I car pool and Friday was my day to drive so I drove him home from work and I arrived at his house right around 5:30."

The first response offers a definitive response to the investigator's question: The investigator knows exactly what time the subject is claiming to have last seen the victim. However, the second response merely *implies* that the last time the subject saw the victim was 5:30. This subject's response leaves open the possibility that he saw the victim later that night, that he came into the victim's house with him, or that he never actually dropped the victim off. Deceptive subjects rely extensively on implication during verbal responses. The subject hopes that the investigator will make unwarranted assumptions about what he probably meant or intended to say. A rule we have previously presented is worth reiterating: If the subject does not state that something happened, the investigator should not make the assumption that it did.[8]

A second common type of evasive response is answering a question with a question. When a subject responds, "Why would I do that?" "Do you think I would risk going to jail by doing that?" or "Don't you think that would be a little ridiculous of me?" the investigator must recognize that the subject has not offered a definitive denial.

lying by referral a response based on an earlier communication in order to avoid lying.

A final type of evasive response is called **lying by referral.** Consider the following dialogue, in which the subject is guilty of stealing a car:

Q: "Did you steal a blue Monte Carlo last Saturday night?"

R: "That other cop already asked me that. Like I told him, I don't know nothing about this."

Even though this subject did steal the car, he has not lied at all during his response. Another police officer did ask him that question, and the subject told the officer that he didn't know anything about the stolen car. What the suspect failed to include in his response is that he lied to the other officer. Whenever a response is predicated on some earlier communication, such as, "Like I wrote in my statement," "As I previously testified," or "You already asked me that and I told you before," the investigator should suspect lying by referral.

Truthful Subjects May Deny Broadly; Deceptive Subjects May Offer Specific Denials

A truthful subject feels much more confident using broad and descriptive language during a denial than a deceptive subject does. Therefore, the following phrases would more often be used by truthful subjects:

"I'm absolutely sure"	"I didn't steal anything"
"I'm positive"	"I've never raped a woman in my life"
"There's no way"	"I had nothing whatsoever to do with this robbery"

As a caveat to this statement, it should be recognized that this behavior symptom only applies to spontaneous interview situations. Prepared statements containing broad language, such as those delivered to a media interviewer (e.g., "I had absolutely nothing whatsoever to do with this heinous crime!") may be nothing more than a guilty suspect's carefully thought-out (or prompted) rehearsed response.

During a spontaneous interview, deceptive subjects, on the other hand, may deny some **narrow aspect** of the interviewer's question. It must be remembered that the deceptive subject knows exactly what the truth is. If he can truthfully deny some narrow aspect of the crime, thereby implying total innocence, he will. The investigator should listen carefully to what the subject is *not* denying. The following are examples of specific denials heard from the guilty:

The investigator should listen carefully to what the subject is not denying.

Q1: "Did you steal that night deposit?"

R1: "I did not steal that deposit bag!"

Q2: "Did you steal money from a man outside of the Stop and Go?"

R2: "I don't have that man's money!"

Q3: "Did you point a handgun at a man outside the Stop and Go?"

R3: "I don't even own any handguns!"

In the first example, the subject may very well have disposed of the deposit bag after the theft. He is not denying stealing the money inside the bag. The subject in the second example probably spent the money and is therefore telling the truth when he denies having any of it. In the third example, the subject may have stolen the handgun or borrowed it from a friend. He is not denying using the handgun, only that he owns one.

Truthful Subjects Offer Confident and Definitive Responses. Deceptive Subjects May Offer Qualified Responses.

A truthful denial will stand on its own, and it will be clear that the subject is accepting full responsibility within his response. On the other hand, deceptive subjects may use phrases that qualify the response, thereby weakening it. One type of **qualified response** is called a **generalization statement**. If the investigator specifically asks the subject what he did at a particular point in time, the deceptive subject may use the following phrases to make the response truthful:

qualified response phrase added to a response to weaken it.

generalization statement one type of qualifying phrase used to respond truthfully but deceptively to a question about a particular point in time. These statements often begin with phrases such as "As a rule" or "Generally."

"As a rule"	"Generally"
"Typically"	"As a matter of habit"
"I like to"	"The policy states"

Consider the subject who is asked, "Were you inside the B&B tavern at all on Saturday night?" and responds, "When I go out on Saturdays I usually go to the Breakaway because that's where most of my friends hang out." Because the subject's response includes the generalization statement "usually," he has avoided lying to the investigator.

A second category of qualifying phrases is **memory qualifiers**, which blame memory. Because memory does not exist in a measurable sense and, of course, cannot be seen, a deceptive subject may reduce anxiety by blaming a poor memory. He realizes that it is impossible to prove what a person did or did not remember at a particular point in time. Some common phrases within this category include the following:

memory qualifier another type of qualifying phrase that blames a poor memory in order to bend a response in the subject's favor. These answers often begin with phrases such as "As far as I recall" or "At this point in time."

"As far as I recall"	"At this point in time"
"To the best of my knowledge"	"If my memory is correct"
"As far as I know"	"I can't recall whether"

With respect to memory qualifiers, the investigator must evaluate these phrases relative to the question asked. If the question requires the subject to rely

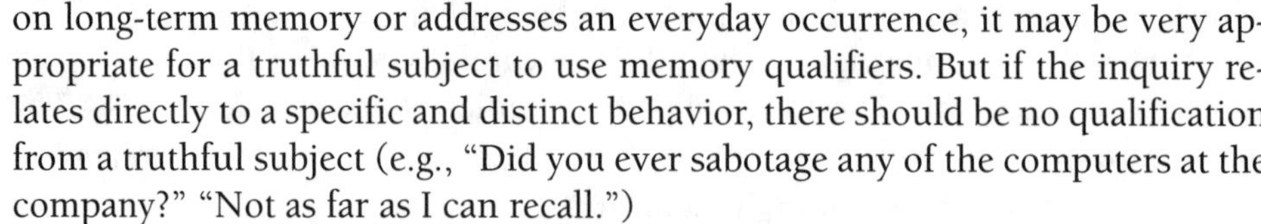

on long-term memory or addresses an everyday occurrence, it may be very appropriate for a truthful subject to use memory qualifiers. But if the inquiry relates directly to a specific and distinct behavior, there should be no qualification from a truthful subject (e.g., "Did you ever sabotage any of the computers at the company?" "Not as far as I can recall.")

omission qualifier qualifying phrase indicating that the subject is omitting part of his answer within his response. Examples of omission qualifiers include "Hardly ever" and "Not often."

A third category of this type of response is **omission qualifiers**. These phrases indicate that the subject is omitting part of his answer within his response. Examples of omission qualifiers include the following:

"Hardly ever"	"Not often"
"Not really"	"Mostly"
"Rarely"	"Nothing much"
"Pretty much"	"Nothing of significance"

When an investigator asks the subject, "Did you and Gloria have an argument last Friday night?" and the subject responds, "We rarely argue," not only has the subject evaded a direct response but he has also acknowledged that, at least occasionally, he and Gloria do argue.

As a final category of qualifying phrases, consider the following two statements:

"I would have to say no"

"My answer would be that I did not."

estimation phrase phrase that tells the investigator that the subject is providing an estimation, rather than an exact statement. These may be appropriately heard from truthful or deceptive subjects.

These are called **estimation phrases** because they tell the investigator that the subject is providing an estimation, rather than an exact statement. Estimation phrases may be appropriately heard from truthful or deceptive subjects. The key is to evaluate the response in relation to the type of question asked. For example, if the investigator asks, "What time did you arrive home last night?" the subject might respond, "I would have to say 10:15." This phrase becomes inappropriate when the subject uses it in responding to a more concrete question, such as, "Were you inside a stolen car at all last night?" to which the subject responds, "My answer would be no." The subject should know whether or not he was inside a stolen car, and the fact that he is estimating that he was not should be viewed suspiciously.

A Deceptive Denial May be Bolstered to Make it Sound More Credible

A truthful denial will be vocalized, such as, "I didn't have anything to do with starting that fire." A deceptive denial, on the other hand, may be merely implied, where the subject offers a weak, "Uh, huh" or just shakes his head "no" and denies on the nonverbal level only.

Sometimes a deceptive subject feels the need to strengthen or bolster his denial to make it sound more convincing. A truthful subject will allow his denial to stand on its own. The following phrases are commonly used to bolster a deceptive denial:

"As God as my witness"	"I swear"
"On my mother's grave"	"Honestly!"

statement against self-interest statement that decreases anxiety by alerting the investigator to the true intent behind a statement.

Another strategy the deceptive subject may use to reduce anxiety within a false statement is to introduce the lie with a **statement against self-interest**. Each of us has been in a conversation where the other person makes the statement, "Not to change the subject, but . . ." It is very clear what this person is about to do—change the subject. Declarations against self-interest are used to ease the guilt or anxiety that would otherwise result from the statement the person is planning to make. Consider each of the following:

"As crazy as it sounds . . ."

"Not to evade your question, but . . ."

"I don't know if this is true, but . . ."

"I don't want to implicate anyone, but . . ."

"You may not believe this, but . . ."

Statements against self-interest decrease anxiety by alerting the investigator to the true intent behind a statement. For example, in the last statement the subject is explaining to the investigator that the response he is about to make is not credible; therefore, the subject feels less anxiety when offering the lie.

Truthful Subjects Will Offer Spontaneous Responses. Deceptive Subjects May Offer Rehearsed Responses

In preparation for an interview, truthful and deceptive subjects engage in different thought processes. As explained in the section on evaluating attitudes, the truthful subject's thoughts are focused on such things as who may have committed the crime, what that person's motivation may have been, and how the crime was committed. On the other hand, the deceptive subject's thoughts are oriented toward concerns about what evidence he may have left behind, what other people may have said about him, and whether or not he can lie convincingly. With respect to his ability to avoid detection, the deceptive subject may spend considerable time before the interview mentally rehearsing his responses. There are two verbal behaviors associated with rehearsed responses.

noncontracted denial a verbal behavior associated with rehearsed responses in which the subject does not use verb contractions when giving answers to questions.

The first of these is a **noncontracted denial**. During spontaneous dialogue, it is customary to contract verbs. For example, "No I didn't," "I don't know," or "I wouldn't have." On the other hand, when the subject responds with noncontracted denials, especially on multiple occasions during the interview, this is indicative of a rehearsed response, as the following excerpt from an interview of a confessed arsonist illustrates:

Q: "Did you start that fire at the Dungeon Lounge?"

R: "No, I did not."

Q: "Do you know who started that fire?"

R: "No, I do not."

Q: "Were you at the Dungeon Lounge at all last Sunday morning?"

R: "No, I was not."

listing using a response that is offered as a list of possibilities—(a), (b), (c) or (1), (2), (3)— indicating that the subject has anticipated the question and spent time formulating credible explanations, particularly if it occurs during the initial interview.

A second example of a rehearsed response is called **listing**. A response that is offered as a list of possibilities—(a), (b), (c) or (1), (2), (3)—is an indication that the subject has anticipated the question and spent time formulating credible explanations, particularly if it occurs during the initial interview. In the previous arson example, which was taken from an actual interview, the subject was asked, "Why wouldn't you start this fire?" The subject's response was, "Well, number one, the owners of the bar are friends of mine. Second, I'm already on probation and don't need more trouble from the police, and third, I'd have nothing to gain by doing it, that I know of." Following an interrogation, the subject confessed to starting the fire after the son of the tavern owner agreed to pay him from the insurance settlement.

Evaluation of Paralinguistic Behavior

There are a number of speech characteristics during a subject's verbal response that can alter the meaning of the words. As a common example of this, we have all heard a friend or co-worker make a sarcastic remark. Based on the pitch or tone of the comment, we know that the person does not really mean what was said. The paralinguistic channel of communication is under less conscious control than the verbal channel. It also is not as easily contaminated by outside factors as the nonverbal channel is. Consequently, paralinguistic cues during an interview may be the best source of detecting deception for a criminal investigator.

Paralinguistic cues may be the best source of detecting deception for a criminal investigator.

response latency the length of time between the last word of the interviewer's question and the first word of the subject's response.

Response Latency

Response latency is defined as the length of time between the last word of the interviewer's question and the first word of the subject's response. During the earlier-mentioned study, response latencies were measured; the average latency for truthful subjects was 0.5 second, whereas the average latency for deceptive subjects was 1.5 seconds. Clearly, delayed responses to a straightforward question should be considered suspicious. A subject should not have to deliberate on how to respond to a question such as "Did you have sexual contact with any of your stepchildren?"

Because normal response latencies vary with different subjects, the investigator should establish at the outset of the interview how long it takes the subject to respond to straightforward questions such as his address, the name of his employer, and the number of children he has. Once the subject's "normal" latency has been established, the investigator can identify latencies that are abnormally long for the particular subject.

Deceptive subjects are often aware of their delayed latencies to the interviewer's questions and may attempt to disguise the delay through stalling tactics. A common strategy in this regard is to repeat the interviewer's question or to ask for a simply worded question to be clarified. The following dialogue illustrates this behavior:

Q: "Did you have sexual contact with any of your stepchildren?"

R: ". . . Did I have sexual contact with them? Um, no."

Q: "Did you show them photographs of nude girls?"

R: "Um . . . what, what exactly do you mean?"

During both of these responses, the subject has bought time to formulate exactly how he should respond to the interviewer's question. A truthful suspect would not attempt to buy such time.

Early Responses

Another category of paralinguistic behavior related to timing is a response offered before the interviewer finishes asking the question. A truthful subject who is somewhat nervous may offer early responses, especially at the beginning of the interview. This is simply the result of the subject's general anxiety. Such early responses from the truthful subject will be repeated after the interviewer finishes asking the question.

Early responses from the deceptive subject are often not repeated. Once the subject voices his denial, in the subject's mind he has answered the question, even though the investigator has not completely finished asking it. It is an especially reliable sign of deception when an early response occurs during the middle or end of an interview; by that time, general nervous tension from the truthful subject should have subsided and any early response is likely coming from the deceptive person anxious to get a prepared lie out of his mouth.

Response Length

Statistically, truthful subjects offer longer responses to interview questions than deceptive subjects do. The truthful subject wants to respond completely to the question and often volunteers more information than the question calls for. The content of the truthful subject's more lengthy response will stay on track with the interviewer's question; he doesn't start out saying one thing and divert the interviewer's attention away from his initial response by talking off the subject.

Some deceptive subjects, on the other hand, may offer the minimal amount of information within their response—just enough to satisfy the investigator's question. Such a subject is concerned that if he offers too much information he may contradict himself or other evidence that exists. Talking is a natural behavior to relieve anxiety, and some deceptive subjects may ramble on in their response. In this instance, the subject's answer is likely to get off track by the time the response is complete. The following two actual responses, the first from a truthful subject and the second from a deceptive one, illustrate this tendency.

> Q: "What is your understanding of the purpose of the interview with me today?"
>
> A1: "Well, on the 25th I balanced my cash drawer and it was $1,000 short. I went through all of my transactions but couldn't find an error. I then called over Peter, my supervisor, and together we reviewed everything. I even took the back of the drawer apart to see if money somehow got stuck behind it, but we couldn't find it. At this point I think someone stole it. They need to know if I'm being honest with them. And that's why I'm here. It's not that they don't trust me, its just, actually, I'm kind of happy this is being done because I can prove to them that I didn't steal it."
>
> Q: "What is your understanding of the purpose of the interview with me today?"
>
> A2: "Some money was missing out of Keith Jones' drawer and they're just interviewing everyone who worked that day."

Response Delivery

The subject's rate, pitch, and clarity during a response can be either consistent or inconsistent with the verbal content of what is said. A response said in sincere

clipped words a behavior symptom indicative of truthfulness where a response is delivered in staccato fashion, emphasizing each word.

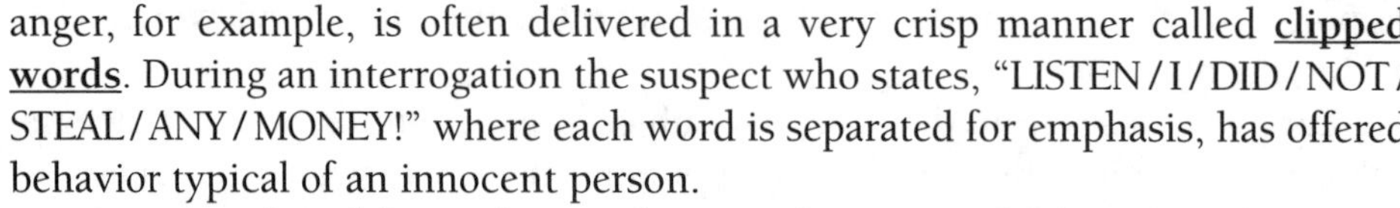

anger, for example, is often delivered in a very crisp manner called **clipped words**. During an interrogation the suspect who states, "LISTEN / I / DID / NOT / STEAL / ANY / MONEY!" where each word is separated for emphasis, has offered behavior typical of an innocent person.

As a general guideline, when a subject is relating a truthful emotional account, his rate and pitch will increase as the subject relives the event. On the other hand, when rate or pitch decrease this may mean the subject is editing information or is uncertain of what actually occurred. An alleged victim of a home invasion who relates the crime in a monotone, or even slows down his response delivery at certain points, is not offering a spontaneous account, and fabrication or omission should be suspected.

As a general guideline, when a subject is relating a truthful emotional account, his or her rate and pitch will increase as the subject relives the event.

A truthful subject wants the investigator to understand his responses and, therefore, will speak clearly and at an appropriate volume level. On the other hand, a deceptive subject may mumble during a response or talk so quietly that the investigator has difficulty hearing the response.

Continuity of the Response

stop-and-start behavior a significant paralinguistic behavior of deception, in which the subject begins a response in one direction but abruptly stops it and starts over again in a different direction.

A truthful response is spontaneous and free-flowing but will maintain continuity, in that one sentence or thought will naturally stem from the earlier one. A significant paralinguistic behavior of deception, however, is **stop-and-start behavior** in which the subject begins a response in one direction but abruptly stops it and starts over again in a different direction. The following is an example of stop-and-start behavior from the previously mentioned arson suspect:

> Q: "You understand the police are saying that you were asked to do this."
>
> R: "They [the police] told me that supposedly me and Thomas both done it which is a lie. I never even // I did not see Thomas on Saturday night."

We cannot be certain what the subject was about to say—perhaps "I never even started that fire" or "I never even saw Thomas at all." What we do know is that the subject did not feel comfortable completing that statement. To reduce anxiety within his intended response, he abruptly stopped and changed his statement to make it a specific denial that he did not see Thomas on Saturday night, which, as it turns out, was the truth. The subject met up with Thomas at a bar around 3:00 a.m. Sunday. Thomas agreed to pay him $2,000, and the suspect started the fire at 4:30 a.m.

Erasure Behavior

erasure behavior paralinguistic behavior that has the effect of "erasing" the implied connotation of the statement.

There are nonverbal behaviors we all use to send the listener the message, "I'm only kidding—don't take my statement seriously." A couple of these are the wink and the smile. The wink or smile has the effect of "erasing" the implied connotation of the statement. If a co-worker makes the remark, "I heard you coerced another innocent suspect to confess last night," the speaker's facial expression will tell the investigator whether or not the statement was said in jest.

Within paralinguistic communication there are specific **erasure behaviors** that can have the same effect as a wink or smile. These behaviors are laughs, coughs, or clearings of the throat immediately following a significant denial. The following dialogue is from a bank employee who eventually confessed to stealing $4,600 from cash deposits from the same customer.

Q: "Did you steal that customer's $4,600?"

R: "No." (laugh)

Q: "Do you know who did steal it?"

R: "I don't even know that it was stolen." (laugh)

Q: "Do you think a bank employee did steal this money?"

R: "That's hard to say, you know. The customer may have just made a mistake on his deposit slip, you know." (clear throat)

Q: "How do you think the results of our investigation will come out on you?"

R: "Well I hope it will come out, you know, okay . . . Because I know I didn't take that money." (laugh)

These laughs and clearings of the throat are significant only because they follow important denials the suspect made within his response. Certainly, truthful subjects will engage in laughter, clearing of the throat, or coughing during an interview for a variety of reasons, ranging from general nervousness to cold symptoms. These behaviors should only be considered a possible symptom of deception when they immediately follow a significant denial.

Evaluation of Nonverbal Behavior

As mentioned earlier, during deception, internal anxiety is experienced by the liar. The mind and body work together to relieve this anxiety. Physically, a person has three responses to a threatening situation: He can fight it, flee from it, or freeze, presumably to wait for the threat to pass. The first two responses (fight or flight) involve relieving anxiety through physical activity. The benefit of exercise for reducing general stress levels is a good example of physical activity relieving anxiety. The physical activity of exercise in some way appears to displace internal anxiety. A freeze response, wherein the person under stress experiences a feeling of numbness and emotional detachment, is also common during an intense threat. In this situation, the mind "turns the body off" so as to focus all efforts on intellectual activity. The result is a person who communicates only on the verbal level.

The true meaning of the spoken word may be amplified or modified by any one or more of many nonverbal cues, such as posture, gestures, facial expressions, and other bodily activities—hence, the commonplace expressions "Actions speak louder than words" and "Look me straight in the eye if you're telling the truth." In fact, according to various social studies, as much as 70% of a message communicated between persons occurs at the nonverbal level.

This statistic does not mean that the interpretation of nonverbal behavior is significantly more accurate than other channels; only that, in comparison to the other channels, nonverbal behavior contributes disproportionately to the ultimate message being communicated. Because nonverbal communication is most distantly removed from the verbal content of a message, it serves as a double-edged sword with respect to behavior analysis. On one hand, even practiced liars may be unable to control their deceptive nonverbal behaviors. But on the other hand, nonverbal behaviors are most subject to misinterpretation and may provide misleading clues, especially if read in isolation from the verbal content of the speaker's message.[9]

Evaluating Posture

During an interview, a subject's posture reveals his emotional involvement, confidence, and level of interest. A truthful subject should maintain a high level of emotional involvement, interest, and, of course, confidence in his statements. The truthful subject's posture will be upright in the chair, and he will align his body with the interviewer so as to assure direct communication. During important statements, the truthful subject may lean toward the interviewer to emphasize the statement. While the truthful subject may cross his legs, it will appear to be comfortable and natural, with relaxed muscles. During the course of a 30- or 45-minute interview, the truthful subject will assume a number of different postures. The transition from one posture to the next will appear to be very casual.

Figures 7-3 to **7-5** depict postures typical of truthfulness during interviews conducted in a nonsupportive environment. Note that if the environment is supportive to the subject, such as his home or office, the interpretation of the subject's posture may be less clear.

A deceptive subject, on the other hand, may slouch in the chair and appear somewhat distant and disinterested in the interviewing process. He may turn his torso away from the interviewer in a nonfrontally aligned posture. Some deceptive subjects may retreat from the interviewing environment and actually move their chair away from the interviewer's chair. A variation of this "retreating" posture is to tuck the feet under the chair or to sit on one's hands. The deceptive subject may cross his arms or legs in a tight fashion in which muscles are con-

Figure 7-3 Truthful forward posture.

Figure 7-4 Truthful frontally aligned posture.

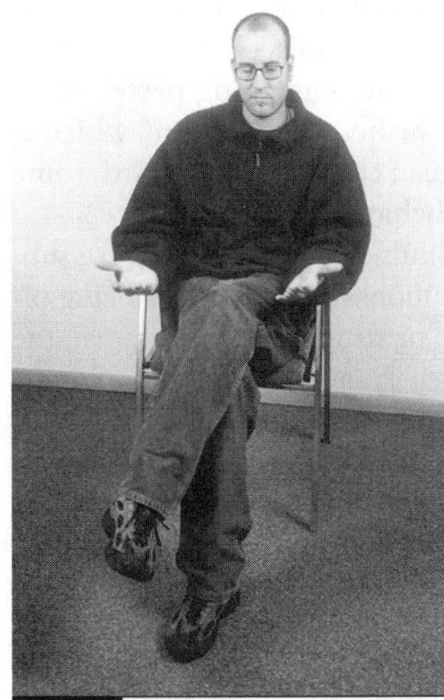
Figure 7-5 Truthful comfortable posture.

Figure 7-6 Deceptive nonfrontal alignment.

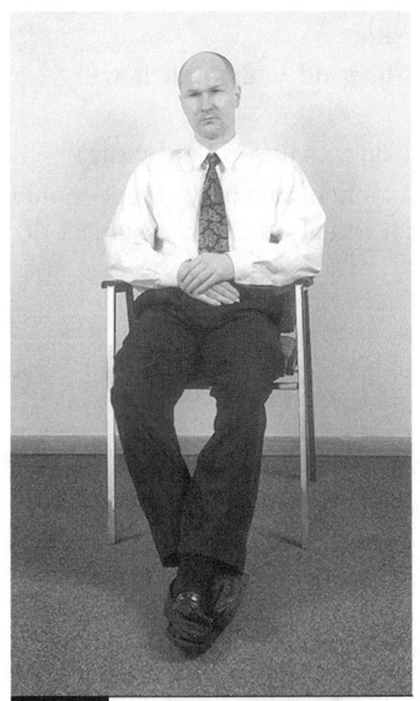
Figure 7-7 Deceptive slouching.

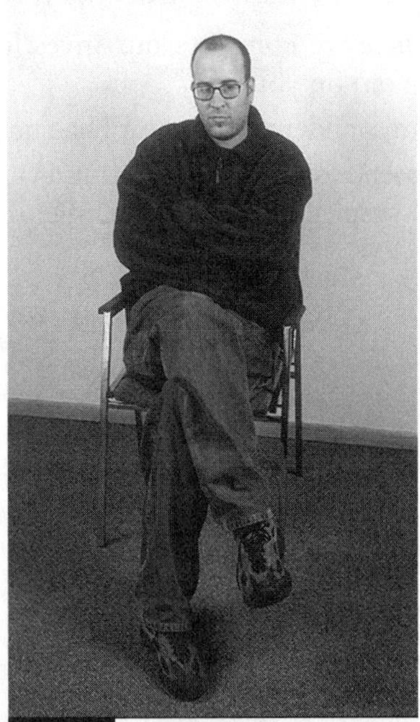
Figure 7-8 Deceptive barrier posture.

tracted. This crossing behavior forms a physical barrier against the interviewer because the subject feels vulnerable. One of the most telling behaviors of deception relating to posture is a static posture. In this instance the subject assumes an initial posture during the interview and remains essentially in it throughout the course of the interview. **Figures 7-6** to **7-8** depict some common deceptive postures.

Evaluating Hands

illustrating moving the hands away from the body and gesturing.

adaptor behavior putting the hands in contact with some part of the body.

hand shrug an illustrator with the specific meaning of "I don't know" or "I don't care." This behavior may involve one or both hands being slightly extended from the body with the palms turned upward.

During a response, a subject's hands can do one of three things. They can remain uninvolved and unmoving, which can be a sign that the subject lacks confidence in his verbal responses or is simply not talking about something perceived as very significant. The hands can move away from the body and gesture, which is called **illustrating** (**Figure 7-9**). Finally, the hands can come in contact with some part of the body, which is referred to as **adaptor behavior** (**Figure 7-11**).

Illustrators are more often associated with truthfulness. Especially when a subject is explaining a physical activity during an emotional event, such as being offered a bribe, raising an arm to thwart off a punch, or struggling with a rapist, the investigator should expect to see illustrators. In essence, the subject is not only verbally communicating what happened, but is also reliving the incident nonverbally.

The **hand shrug** (**Figure 7-10**) involves an illustrator with the specific meaning of "I don't know" or "I don't care." This behavior may involve one or both hands being slightly extended from the body with the palms turned upward. Often the subject's shoulder will also rise. The hand shrug may reinforce the subject's verbal response or contradict it. Consider the following two verbal responses, each accompanied with a hand shrug. The first would be indicative of truthfulness, the second of deception.

I: "Why do you think she's saying you did this to her?"

S: "I have no idea whatsoever." (hand shrug)

I: "Once we complete our investigation, how do you think it will come out on you?"

S: "I'm confident it will show I had nothing to do with this." (hand shrug)

The absence of illustrators during a victim's account of a robbery or rape should be viewed suspiciously.[10] For example, during an actual interview a subject de-

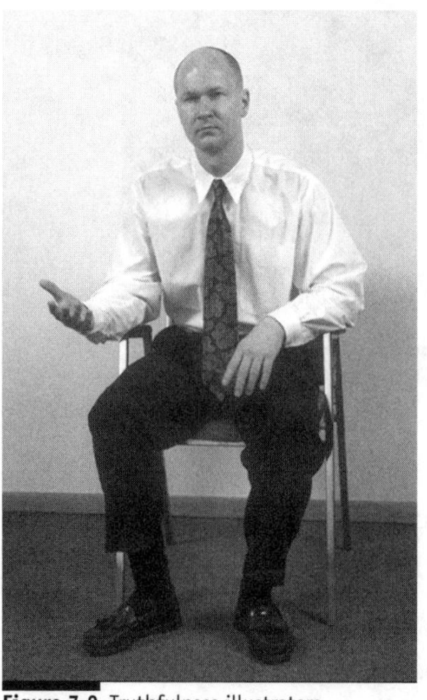

Figure 7-9 Truthfulness illustrators.

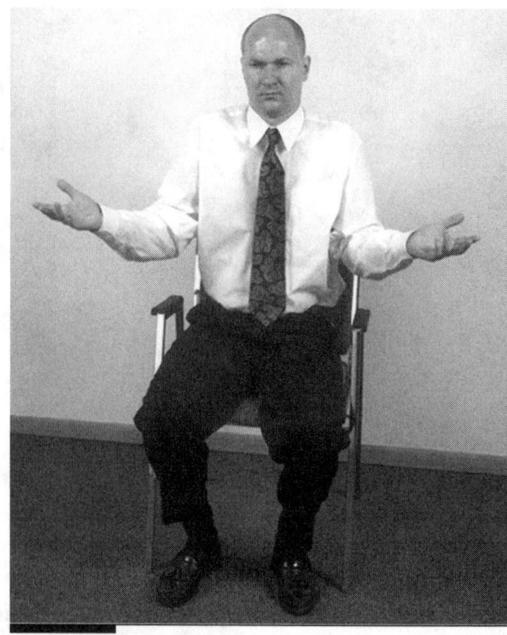

Figure 7-10 Hand shrug.

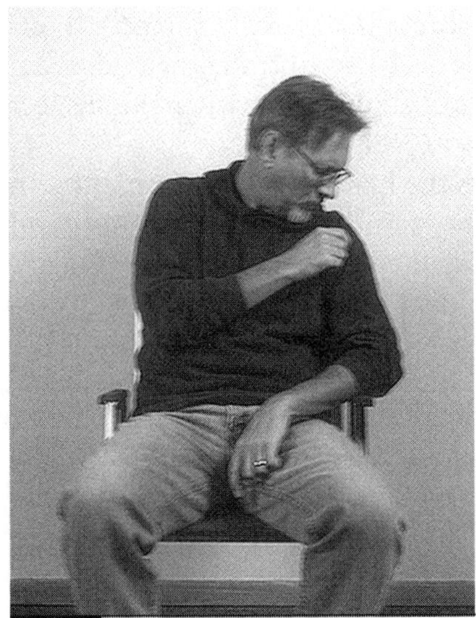

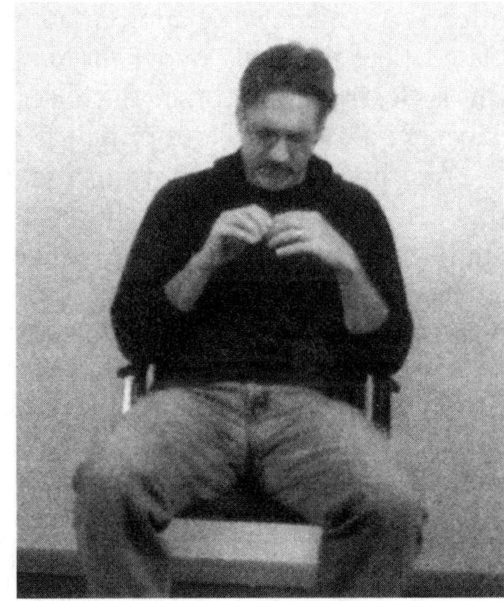

Figure 7-11 Deceptive adaptor behaviors.

scribed how a man approached his vehicle and demanded the cash deposit he was taking to the bank. The subject explained how he first tried to put the car in reverse and later held onto the door handle to prevent the robber's entry. Once the robber opened the door, the subject said, he and the man fought over the bank bag. Throughout this very emotional statement, the subject's hands remained passively uninvolved in his lap. Following an interrogation, the subject explained that he made up the story about being robbed and that he stole the cash deposit himself.

Adaptor behaviors are divided into a number of different categories. The first of these are called grooming gestures because they involve, in some manner, the subject's appearance. Examples of grooming behavior include picking lint from clothing, dusting clothing, inspecting fingernails, straightening hair, or pulling up socks. None of these behaviors, in and of themselves, means anything. However, when grooming behaviors occur in conjunction with a verbal response, the timing of the behavior can make it significant. A number of comedians, including Rodney Dangerfield and Johnny Carson, adjust the knot in their neck tie to emphasize the stress they are feeling. The gag works because of its timing.

grooming gestures adaptor behaviors that involve, in some manner, the subject's appearance.

personal gestures a gesture, which may involve the hand coming in contact with the body, that reflects the subject's own unique nonverbal manner of relieving anxiety.

A second category of adaptor behavior is called personal gestures. These gestures satisfy a biological need of some sort—for example, scratching, rubbing, wringing the hands, knuckle-popping, drumming fingers on a desk top, or pulling an ear lobe. The timing of such personal gestures may indicate that the subject is uncomfortable with his response or with the interviewer's question. These various nonverbal behaviors are termed "personal" because they tend to be unique to each person. When experiencing anxiety some people may pull their earlobes, others may bounce their foot and yet others may scratch the back of their neck. Because personal gestures are individually defined, an investigator must first establish a normative baseline for each suspect to identify how that particular person nonverbally responds during stress or anxiety.

The final category of adaptor behavior is called protective or supporting gestures. Supporting gestures bring the hand into contact with the face. In one such posture, the subject supports his head on the palm of his hand, resulting in a leaning posture. It reflects the subject's emotional detachment during the

protective or supporting gestures a final category of adaptor behavior involving gestures that bring the hand into contact with the face.

interview. This may be appropriate midway through a truthful subject's interview where the topic under discussion is relatively nonthreatening. However, this is clearly inappropriate during early stages of an interview when the suspect is being questioned about principal involvement in an offense.

Another example of a protective gesture is the hand covering the mouth. In this case, the subject, literally, is speaking through his fingers, as if his hand could grab, out of thin air, incriminating words the subject might utter. Finally, a deceptive subject may disguise poor eye contact by covering his eyes or rubbing his eyebrows with a hand while speaking.

Evaluating Feet

When a subject has his legs crossed with one knee over the other, he may bounce his foot. Ongoing foot-bouncing during an interview simply means the subject is generally anxious and should not be considered as an indication of deception. However, changes in foot-bouncing behavior—whether it be starting or stopping—that occur in conjunction with a verbal response can be a significant indication of deception. The behavior will last a second or two, and the subject will then resume his normal activity with his feet.

The feet are also involved in significant posture changes called *shifts in the chair.* With this behavior, the subject plants his feet and literally pushes his body up, slightly off the chair, to assume a new posture. Significant shifts in the chair of this nature are good indications of deception when they immediately precede or occur in conjunction with a subject's verbal response.

Facial Expressions and Eye Contact

A variety of facial expressions may be caused by a guilty suspect's fear of detection, uncertainty of success at evading detection, or perhaps an awareness that his deception has already been revealed and, therefore, he might just as well confess. The mere existence of variation of expressions may be suggestive of untruthfulness, whereas the lack of such variation may be suggestive of truthfulness. Of all the facial expressions, one of the most difficult to evaluate is that which reveals anger. (It is the subject of discussion in the following chapter.)

mutual gaze maintained eye contact.

One of the most important transmitters of nonverbal behavior symptoms is the degree of eye contact the suspect maintains with the investigator. In Western culture, **mutual gaze** (maintained eye contact) represents openness, candor, and trust. Deceptive suspects generally do not look directly at the investigator; they look down at the floor, over to the side, or up at the ceiling as if to beseech some divine guidance when answering questions. They feel less anxiety if their eyes are focused somewhere other than on the investigator; it is easier to lie while looking at the ceiling or floor. Consequently, they either try to avoid eye contact with the investigator by making compensatory moves or else they overact by staring at the investigator in a challenging manner.

Truthful suspects, on the other hand, are not defensive in their looks or actions and can easily maintain eye contact with the investigator. Even though they may be apprehensive, they show no concern about the credibility of their answers. Although attentive, their casual manner is unrestrained. They need no preparation because their answers are truthful. **Table 7-2** provides further guidelines regarding eye contact.

Table 7-2 Guidelines for Using Eye Contact to Assess a Suspect's Veracity

- **Generally speaking, a suspect who does not make direct eye contact is probably withholding information.** However, some consideration should be given to the possibility of an eye disability, inferiority complex, or emotional disorder, any of which may account for the avoidance of eye contact. Also, some cultural or religious customs consider it disrespectful for a person to look directly at an "authority figure." Background information on the suspect, of course, may alert the investigator regarding these or similar nondeceptive reasons for a lack of eye contact.
- **Under no circumstances should an investigator challenge the suspect to look him "straight in the eye."** Many lying suspects will accept the challenge and will very promptly do precisely that; they may even continue to stare at the investigator throughout the interrogation. Thus, the challenge and follow-up stare will destroy the chance for the display of any further meaningful behavior symptoms and may even render futile a continuation of the interrogation.
- **Instead of staring at the suspect, the investigator should somewhat casually observe his eyes and other behavior symptoms to avoid making the suspect feel uncomfortable.** A casual glance or two at the suspect's eyes followed by a sharp change in eye contact by the suspect will be sufficient to determine that he is purposely avoiding a direct look. It provides an effective method for observing eye movement without making the suspect aware that his behavior is being studied; otherwise, the individual may become more guarded in his actions, thus depriving the investigator of the observation opportunity.
- **An investigator should not expect a suspect to constantly look at him; in fact, it is unnatural for either party in a normal conversation to stare at each other with consistency.** It is very important, however, for the investigator to maintain casual eye contact with the suspect because the lying suspect himself may be watching the investigator for indications of insecurity or lack of confidence.
- **A suspect should not be permitted to wear dark glasses during the interview or interrogation unless there is a medical condition requiring their use indoors.** A suspect wearing dark glasses should be asked to remove them at the outset, and the investigator should then set them off to the side, out of reach. Dark glasses during an interview will conceal eye contact and thereby permit the suspect to develop a feeling of confidence in the effort to avoid detection. Most certainly, the investigator should not wear dark glasses because the suspect should be able to observe the appearance of sincerity and interest in the investigator's eyes, especially during an interrogation.
- **In general (and in loosely phrased terminology), a lying suspect's eyes will appear foggy, puzzled, probing, pleading (as though seeking pity), evasive or shifty, cold, hard, strained, or sneaky.** On the other hand, a truthful person's eyes will appear clear, bright, alert, warm, direct, easy, soft, and unprobing.

  The investigator should bear in mind, of course, that if the suspect's eyes look tired, this may be attributable to his having worked all night or, if guilty, to having lost much sleep by worrying or by rehearsing his story to avoid detection. Ordinarily, an innocent person who has worried about being questioned and thereby has lost sleep will probably reveal that fact to the investigator without being prompted to do so. A liar, on the other hand, is not apt to reveal his apprehension because of a concern about opening up another facet of suspicion to the investigator's scrutiny.

KEY POINTS

- People communicate through verbal, paralinguistic, and nonverbal channels. The investigator should carefully observe a subject's behavior in all three areas simultaneously.
- Physical activities of the lying suspect may be categorized into the following general types: Significant body movements, grooming gestures and cosmetic adjustments, and supportive gestures.
- When a suspect repeatedly engages in any of the foregoing nonverbal reactions in conjunction with verbal responses, that fact is a strong indication that the verbal response may not be truthful.
- It is exceedingly important—indeed critical—that a suspect's behavior symptoms be assessed in accordance with the following general guidelines: (1) Look for deviations from the suspect's normal behavior, and (2) evaluate all behavioral indications on the basis of when they occur (timing) and how often they occur (consistency).
- To be reliable indicators of truth or deception, behavioral changes should occur immediately in response to questions or simultaneously with the suspect's answers. Furthermore, similar behavioral responses should occur on a consistent basis whenever the same subject matter is discussed.
- As a subject's responses move further from the truth, the subject experiences more and more internal anxiety.
- Deceptive subjects may answer questions with evasive, qualified, or rehearsed responses, or they may offer specific denials rather than broad ones.
- Behavior areas to watch include the following: response latency, early responses, response length, response delivery, continuity of response, and erasure behavior.

KEY TERMS

adaptor behavior Putting the hands in contact with some part of the body.

attitude A predisposed expectation toward a situation or event; during an interview with a criminal investigator, it is based on the subject's knowledge of his guilt or innocence with respect to the issue under investigation.

clipped words A behavior symptom indicative of truthfulness where a response is delivered in staccato fashion, emphasizing each word.

deceptive response A response that is associated with the greatest level of internal anxiety.

erasure behavior Paralinguistic behavior that has the effect of "erasing" the implied connotation of the statement.

estimation phrase Phrase that tells the investigator that the subject is providing an estimation, rather than an exact statement. These may be appropriately heard from truthful or deceptive subjects.

evasive response A response that implies innocence without stating it.

generalization statement One type of qualifying phrase used to respond truthfully but deceptively to a question about a particular point in time. These statements often begin with phrases such as "As a rule" or "Generally."

grooming gestures Adaptor behaviors that involve, in some manner, the subject's appearance.

hand shrug An illustrator with the specific meaning of "I don't know" or "I don't care." This behavior may involve one or both hands being slightly extended from the body with the palms turned upward.

illustrating Moving the hands away from the body and gesturing.

listing Using a response that is offered as a list of possibilities—(a), (b), (c) or (1), (2), (3)—indicating that the subject has anticipated the question and spent time formulating credible explanations, particularly if it occurs during the initial interview.

lying by referral A response based on an earlier communication in order to avoid lying.

memory qualifier Another type of qualifying phrase that blames a poor memory in order to bend a response in the subject's favor. These answers often begin with phrases such as "As far as I recall" or "At this point in time."

mutual gaze Maintained eye contact.

noncontracted denial A verbal behavior associated with rehearsed responses in which the subject does not use verb contractions when giving answers to questions.

nonverbal channel Posture; arm and leg movements; eye contact; and facial expressions.

omission qualifier Qualifying phrase indicating that the subject is omitting part of his answer within his response. Examples of omission qualifiers include "Hardly ever" and "Not often."

omissive response A response that may consist of a nonverbal response alone or a verbal answer that accepts physical responsibility for an act but denies criminal intentions.

paralinguistic channel Characteristics of speech falling outside of the spoken word.

personal gestures A gesture, which may involve the hand coming in contact with the body, that reflects the subject's own unique nonverbal manner of relieving anxiety.

personality Fairly rigid and inflexible traits that are not condition specific.

protective or supporting gestures A final category of adaptor behavior involving gestures that bring the hand into contact with the face.

qualified response Phrase added to a response to weaken it.

response latency The length of time between the last word of the interviewer's question and the first word of the subject's response.

statement against self-interest Statement that decreases anxiety by alerting the investigator to the true intent behind a statement.

stop-and-start behavior A significant paralinguistic behavior of deception, in which the subject begins a response in one direction but abruptly stops it and starts over again in a different direction.

truthful response A statement that reflects the truth and, therefore, does not cause any internal anxiety as a result of deception.

verbal channel Word choice and arrangement of words to send a message.

ENDNOTES

1. For a detailed discussion of a similar later study, see Reid and Arther, *Behavior Symptoms of Lie Detector Subjects*, 44 J. Crim L., C. & P. S. (1953), and Horvath, *Verbal and Nonverbal Clues to Truth and Deception During Polygraph Examinations*, 1 J. Police Sci. & Adm. 138-152 (1973).
2. Horvath, F. & Jayne, B. "A Pilot Study of the Verbal and Nonverbal Behaviors of Criminal Suspects During Structured Interviews" NSA grant No. 89-R-2323, 1990; Horvath, F., Jayne, B. & Buckley, J. "Trained Evaluators' Judgments of Behavioral Characteristics of Truthful and Deceptive Criminal Suspects During Structured Interviews" NSA grant 904-90-C-1164, 1992.
3. Horvath, F., Jayne, B. & Buckley, J. "Differentiation of Truthful and Deceptive Criminal Suspects in Behavior Analysis Interviews," *Forensic Journal of Science,* Vol. 39 No. 3 May, 1994 793-806.
4. Blair, J.P. & McCamey, W.P. "Detection of Deception: An Anaylsis of the Behavioral Analysis Interview Technique," *Law Enforcement Executive Forum,* 2(2), 2002 164-169.
5. "On the Line: The Deceptive Judgments of Customs Inspectors and Laymen" *Journal of Personality and Social Psychology* (1980) 39 784-798.
6. "Training Police Officers to Detect Deceptive Eye-witness Statements: Does It Work?" *Social Behavior* (1987), 2 1-7.
7. "Who Can Catch a Liar?" *American Psychologist* (1991) Sept. 913-919.
8. For research investigating evasion, see Rudacille, W., *Indentifying Lies in Disguise*, Dubuque: Kendall/Hunt, 1994, pp. 59-76.
9. One of the conditions in the previously mentioned NSA sponsored study involved trained evaluators making judgments of a suspect's truthfulness after hearing the interviewer's question and then only being exposed to the suspect's nonverbal response (the audio channel was not recorded). Under this condition, the evaluator's mean accuracy of detecting truth or deception was 72.5%.
10. If a crime victim is still in shock or experiencing psychological or emotional trauma as a result of the event, extreme caution should be used in any attempt to assess the verbal or nonverbal behaviors as indications of truth or deception.

EXERCISES

Determine whether these responses to the following interview questions are more typical of a truthful or deceptive suspect:

Q: "Did you steal a car from the Ford dealership?"

A: "Absolutely not!" [Direct eye contact, on time.]

____

Q: "Do you know who stole that car from the dealership?"

A: "I'm not even certain it was stolen (laugh)." [Slight delay, sitting back in chair.]

____

Q: "Has anyone ever approached you, asking you to help them take a car from the dealership?"

A: "Has anyone ever approached me? No." [On time, hand to mouth, eyes to ceiling.]

____

Q: "Have you ever just thought about taking a car from the dealership?"

A: "No way." [Forward lean, direct eye contact.]

____

Q: "Over the weekend were you inside a stolen car?"

A: "I would have to say no."

____

Q: "How do you feel about being interviewed concerning this stolen car?"

A: "It doesn't bother me. I know you're just doing your job." [The subject crosses his legs and bounces his foot.]

____

Q: "Once we complete our entire investigation, how will it come out on you?"

A: "It better show that I'm not the person who stole that car." [The subject has direct eye contact and extends his hand toward the investigator.]

____

____

8

Behavior Symptoms of Truthful and Untruthful Subjects

Chapter Objectives

Upon completion of this chapter you will be able to:

- Explain the initial assessment of the subject
- Describe behaviors common to both truthful and deceptive subjects
- Discuss factors that may lead to misinterpretation of behavior symptoms

Perspective

Although behavior symptoms can be very helpful in differentiating truth from deception, they are not to be considered determinative of the issue. This is also true with respect to any diagnostic effort respecting human behavior, whether in psychiatry or medicine. To be meaningfully interpreted, a subject's behavior must be considered along with investigative findings and the subject's background, personality, and attitudes.

This chapter first presents attitudes common to both truthful and deceptive subjects and then discusses factors that can influence the misinterpretation of behavior symptoms. Once an investigator has carefully evaluated the potential impact of these variables on the subject's behavior symptoms, he can determine how confident he can be in behavioral assessments of the subject used to eliminate the subject from further suspicion or to proceed with an interrogation.

Initial Assessment of the Subject

range of normalcy a "normal range" relative to emotional, mental, cognitive, and physical health.

The inferences an investigator draws from a subject's behavior during questioning are based on an assumption that the subject is operating within a "**normal range**" relative to emotional, mental, cognitive, and physical health. While the range of normalcy in these areas is quite wide, investigators need to be cognizant of the potential effects these variables can have on a subject's behavior.

With this in mind, it is important to establish a subject's normal behaviors at the outset of the interview (see **Table 8-1**). This should be done by asking non-threatening background questions.

Table 8-1 Establishing a Subject's Normal Behaviors

Examples of areas to initially evaluate include the following:

- Intelligence: Verbal communication skills, vocabulary, comprehension
- Influence of drugs: Slurred speech, pupil dilation or constriction, disorientation, inappropriate emotional affect
- General nervous tension: Frequent posture changes, nervous laughter, rapid changes in eye movement, hand-wringing, repetitive hand or foot gestures
- Neurological disorders: May manifest themselves through facial tics, rapid blinking, or hand tremors

Behaviors Common to Both Truthful and Deceptive Subjects

reticence being silent or relatively uncommunicative except for a few brief comments.

Reticence

Being **reticent** at the beginning of an interview is a behavior symptom common to both guilty and innocent subjects. A guilty subject who is afraid to speak for fear of being trapped will find it much easier to defend himself by being as nontalkative as possible. Any comments at all will usually be very brief. Questions may be answered with a succinct "No," "I don't know," or "I couldn't say," and the subject may attempt to seem casual about it, often not giving the question adequate thought. On the other hand, a truthful subject may be reticent because of an apprehension about being mistaken as guilty or because of fear of being unable to articulate his position properly. If the investigator is patient and understanding, even the most reticent truthful subject will become less apprehensive and more naturally responsive over time.

Nervousness

It is not uncommon for innocent as well as guilty subjects to exhibit signs of nervousness when questioned by a law enforcement or security investigator. Innocent persons may be nervous for several reasons: (1) the possibility of being erroneously considered guilty, (2) a concern as to the treatment they may receive, or (3) a concern that questioners may discover some previous, unrelated crime or act of indiscretion the subject committed. The third reason would be particularly true in an instance in which the previous crime was of a more serious nature than the present one.

On the other hand, the nervousness of guilty persons would be attributable to awareness of their guilt regarding the present crime, the possibility of it being detected, and the prosecution and punishment that may follow.

The principal difference between the nervousness of the innocent and that of the guilty is in the *duration* of nervous symptoms. As the interview progresses and the innocent subject understands that the questioning is nonaccusatory, he becomes more relaxed and composed. Conversely, the deceptive subject's nervousness is maintained or sometimes actually increases during the course of the interview.

Impertinence

impertinence reactions exhibiting anger and rudeness; insolence.

Impertinence may be displayed by both truthful and untruthful subjects. This reaction is usually confined to youthful subjects, who may resent authority in general and who may attempt bravado, especially if questioned when their peers are present or know of the investigation. Consequently, little significance can be placed upon this particular behavior as to whether such persons are lying or telling the truth. As for adults, an act of impertinence by a subject can be a shield to fend off questions presented by the investigator. This trait is seldom displayed by a truthful subject. On the other hand, a lying adult may be impertinent because of the awareness of being caught and the feeling of a need to show defiance and lack of fear.

Anger

A very difficult behavioral reaction to evaluate is anger. For instance, a resentful scowl may result from a guilty subject's feigned anger, but it may also be the genuine reaction of an innocent person. Although making a differentiation presents a problem for the investigator, it can usually be resolved by an awareness that a guilty person's "anger" is more easily appeased than the true anger of an innocent person. The innocent person will persist with his angry reaction, whereas a guilty person will usually switch to a new emotional state when he realizes that feigned anger has not deterred the investigator.

Whenever a subject is resentful of the fact that he is under suspicion, the investigator should allow for a vent of that feeling. This has the desirable effect of establishing more open communication as the subject realizes that the investigator is concerned about his emotional state. The investigator should respond to such resentment by rationally explaining why it is necessary to talk to the subject, and, if possible, by explaining that no decision as to the subject's involvement in the offense has been made.

It is not uncommon for an innocent subject to express sincere resentment because of the belief that he is being singled out as the obvious guilty person. The investigator should assure such a subject that he is only one of many people being interviewed concerning the issue under investigation. In other instances, the subject may express resentment about treatment by others prior to the interview, for example, being taken away in handcuffs in front of family and neighbors, or perhaps being subjected to derogatory and abusive questioning by another investigator. When appropriate, the investigator should empathize with the subject's feeling and distance himself from the "other people" who caused the embarrassment or mistreatment.

Despair and Resignation

If a subject adopts an attitude of despair and resignation (which is usually more common with the guilty) and says something like "I don't care whether you believe me or not; I'd just as soon go to jail; there's nothing for me to look forward to anyway," he should be invited to talk about his general troubles and misfortunes. The investigator should then listen and console the subject with sympathetic understanding. The investigator may say, "Joe, I guess life has treated you rather roughly, hasn't it?" Such a question will very likely "open up" the subject. He will probably begin with a simple "yes" answer, after which the investigator can delve into the matter with specific questions regarding childhood difficulties and so forth. After a relatively brief period of attentive listening, the investigator can shift the discussion toward the offense itself.

The gravity of the offense under investigation will, of course, have a bearing on the extent and quality of a subject's behavior symptoms. For instance, a guilty subject will display greater and more reliable symptoms when questioned about a rape than when questioned about a petty theft or other relatively minor offense.

Factors That May Lead to Misinterpretation of Behavior Symptoms

Overwhelming Investigative Findings

Many of the previously discussed behavior symptoms of guilt are a product of the subject's psychological efforts to avoid detection of deception. In essence, during the course of an interview the guilty subject is actively trying to "get away with the crime," and these efforts can result in tell-tale signs of deception. However, we have encountered instances in which guilty subjects have psychologically "given up," to the extent that they do not display attitudes common to the guilty, nor are their behavior symptoms necessarily indicative of deception. Case 8-1: The Crooked, but Confident, Bank Teller is such an instance.

Case 8-1: The Crooked, but Confident, Bank Teller

A theft investigation involved a bank employee who reported a $2,100 shortage in her cash drawer. All of the evidence clearly indicated that this employee simply grabbed the $2,100. There was no attempt to disguise the theft or to make the theft difficult to trace back to her. Despite the overwhelming evidence presented by her employer, she maintained that she was not involved in stealing the funds.

During this employee's interview in our office, she came across as fairly sincere and realistic; she openly acknowledged that she would have had the best opportunity to steal the money. She stated that the person who stole it should be fired and possibly prosecuted and that she would not give the person who stole the money a second chance. Other than appearing quiet and withdrawn, there were no clear indications of deception evident during her interview. Yet, based on the overwhelming evidence against her, she was interrogated and she confessed shortly after the initial confrontation. Because of the inconsistent behavior displayed during her interview, the investigator conducted a post-confession interview of this subject.

During this interview the investigator learned that the same night she stole the money, she told her husband about the theft and he was supportive of her motives (being behind on bills). She also stated that she believed she would never get away with the theft but that she felt entitled to the money. Even though it was explained to her that prosecution was a real possibility, she doubted that the bank would prosecute.

The lesson Case 8-1 teaches is that the investigator should not allow behavior analysis to outweigh the evidence and case facts. This is especially true when the subject knows that there is significant evidence indicating his guilt. In that circumstance the subject may not be operating psychologically from the position of trying to actively avoid detection of deception, and the standard guidelines for behavioral assessments may not apply.

The investigator should not allow behavior analysis to outweigh the evidence and case facts.

Use of Medications

The legitimate use of medication for physical or psychological problems can distort an innocent subject's behavior. For example, a sedative prescribed to reduce nervous tension can cause a person to appear withdrawn and disinterested. Also, intentional abuses of other medication, drugs, or alcohol may cause an innocent subject to seem confused or disoriented in offering an alibi or some other disclosure, such as the sequence of events. Similar factors might also cause a display of misleading behavior symptoms. For example, withdrawal effects from drug addiction may cause a subject to appear nervous, sweaty, or shaky. The use of some drugs (whether for medical or nonmedical reasons) may cause dry mouth, and certain prescribed drugs can cause users to have a clicky dry mouth. The same drugs may also affect the activity of the Adam's apple, causing it to move up and down. These reactions should be carefully evaluated to avoid misinterpreting them as indicative of deception.

Mental Illness

Investigators should be highly skeptical of the behavior symptoms of a person with a psychiatric history. No matter how clear-cut the symptoms are, extreme caution should be exercised. Such a person who has committed a criminal act may display behavior suggestive of innocence; on the other hand, an innocent person with a psychological affliction may appear to be

The investigator should be aware of the effects of clinical depression on a subject's behavior and thought processes.

guilty. In particular, the investigator should be aware of the effects of clinical depression on a subject's behavior and thought processes. Even though innocent, the severely depressed subject may appear lethargic, disinterested, immobile, and inattentive during an interview. His responses to interview questions may be disorganized or lack spontaneity. This is not to suggest that clinical depression should be associated with truthfulness. Indeed, we have elicited valid confessions from many guilty subjects with this diagnosis; in some of those cases, the depression may have contributed to, or even have manifested itself because of, the subject's criminal behavior (child abuse, arson, theft, etc.).

In instances in which a subject has a mental history of delusions or hallucinations, obviously little weight should be placed on that subject's behavior symptoms. Case 8-2: Deceiving Appearances illustrates the risk that may be occasioned by such factors.

Case 8-3: Deceiving Appearances – Version 2 illustrates the opposite effect.

Case 8-2: Deceiving Appearances

A young woman reported to the police that she had received several indecent phone calls, and finally an invitation was received to visit the caller in his hotel room. The police advised her to go to the hotel room and said they would follow her and afford her adequate protection. She went to the room, knocked on the door, and was let in by a man. Soon thereafter, the police entered and arrested him. He vehemently denied having made the phone calls and said that he had been under the impression that the woman who had knocked on his door was a prostitute and he had been interested in procuring her services. The man was a member of a prestigious businessmen's club and an employee of a reputable oil company, and his fellow club members and officials of the company came to his defense, assuring the police that he could not possibly be the person who had made the phone calls.

When he was subjected to an interrogation, his behavior symptoms were indicative of truth-telling, and he persisted in his protestations of innocence. In view of the circumstantial evidence, however, the police investigators were advised to conduct a thorough investigation of his background. It revealed that he had a history of making sexually motivated phone calls of the type in this case, and indeed, had been in several mental institutions for treatment. None of this, of course, had been known by the individuals who had vouched for his good character. On the basis of the new information, the accused was again interrogated. When confronted with his past record, he confessed to making the calls in the present case.

Case 8-3: Deceiving Appearances – Version 2

A policewoman was suspected of making obscene calls to a Catholic convent. The basis for the suspicion was a nun's report to the police department that very soon after the policewoman visited the convent as the investigator assigned to the case, another call had been received from a woman whose voice sounded like that of the policewoman herself. On the basis of this and other circumstances that did not rule out such a possibility, the policewoman was interrogated. She seemed to be highly nervous and so distraught emotionally that the interrogation had to be suspended temporarily, despite some behavior symptoms of untruthfulness. Shortly thereafter, another call was traced to a different person, who admitted being responsible for all of the calls. The policewoman's past history revealed an "unstable personality," which undoubtedly accounted for the misleading behavior symptoms.

A professional interviewer/interrogator should be familiar with the field of psychopathology, not to diagnose such disorders but to recognize their symptoms and thereby evaluate the suitability (and possible credibility) of individuals suffering from mental illness. In particular, investigators should be alert to witnesses or victims who may relate delusional accounts as a result of paranoid schizophrenia or untreated bipolar disorders (e.g., manic depression). Such individuals are naturally attracted to people in authority, such as criminal investigators or polygraph examiners. We have had numerous encounters with such individuals, who demand to be examined on important criminal issues. Actual examples include relating physical and sexual abuse suffered as a youngster (most common), witnessing the governor of Wisconsin sell illegal drugs, exposing a crime syndicate working out of the University of Michigan, and reporting a dentist who was slowly poisoning patients.

When such individuals come forward with their stories, behaviorally they are quite credible. After all, in their mind, they are relating what they believe to be the truth. It is only the process of patient questioning that brings to light the delusion. In this regard, it is an effective technique to ask a person suspected of suffering from delusions whether or not he has further information concerning other unsolved crimes or criminal activity. Frequently, the individual will offer, again in a credible manner, detailed information of an entirely unrelated event that is equally serious. Another productive question to ask such a person is whether or not he has ever been wrongly accused by someone in authority (parent, police, judge, etc.). Many delusions, in one way or another, center around the person perceiving himself as a helpless victim, and this question often opens doors to further useful information.

Intelligence, Social Responsibility, and Maturity

The evaluation of behavior symptoms in terms of truth or deception should take into general consideration the subject's intelligence, sense of social responsibility, and degree of maturity. As a rule, the more intelligent a subject is, the more reliable behavior symptoms will be. The intelligent individual will usually possess a higher concern over the importance and consequences of the investigation; his appraisal of right and wrong will be more acute; and if the person is deceptive, she will experience a greater degree of internal conflict and anxiety.

Social responsibilities, such as the person's family, job, and reputation, will affect the subject's degree of emotional involvement in the interview process. Such emotional involvement may be generally lacking or prevail to a lesser degree in a person who is without such responsibilities. This will be especially true among subjects who have had a dependency upon alcohol or drugs. People without the usual values have very little at stake and will exhibit fewer emotional reactions and behavior symptoms from which the investigator may assess guilt or innocence. Similar characteristics prevail in youthful subjects or others who lack maturity. Ordinarily, it seems to matter rather little to these subjects whether what they say is truthful or untruthful; they tend to envision themselves as socially unaccountable for their conduct. As a consequence, their behavior symptoms tend to be unreliable.

Behavior Analysis in Young Children

Particular caution must be applied when evaluating the behavior symptoms of a young child (less than 9 years old). Children in this age group are generally not interviewed as suspects in an investigation, but rather as possible victims of physical or sexual abuse or as witnesses to another person's actions. As any parent knows, young children can tell a very convincing and persistent story that later turns out to be totally fabricated. The psychological basis of these fabrications can range from fantasies to misinterpreting events. Because of this, such fabrications may not constitute a conscious effort on the part of the child to give false information (lying).

Just as some false stories that children tell appear to be very credible, other true stories a child tells may appear to be false based on behavioral observations. A child may display misleading behaviors resulting from feelings of guilt, uncertainty in discussing unfamiliar or sensitive topics, or inadequate communication skills. Statements from young children, therefore, present a dilemma both with respect to false-positive and false-negative evaluations. Consequently, the veracity of a young child's statements should not be assessed solely on the basis of the child's behavior.

Emotional Condition

In addition to precautions regarding the behavior symptoms of suspects, where doubt arises as to the validity of a reported crime, the investigator must consider that the traumatic experience of the crime itself may produce reactions of nervousness or instability that might be misinterpreted as indications of falsity. For example, a normally nervous victim who has just been robbed at gunpoint may be honestly confused or disoriented by the experience, and consequently may seem to be untruthful about the report of the incident. Or, a wife whose husband has been shot to death in her presence may have been so shocked by what she observed that her version of the incident soon thereafter may appear to be untruthful, when in fact she truthfully reported what occurred.

Another example of how misleading behavior symptoms may surface is one in which a male friend of a female murder victim was interrogated about her death. According to the initial investigators, he displayed a number of guilty symptoms. It was reported that he could not look them straight in the eye, that he sighed a lot, that he had a disheveled appearance, and that he seemed to be going through a great deal of mental anguish. An investigator reported, "He looked guilty as hell!" During a subsequent interview conducted by a professionally competent investigator, however, it was ascertained that the subject was emotionally upset because of the young woman's death and that he had been crying uncontrollably over it. He simply had not verbally or demonstrably disclosed to the other investigators the extent of his grief. The investigators mistakenly confused his emotional behavior as indicative of guilt, and therefore, he became the prime suspect. Later developments in the case produced factual evidence that totally exonerated him from any part in the murder.

Cultural Differences

Some behavior symptoms are directly caused by physiological changes occurring within the body as a result of an intense emotional state (skin blanching, tremor, pupil dilation), and others appear to be genetically encoded (grooming behaviors, protective gestures, a freeze response). However, other behaviors are clearly learned and therefore have cultural roots. An example is eye contact. Individuals raised in Eastern cultures are taught that it is disrespectful to establish direct eye contact with a person in authority. Western culture, conversely, teaches that direct eye contact represents candor, sincerity, and truthfulness.

Social space is also culturally learned. Western society teaches that interaction between two strangers is comfortable at about three to four feet. Individuals raised in the Middle East will interact with strangers from between one and two feet away. Unaware of cultural differences, an investigator may easily misinterpret this closeness as a challenge or an indication of anger.

An investigator, therefore, must be aware of possible cultural influences on a subject's behavior. As with many of the factors that influence a subject's behavior, establishing a behavioral baseline is central to the accurate assessment of a subject's behavior. If a subject exhibits poor eye contact while providing background information, the lack of eye contact when discussing the issue under investigation should certainly not be considered a symptom of deception.

Conclusion

Although the verbal and nonverbal behavior displayed by a subject during an interview may provide very valuable and accurate indications of possible innocence or guilt, the investigator should evaluate the behavior according to the guidelines stated in Chapter 7. Furthermore, the following factors that may affect the validity of behavior symptoms should be considered: the perceived seriousness of the offense; the mental and physical condition of the subject; underlying psychiatric or personality disorders; level of intelligence; degree of maturity; cultural influences; and the extent or absence of social responsibilities.

KEY POINTS

- It is important to establish a subject's normal behaviors at the outset of the interview. Thus, the investigator should evaluate the subject in the areas of intelligence, sense of social responsibility, degree of maturity, possible influence of drugs, general nervous tension, emotional condition, cultural differences, and preexisting neurological disorders.
- The initial evaluation should be done by asking nonthreatening background questions.
- Both truthful and deceptive subjects can exhibit reticence, nervousness, impertinence, and anger. Signs of despair and resignation are more common in guilty subjects.
- The investigator should not allow behavior analysis to outweigh the evidence and case facts.
- Investigators should be highly skeptical of the behavior symptoms of a person with a psychiatric history.
- An investigator must keep in mind the many factors that can influence the misinterpretation of behavior symptoms.

KEY TERMS

impertinence Reactions exhibiting anger and rudeness; insolence.

range of normalcy A "normal range" relative to emotional, mental, cognitive, and physical health.

reticence Being silent or relatively uncommunicative except for a few brief comments.

EXERCISES

Identify a cause other than deception for the following behavior symptoms:

1. The subject exhibits very little eye contact throughout the course of the interview.

   ____

2. The suspect appears defeated throughout the interview and many of his responses are delayed.

   ____

3. When relaying what happened to him, the person exhibits very little eye contact, and talks slowly and at a low volume. The person also exhibits a collapsed posture throughout the interview.

   ____

II

Employing the Reid Nine Steps of Interrogation

9

Overview of and Preparation for the Reid Nine Steps

Chapter Objectives

Upon completion of this chapter you will be able to:

- Explain the difference between emotional and nonemotional offenders
- List and briefly explain the Reid nine steps of interrogation
- Describe preparations for applying the nine steps

Perspective

The authors again wish to make clear that the word *guilt* as used in this text only signifies the investigator's opinion. In no way does it connote legal guilt based upon proof beyond a reasonable doubt. It is in that context that this part of the text presents the tactics and techniques for the interrogation of suspects whose guilt, *in the opinion of the investigator,* seems definite or reasonably certain. Among these techniques are the nine steps of interrogation.

General Classification of Offenders

The selection of interrogation procedures depends to a considerable extent on the personal characteristics of the suspect, the type of offense, the probable motivation for the crime, and the suspect's initial behavioral responses to questioning. On the basis of these considerations, criminal offenders are subject to a

emotional offender one who would predictably experience a considerable feeling of remorse, mental anguish, or compunction as a result of his offense.

nonemotional offender a person who ordinarily does not experience a troubled conscience as a result of committing a crime.

rather broad, yet flexible, classification as either emotional offenders or nonemotional offenders.

An emotional offender is one who would predictably experience a considerable feeling of remorse, mental anguish, or compunction as a result of his offense. This person has a strong sense of moral guilt—in other words, a "troubled conscience." Emotional offenders can be identified behaviorally during an interrogation because they tend to be emotionally moved by the investigator's words and actions. As the interrogation progresses, the emotional offender may develop watery eyes, and his body posture will become less rigid and more open, without crossed arms and legs. The subject's eye contact with the investigator will become less frequent, eventually becoming a vacant stare at the floor. Because of the "troubled conscience" feeling, it is most effective to use sympathetic interrogation tactics and techniques on such a suspect—expressions of understanding and compassion with regard to the commission of the offense as well as the suspect's present difficulty.

A nonemotional offender is a person who ordinarily does not experience a troubled conscience as a result of committing a crime. This emotional indifference may be the product of an antisocial personality disorder; it may be a conditioned response where the suspect has experienced repeated prior success in escaping punishment through lying; or it may be a manifestation of the career criminal, who perceives committing crimes as a business in much the same way a legitimate businessperson sells a product. In the latter case, the suspect approaches arrest, prosecution, and possible conviction as an occupational hazard and experiences no regret or remorse as a result of exploiting victims—he is psychologically insulated from his victims.

The motive for a nonemotional offender to commit a crime may involve emotionality, but when interviewed he typically expresses an unconcerned, detached attitude. During interrogation, the nonemotional offender may offer token, weak denials of guilt that are stopped easily. (In the suspect's mind, the interrogation is a game and he readily accepts the investigator's premise of his guilt.) The nonemotional suspect is quite content to allow the investigator to talk, but the words fall on seemingly deaf ears as the suspect maintains a defensive, closed posture, including crossed arms, erect head, and a cold, hard stare. A remarkable characteristic of the nonemotional offender is a resistance to becoming emotionally involved in the interrogation.

It is most effective to use factual-analysis tactics and techniques on the nonemotional offender. This means appealing to the suspect's common sense and reasoning rather than to his emotions; it is designed to persuade him that his guilt is established or that it soon will be established and, consequently, the intelligent choice to make is to tell the truth.

A common mistake many investigators make when formulating an interrogation strategy is to assume, based on the offender's criminal record or demeanor during the interview, that he must be a nonemotional offender. As a general rule, the majority of all offenders, emotional and nonemotional, possess emotional traits to some degree. For this reason, the sympathetic and factual-analysis approaches should often be intermingled. Greater emphasis will be placed, however, on one or the other depending on the type of offender.

Regardless of the interrogation approach used, the investigator's goal is to persuade a suspect to tell the truth. Largely because of movie and television portrayals of interrogation, the average citizen has little appreciation for the persuasive efforts required to convince a guilty suspect to offer admissions against self-interest.

Brief Analysis of the Nine Steps of Interrogation

As a result of many years' experience, primarily on the part of the staff of John E. Reid and Associates under the guidance of the late John E. Reid, the interrogation process has been formulated into nine structural components—the nine steps of criminal interrogation. These nine steps are presented in the context of the interrogation of suspects whose guilt seems definite or reasonably certain.[1] It must be remembered that none of the steps is apt to make an innocent person confess and that all of the steps are legally as well as morally justifiable. For those investigators who have qualms or reservations about utilizing some of the steps, our discussion of the interrogation process will include explanations as to why these approaches are necessary to persuade a guilty person to tell the truth, and why they would not be likely to cause an innocent suspect to confess.

Step 1 involves a direct, positively presented confrontation of the suspect with a statement that he is considered to be the person who committed the offense. At this stage, the investigator should pause to evaluate the suspect's verbal and nonverbal response. A suspect who says nothing and looks down to the floor will be approached somewhat differently than a suspect who crosses his arms and leans back in his chair while stating, "You're crazy. I swear, I didn't do it." Regardless of the suspect's initial response to the direct, positive confrontation, the investigator will proceed to offer a reason as to why it is important for the suspect to tell the truth. This *transition statement* introduces the interrogation theme.

In **Step 2**, the investigator introduces an interrogation theme by putting forward a supposition about the reason for the crime's commission. In effect, the suspect is being offered a possible moral excuse for having committed the offense. To accomplish this, the investigator should generally attempt to affix moral blame for the offense on some other person (e.g., an accomplice, the victim) or some particular circumstance, such as an urgent monetary need of the suspect or his family. If a suspect seems to listen attentively to the suggested "theme" or seems to be deliberating about it, even for a short period of time, that reaction is strongly suggestive of guilt. On the other hand, if the suspect expresses resentment over the mere submission of such a suggestion, this reaction may be indicative of innocence. During development of the interrogation theme, a guilty person, as well as an innocent one, can be expected to offer denials of involvement in the offense.

The investigator should then embark upon **Step 3**, which consists of handling the initial denials of guilt by discouraging the suspect's repetition or elaboration of the denial and returning to the moral excuse theme begun in Step 2. An innocent person will not allow such denials to be cut off; furthermore, he will attempt more or less to "take over" the situation rather than submit passively to continued interrogation. On the other hand, a guilty person will usually cease to voice a denial, or else the denials will become weaker, and he will submit to the investigator's return to a theme.

Step 4 involves overcoming the suspect's secondary line of defense after the initial denial—that is, the suspect offering reasons as to why he would not or could not commit the crime. These excuses will consist of what may be viewed as "objections" from the suspect, presented in the form of explanations oriented around economic, religious, or moral reasons for not committing the crime. These excuses are normally offered by only the guilty suspect, especially when they come after the denial phase of the interrogation. They are significant in that they are evasions of a bold denial by the substitution of the less courageous statement as to why the suspect did not or could not commit the offense under investigation. Such an objection causes less internal anxiety than the utterance of an outright denial.

When a guilty suspect's verbal efforts (denials and objections) are ineffective in dissuading the investigator, the suspect is likely to mentally withdraw and "tune out" the investigator's theme. Unless the investigator now gets and retains the suspect's full attention, the interrogation may amount to no more than an exercise in futility. During **Step 5**, the investigator will clearly display a sincerity in what he says. Helpful in achieving this is an increase in the closeness of the previously described seating arrangement between investigator and suspect and physical efforts by the investigator to maintain eye contact with the suspect.

Step 6 involves recognizing the suspect's passive mood. During this stage the suspect is weighing the possible benefits of telling the truth, and this is generally reflected in changes within the suspect's nonverbal behavior (tears, a collapsed posture, eyes drawn to the floor).

Step 7 is the use of an alternative question—a suggestion of a choice to be made by the suspect concerning some aspect of the crime. Generally, one choice is presented as more "acceptable" or "understandable" than the other. This choice will be in the form of a question such as "Was this the first time, or has it happened many times before?" Whichever alternative is chosen by the suspect, the net effect of an expressed choice will be the functional equivalent of an incriminating admission.

In **Step 8** the investigator has the suspect orally relate the various details of the offense that will serve ultimately to establish legal guilt. These details can include where the fatal weapon was discarded, where the stolen money was hidden, and the motive for the crime's commission.

Step 9 is the confession itself. This step involves the recommended procedure for converting an oral confession into a written one.

Preliminary Preparations for Applying the Nine Steps

Before applying any of the nine steps, the *Miranda* warnings must be given to a custodial suspect, and a waiver of these rights must be obtained. In custodial cases, this must occur before the interview. Unless the investigator knows that this has already been done by the person who presented the suspect for the interview, or by someone else in authority prior to the interview, the investigator should give the warnings and obtain the waiver. It is preferable, however, that the investigator be spared this responsibility so that he may immediately proceed with the interview and interrogation without the diversion occasioned by the warning procedure.

Before the interrogation, allow the suspect to sit in the interview room alone for about five minutes. A guilty suspect will rapidly try to review everything that is going to be said, and this preparation will cause him to become insecure. Additional doubts and concerns will arise in the suspect's mind and thereby further disorganize efforts at deception. Some guilty suspects will be so deep in thought and so concerned with their plight that when the investigator enters the room, they will become startled and immediately indicate by their eyes and general appearance that they expect their deception to be revealed. On the other hand, an innocent suspect, even though somewhat apprehensive, will usually turn easily toward the investigator when he enters; although understandably interested, there will be an "at ease" look in the suspect's eyes, and the appearance will be a favorable one.

Before entering the interview room, the investigator should prepare and have on hand an evidence case folder, or a simulation of one. At the outset of the interrogation, and also at appropriate times during the various steps that follow the initial confrontation, the investigator can make visual reference to the evidence folder. The purpose for doing so is to lead the suspect to believe that it contains information and material of incriminating significance, even though, in fact, the file may contain nothing but blank sheets of paper. The mere sight of the file has a desirable effect on both guilty and innocent suspects because of the impression of preparedness on the part of the investigator.

In addition to an evidence file, depending on the nature of the case, the investigator may consider bringing other visual props, such as a video or audio tape, a fingerprint card, an evidence bag containing hair or other fibers, spent shell casings, vials of colored liquid, and so forth.[2] No verbal reference needs to be made at all concerning these items of apparent physical evidence. The visual impact of seeing the implied evidence can have a very desirable effect on a guilty suspect.

After the suspect has been waiting about five minutes, the investigator's entrance into the interview room should be very deliberate and should be accompanied by an air of confidence. The success or failure of an interrogation depends to a large extent upon the investigator's initial approach and the first impression created. If the suspect is not seated, the investigator should direct him to do so. On the other hand, if the suspect is seated and starts to rise, there should be a direction to remain seated.

One of the advantages of conducting a nonaccusatory interview before an interrogation is that the investigator can contrast his friendly, approachable demeanor displayed during the interview to a much more serious and firm demeanor at the outset of an interrogation. This apparent contrast in the investigator's comportment will help instill a sense of confidence and sincerity that is fundamental to a successful interrogation.

The investigator should be polite, of course, but at the same time should maintain a degree of professional detachment as he enters the room. It is well to emulate somewhat the conduct and behavior of a busy medical specialist who calls upon a hospitalized patient to whom the specialist has been previously identified and who anticipates the specialist's arrival. Although the specialist will extend a brief greeting, usually no handshaking or other social gestures occur. The physician proceeds with his professional duties, such as examining the patient's chart and then interviewing and examining the patient. It is strictly a professional event.

In those rare instances where no interview precedes the interrogation, once the investigator enters the interview room he should still not volunteer any handshaking. If, however, the suspect extends his hand to the investigator, the response should be a very casual handshake. If the suspect inquires about the investigator's name, only the last name should be mentioned (e.g., Mr. Kingston). If the investigator were to include an authoritative title, such as Detective Kingston, it would remind the suspect of the seriousness of his crime and psychologically put the investigator on a different level than the suspect—both effects are undesirable. Furthermore, if the investigator identifies himself as Jack Kingston, this may encourage the suspect to refer to him as "Jack," thereby establishing an emotional familiarity that will serve as a psychological handicap to the investigator.

We would like to emphasize that an investigator need not utilize the steps in the exact order in which they appear in this text. In fact, it would be impossible to do so in any given case situation, since various developments in the early stages of an interrogation may require shifting the sequence of the remaining recommended steps. Moreover, there may be times when two or more steps will have to be intermingled so that they may seem to represent only a single step.

KEY POINTS

- Criminal offenders are subject to a rather broad, yet flexible, classification as either emotional offenders or nonemotional offenders.
- An emotional offender is one who would predictably experience a considerable feeling of remorse, mental anguish, or compunction as a result of his offense. It is most effective to use sympathetic interrogation tactics and techniques on such a suspect.
- A nonemotional offender is a person who ordinarily does not experience a troubled conscience as a result of committing a crime. It is most effective to use factual-analysis tactics and techniques on the nonemotional offender.

The Reid Nine Steps of Interrogation

- Step 1: The investigator directly and positively confronts the suspect.
- Step 2: The investigator introduces an interrogation theme.
- Step 3: The investigator handles the initial denials of guilt.
- Step 4: The investigator overcomes the suspect's objections.
- Step 5: The investigator gets and retains the suspect's attention and clearly displays sincerity in what he says.
- Step 6: The investigator recognizes the suspect's passive mood.
- Step 7: The investigator uses an alternative question—a suggestion of a choice to be made by the suspect concerning some aspect of the crime.
- Step 8: The investigator has the suspect orally relate the various details of the offense that will serve ultimately to establish legal guilt.
- Step 9: The verbal confession is converted into a written or recorded statement.

Preliminary Steps

- Before applying any of the nine steps, the *Miranda* warnings must be given to a *custodial* suspect, and a waiver of these rights must be obtained.
- Allow the suspect to sit in the interview room alone for about five minutes before an interrogation is to begin.
- Before entering the interview room, the investigator should prepare and have on hand an evidence case folder, or a simulation of one. At the outset of the interrogation, and also at appropriate times during the various steps that follow the initial confrontation, the investigator can make visual reference to the evidence folder.
- The investigator's entrance into the interview room should be very deliberate and should be accompanied by an air of confidence.

KEY TERMS

emotional offender One who would predictably experience a considerable feeling of remorse, mental anguish, or compunction as a result of his offense.

nonemotional offender A person who ordinarily does not experience a troubled conscience as a result of committing a crime.

ENDNOTES

1. It has been suggested that the reason for this guideline is because the interrogation techniques presented are so psychologically sophisticated that they could induce an innocent person to confess (*20/20, ABC News, June 18, 1999*). This, of course, is not the concern. Rather, the guideline is offered to discourage investigators from using accusatory interrogation techniques as the primary means to establish the truthfulness of a suspect. In most situations, a non-accusatory interview will accomplish that goal.
2. The investigator should not, however, prepare false incriminating documents which appear to have been generated through an official source, e.g., crime lab, FBI. The reason for this is a concern that such falsified documents may find their way into the court system, see *State v. Cayward*, 552 S. 2d. 971 Flo. 1989.

10

Step 1: Direct, Positive Confrontation

Chapter Objectives

Upon completion of this chapter you will be able to:

- Detail the importance of beginning an interrogation with a direct, positive confrontation
- Explain the procedures used in formulating and issuing the direct, positive confrontation
- Discuss the importance of and reason for following the direct, positive confrontation with a behavioral pause
- List and explain various ways in which a transition statement may be formulated

Principles

At the outset of the interrogation, the guilty suspect is closely evaluating the investigator's confidence in his guilt. If the suspect perceives that the investigator is not certain of his guilt, he is unlikely to confess. Consequently, we recommend that the investigator start the interrogation with a direct statement indicating absolute certainty in the suspect's guilt. When an innocent suspect is directly accused of committing a crime, he recognizes immediately that the investigator's statement is incorrect and will offer behaviors helpful in identifying his truthfulness.

During a trial, a defense attorney may argue that approaching his client in this accusatory fashion prevented his client from presenting his side of the story. But when the interrogation followed an interview, the investigator should respond that a nonaccusatory interview was conducted prior to the interrogation, in which the suspect was provided with ample opportunity to tell the truth.

Defense attorneys have also argued that the investigator's presumption of their clients' guilt was improper for the purpose of establishing the truth. The investigator should explain that, based on all the available evidence, he formed an opinion that the suspect was involved in committing the crime and knew from experience that persuasion would be necessary to learn the truth.

direct, positive confrontation starting the interrogation with a direct statement indicating absolute certainty in the suspect's guilt.

transition statement statement that offers a reason for the interrogation other than eliciting a confession.

An important part of the **direct, positive confrontation** is the **transition statement**. This statement offers a reason for the interrogation other than eliciting a confession. (Since the interrogation begins by the investigator telling the suspect that there is no doubt as to his involvement in the crime, the investigator must develop a reason for the interrogation other than eliciting a confession.) An example of a transition statement is saying that the purpose of the discussion (interrogation) is to establish *why* the suspect committed the crime.

Procedures

The Confrontation Statement

In instances in which the investigator has had no prior contact with the suspect, the investigator, while still standing in front of the seated suspect and using the case folder as a prop, should state clearly and briefly something along the following lines: "You're Joe Burns? I'm in here to talk to you about the break-in at Jason's Jewelry Store last week." As that comment is being made, the investigator should finger through the case folder to create the impression that it contains material of an incriminating nature about the suspect.

Although the investigator in this instance has already been insulated from having his own first name used, he has gained a psychological advantage by addressing the suspect by his first name. This is particularly so when the suspect is a person with a professional title or someone of social, political, or business prominence. Such suspects are thereby stripped of the psychological advantage they may assume they have by virtue of their position. It is a very disarming tactic. There are exceptions, however. Whenever there is a significant disparity between an investigator's young age and the older age of the suspect, it may be inappropriate to call the suspect by his first name. However, a psychological gain might accrue to the investigator by addressing a person of low socioeconomic status by his or her last name (prefaced in appropriate instances by Mr., Mrs., or Miss).

The direct, positive confrontation in our hypothetical burglary case should be as follows: "Joe, the results of our investigation clearly indicate that you broke into Jason's Jewelry Store last week." When an investigative interview has been conducted prior to the interrogation, upon returning to the interview room the investigator's statement might be something like this (using a hypothetical arson case): "Mike, I have in this folder the results of our entire investigation. After talking to you and reviewing our results, there is no doubt that you did start the fire in that warehouse." This direct, positive statement should be emphatically expressed in a slow, deliberate, and confident manner. The respective positioning of the investigator and suspect are illustrated in **Figure 10-1.** The phrases "broke into" and "started the fire" have an unmistakable meaning and,

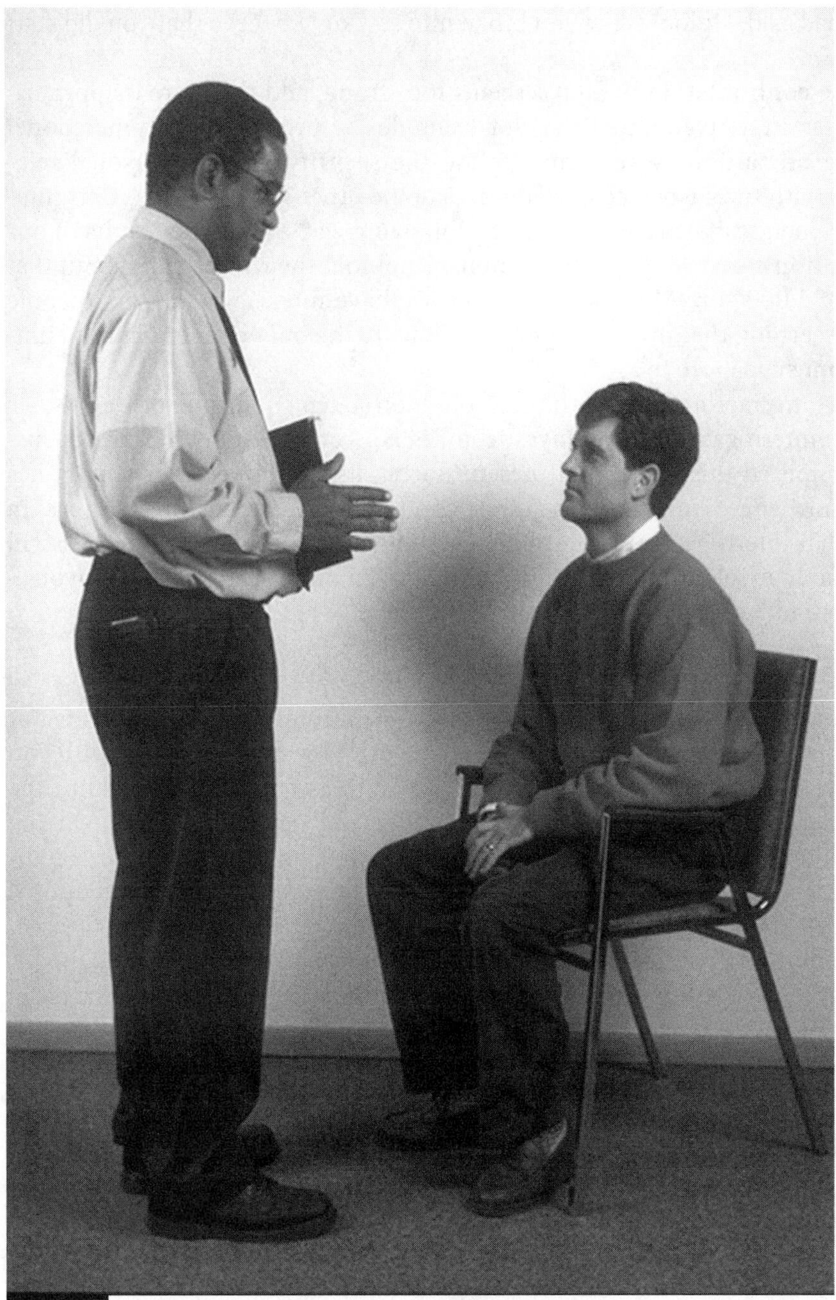

Figure 10-1 Interrogator's position during direct positive confrontation.

at the same time, avoid the legal or realistic terms "burglary" or "arson." (As earlier stated, there is a psychological disadvantage in using words or expressions that conjure up in the suspect's mind the legal consequences of a confession of guilt.)

Note that in the example given of a direct confrontation, the investigator referred to "our" investigation. This carries the implication that several investigators have contributed evidence to the case and share in the belief of the suspect's guilt. The statement, therefore, is more impressive than if the investigator merely had said, "It looks like you broke into . . ." or "I believe that you did start that fire."

If the confrontation in Step 1 seems too strong, and therefore inappropriate for use in a given situation—for example, by private security personnel (because of cautionary company policy, the security officer's personal relationship with the suspected employee, or some other reason)—the confrontation statement can be rephrased in the following ways: "Joe, the results of our investigation clearly indicate that you have not told the whole truth about that missing $2,000" or "Mike, as you know, we have interviewed several people here concerning that fire and right now, you are the only one we cannot eliminate from suspicion."

This same modification of the confrontation statement may also be advisable in police interrogations if the investigator is not certain as to whether the suspect committed the crime, was present during its commission, or simply has guilty knowledge. Similarly, a less direct confrontation statement may be best in a custodial interrogation where the investigator is concerned the suspect will immediately invoke his rights under *Miranda* if a direct accusation of involvement were to be made.

The Behavioral Pause

Immediately following the direct, positive confrontation, the investigator should make a statement similar to the following: "I want to sit down with you so that we can get this straightened out. OK?" While saying nothing further, the investigator should place the evidence folder and any other accompanying props off to the side, and position his chair approximately three to four feet directly in front of the suspect. This activity should create a period of intentional silence called the **behavioral pause**. The pause should only last three to five seconds, even though it may seem longer to the suspect.

behavioral pause a period of intentional silence that follows the direct, positive confrontation and lasts about three to five seconds.

The purpose of this intentional period of silence is to evaluate the suspect's initial reaction to the direct, positive confrontation. The investigator is afforded an initial indication as to whether or not the suspect is, in fact, guilty of the offense under investigation. Just as important, the suspect's initial response to the direct, positive confrontation often provides insight into how the investigator should proceed with the interrogation.

If, after the first accusation, the suspect responds by asking the investigator "What do you mean?" or "What did you say?" he is probably stalling for time or trying to reorganize his thoughts, which were disrupted by the direct accusation. (This inference is, of course, valid only if the accusation was unmistakably clear.) On the other hand, an innocent person will usually have no reason to ask a question as to what the investigator said or meant, and may immediately express resentment over being accused.

During the behavioral pause, a guilty suspect will probably look at the floor or to the side as much as possible, to avoid direct eye-to-eye contact. This will afford the suspect time to develop a verbal response, which, in many instances, may not in fact represent an answer at all. The suspect may at this stage also exhibit physical signs of guilt: shifting posture, crossing legs, brushing clothing as if to remove dust, slouching in the chair, or moving back in the chair to get as far away from the investigator as possible. The innocent suspect, on the other hand, may move forward in the chair, displaying none of the aforementioned gestures. The innocent suspect's face may become flushed, the eyes may concentrate on the investigator, and he may also respond verbally in a very angry, blunt manner. No attempt will be made to conceal resentment over the accusation. Some innocent suspects, however, will seem completely surprised and taken aback by the accusation or will exhibit a moment or two of disbelief. Then, a sincere, spontaneous, and even vehement denial may follow, accompanied by direct eye-to-eye contact. The innocent person may look truly offended and may attempt to stop the false accusation. On the other hand, a guilty person will usually be passive; he may respond with a rather pleading look and answer in the form of a soft denial or a rather vague inquiry to the investigator.

A guilty suspect may attempt to evade detection by employing dramatic physical gestures, such as moving the head back and forth and running fingers through his hair in an effort to create the impression of complete desperation. By this means, the suspect can also avoid looking the investigator straight in the eye. He may speak loudly upon the assumption that this will intimidate the investigator into terminating the interrogation. These pretenses should not be permitted to mislead the investigator.

The Transition Statement

As previously indicated, a guilty suspect will not easily be persuaded to offer incriminating statements that could potentially lead to losing his job or to a prison sentence. The investigator must therefore provide the suspect with a perceived benefit of telling the truth. This benefit can in no way involve a promise of leniency in exchange for a confession. Nor can this benefit center on avoiding inevitable consequences. Consequently, the transition statement, which is offered immediately following the direct, positive confrontation, must offer a legally permissible reason for the suspect to want to tell the truth.

Furthermore, if the investigator appears too anxious to elicit a confession from the suspect, the credibility of the initial confrontation statement will be lost. After all, if there is no doubt as to the suspect's involvement in the crime, the investigator should not require any further statements from the suspect to prove his case. Therefore, not only does the transition statement have to offer a legally permissible reason for the suspect to confess, but it also must establish a pretense for the interrogation other than to elicit a confession. The following are examples of statements that can be used effectively to create a pretense for the interrogation:

- **Comment on the suspect's redeeming qualities.** Regardless of the suspect's background, there is usually something positive that can be said about him. It may be that he does not have a lengthy police record, or that he appears to be decent and intelligent. In other cases, the suspect may be a responsible parent or a hard-working individual. In essence, the investigator tells the suspect that because of these redeeming qualities, he feels obligated to offer the suspect an opportunity to explain his side of the story.

Transition Statement: Example #1

"Mary, at this stage of an investigation, I have a choice. I can turn in my report and allow my supervisors to act on the evidence, or I can sit down with the person who did something and give that person an opportunity for input in my final report. When I deal with someone who has been cooperative in answering my questions and they don't give me a hard time, I feel they deserve a chance to explain their side of the story. That's how I feel about you. You strike me as a decent person and have certainly shown me respect today. On the other hand, if you had come in here with an attitude and were taking the position, 'Hey if you think I did this prove it!' I wouldn't even bother sitting down with you now."

Explain that the only unanswered question is why the suspect committed the crime. Especially when dealing with an emotional offender, the investigator should focus the interrogation on the circumstances that led up to the commission of the crime. The emotional offender is likely to have morally justified the crime in some way and is often responsive to this technique.

Transition Statement: Example #2

"Peter, as I said, there is absolutely no doubt that you did have sexual contact with your stepdaughter. The reason I wanted to sit down and talk with you about this is to find out what the circumstances were surrounding this thing. The reason why someone did something is often much more important than what they did."

Explain that you need to find out what kind of person the suspect is. Even the most hard-core, dishonest suspect perceives himself in a positive manner. No sane person who commits a crime believes he is fundamentally a no-good criminal. The investigator can take advantage of this distorted perception by creating a concern in the suspect's mind that if the truth is not learned, others may believe that the suspect is basically dishonest, a child molester, a thief, or a hard-core criminal.

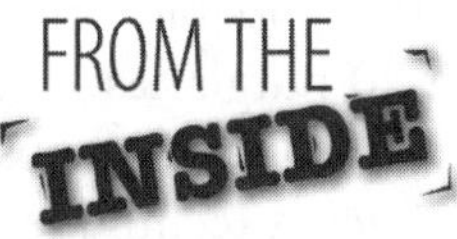

Transition Statement: Example #3

"Sam, in my experience there are two types of people who take money from another person. The first type is a common criminal who is greedy and gives no thought to his actions. He acts impulsively because the only person he cares about is himself. Now the second type of person who would do something like this is basically honest but acts out of character because of pressures in his life. He oftentimes acts spontaneously, on the spur of the moment, and after it happens he feels really bad about what he did. Now Sam, there is absolutely no doubt that you did this. What I need to establish with you right now is what kind of person you are."

Explain that you need to establish the extent or frequency of the suspect's involvement. Especially when the issue under investigation is an ongoing crime, it is effective to use a transition statement that addresses the frequency of the suspect's criminal activity. With this tactic, the investigator credibly exaggerates the suspect's possible involvement in other crimes. The types of cases where this approach would be applicable are burglaries, auto theft, drug sales, and embezzlements.

Transition Statement: Example #4

"Joe, the only reason I'm talking to you now is that we don't know how many other homes in that area you have entered. There's no question that you went into the home on Wilson Avenue last weekend. My concern is that we have over 20 unsolved burglaries within a two-mile radius of that home. These homes were broken into in the same way the Wilson Avenue home was entered, and at about the same time of day. Now if you were involved in all of those other 20 burglaries, quite frankly, I wouldn't expect you to say anything. But, Joe, if you're not involved in all of those others, if it was a lot less than 20, we need to know that because it means that there is someone else out there responsible for those. The last thing I want to have happen is for you to be blamed for something you didn't do. That's why I'm talking to you now."

In establishing the pretense for the interrogation given in Transition Statement: Example #4, the investigator should not mention the possible consequences associated with being potentially charged with all 20 burglaries. This approach is not designed to place the suspect in the dilemma of having to choose between going to jail for 3 years or 15 years, for example. Such a technique is inappropriate and could lead to challenges during a subsequent suppression hearing. Rather, the technique is intended to motivate the suspect to tell the truth by refuting false allegations.

KEY POINTS

- The investigator should start the interrogation with a direct statement indicating absolute certainty in the suspect's guilt. This should be expressed in a slow, deliberate, and confident manner.
- Immediately following the direct, positive confrontation, the investigator should make a statement similar to the following: "I want to sit down with you so that we can get this straightened out. OK?"
- The investigator should then create a period of intentional silence, during which he can evaluate the suspect's initial reaction to the direct, positive confrontation.

KEY TERMS

behavioral pause A period of intentional silence that follows the direct, positive confrontation and lasts about three to five seconds.

direct, positive confrontation Starting the interrogation with a direct statement indicating absolute certainty in the suspect's guilt.

transition statement Statement that offers a reason for the interrogation other than eliciting a confession.

11

Step 2: Theme Development

Chapter Objectives

Upon completion of this chapter you will be able to:

- Explain the principles of theme development
- Discuss procedures for emotional offenders, including approaches to be avoided, third-person themes, and specific themes that can be used
- Discuss procedures for nonemotional offenders

Principles

Immediately after the direct, positive confrontation described in Step 1, the investigator should begin the development of a theme. This involves, in large measure, presenting a "moral excuse" for the suspect's commission of the offense or minimizing the moral implications of the conduct. Some themes may offer a "crutch" for the suspect as he moves toward a confession.

theme a monologue presented by the interrogator in which reasons and excuses are offered that will serve to psychologically justify or minimize the moral seriousness of the suspect's criminal behavior.

Most interrogation themes reinforce the guilty suspect's own rationalizations and justifications for committing the crime. As part of an offender's decision to commit a crime—or, in the case of a spontaneous crime, following it—it is natural for him to justify or rationalize the crime in some manner.[1] The average person can relate to this instinctive mechanism when thinking back over the last time he exceeded the speed limit while driving. The illegal behavior may be explained away by believing that the speed limit signs were poorly posted, or that a perceived emergency existed wherein the driver could not afford to be late to a scheduled appointment. Justification may be rationalized by the fact that the driver was not going that much over the speed limit and other drivers were going much faster than he was, or the driver may blame his passenger for engaging him in conversation, which was distracting. The principle being expressed here is that it is human nature to project blame away from oneself and create excuses for behaviors that cause anxiety, loss of self-esteem, or guilt.

This justification process is one of the most significant differences between innocent and guilty suspects: The guilty suspect has justified the crime in some manner, whereas the innocent person has not. In justifying the crime, the guilty suspect experiences much less of a troubled conscience when he later lies about committing it.

Since most themes reinforce the suspect's own justifications and rationalizations, it is relatively easy to overcome the deceptive suspect's denials during an interrogation because the suspect relates to the theme concepts being presented. On the other hand, the innocent suspect, who has not justified the crime, does not relate to the investigator's suggested justifications and rationalizations; he actively rejects such preposterous statements and becomes stronger and more persistent in his denials. It is imperative, however, that the investigator limit theme concepts to moral justifications or rationalizations concerning the crime. If the theme presents threats of inevitable consequences coupled with promises of leniency, it could jeopardize the validity of the confession. Similarly, an interrogation theme should in no way attempt to convince the suspect that he is guilty of the crime under investigation.

A defense attorney may claim that the interrogation theme was presented in an effort to plant false ideas in his client's mind, similar to brainwashing.[2] As evidenced by the innocent suspect's rejection of the investigator's theme concepts, an interrogation theme does not plant new ideas in a suspect's head. The guilty suspect relates to the theme because these ideas, or ones of a similar nature, have already occurred to him as a natural by-product of committing the crime. Just as an innocent suspect will reject theme concepts because he has not justified the crime, so too a guilty suspect will reject a theme if the investigator's theme does not fit the suspect's justification of the crime.

Procedures for Emotional Offenders

Since emotional offenders often experience shame and guilt, themes centered around excusing their criminal behavior are effective because such themes permit the suspect to accept physical responsibility for committing the crime while relieving his emotional guilt. The selected theme may be based on a simple, commonsense analysis of the suspect's background and the probable motive that triggered the criminal conduct.

Approaches to be Avoided

During the presentation of any theme based on the morality factor, caution must be taken to avoid any indication that the minimization of moral blame will relieve the suspect of *criminal responsibility*. Examples of this include suggesting to a homicide suspect that he "accidentally" killed the victim or that a theft suspect is merely responsible for the missing deposit because he was negligent in leaving the deposit bag in his unlocked car, which allowed someone else to steal it. In short, investigators should generally avoid themes that absolve the suspect of legal consequences for his actions.

Investigators should generally avoid themes that absolve the suspect of legal consequences for his actions.

A mistake criminal investigators frequently make is to reveal, at the outset of the interrogation, all of the specific evidence implicating the suspect. Once the investigator reveals such evidence, the suspect knows the strength (or weakness) of the case against him. If the evidence is extremely convincing and strong, the suspect may psychologically withdraw and take the position, "Go ahead and prosecute me." On the other hand, if the evidence is merely circumstantial, the suspect may argue the insignificance or fallibility of the evidence and thus relieve anxiety through this discussion. Further, the introduction of evidence during the early stage of an interrogation may inhibit the investigator's ability to develop an interrogation theme.

In some instances, it may be advantageous for the investigator to make a passing remark about evidence, but it should not be the focus of the interrogation, nor should the investigator reveal to the suspect all of the evidence known. For instance, in a hit-and-run case, the investigator might comment about the dent in the front fender of the suspect's car and about the fact that human hair and blood have been found around the dent. Once this is brought to the suspect's attention, the investigator should move directly to a theme and discourage the suspect from offering any explanation for the evidence. If the investigator were to build his interrogation around that single piece of circumstantial evidence, the suspect would be likely to excuse away the evidence by claiming that someone else was driving his car, or he might demand to see the crime lab report or state that he wants to talk to an attorney before answering any more questions.

Guilty suspects generally require a face-saving excuse to tell the truth. The (threatening) approach of bombarding them with evidence of their guilt is likely to invoke a fight-or-flight response. If this happens, they might then (1) engage in persistent denials, (2) flee from a formal interrogation by invoking their rights under *Miranda*, or (3) terminate a voluntary interrogation.

Guilty suspects generally require a face-saving excuse to tell the truth.

Interrogations focused on evidence also have the tendency to lead to statements that threaten inevitable consequences or promise leniency. In essence, the investigator tells the suspect that the case against him is ironclad and that he certainly will be found guilty of the crime. The only issue to resolve is the length of sentence the suspect will receive. Under the guise of "offering full cooperation," the investigator tells the suspect that the court will view favorably a confession with respect to sentencing. This statement, of course, could render a subsequent confession inadmissible.

Basic to any theme application is confidence on the part of the investigator and, more important, a conveyance of sincerity in whatever is said. The fact that a suspect has a criminal record, even an extensive one, should not be assumed to present an insurmountable barrier to securing a confession. Persons of that type often are persuaded to tell the truth through the tactics and techniques described in this text. In any event, if an investigator becomes concerned over the fact that the suspect has a criminal record and is probably too "wised up" to confess, the investigator will have encountered defeat before even starting.

The most effective attitude is generally one that reveals a calm confidence, a patient display of a vital, intense interest to learn the truth, and, at the same time, an understanding, considerate, and sympathetic feeling toward the suspect. In conveying a sympathetic, understanding attitude, an investigator must not indulge in fast or glib talk. Except when actually feigning impatience or displeasure, the investigator should talk slowly—even to the point of occasionally hesitating, or even seemingly stuttering, in his attempt to formulate a theme.

Third-Person Themes

third-person theme a real or fictitious event about the interrogator, friend, or other case depicting a similar type of crime and the extenuating circumstances that led to that act.

Following the transition statement in Step 1, the investigator may feel awkward immediately developing a theme directly addressing the suspect's crime. A suggested approach is to initially develop a **third-person theme** in which the investigator talks about some person or situation that is removed from, but similar to, the suspect's present case. This third-person theme provides a foundation for the eventual presentation of a theme related to the suspect's crime. It is also advisable to use a third-person theme for suspects who are quite vocal during Step 1: A suspect is less inclined to offer denials when the investigator talks about a situation not directly relating to his crime.

Developing a Third-Person Theme

"Joe, the reason I want to talk with you today is that you remind me of a fellow we had in here a couple of weeks ago. He was young and ambitious and a real go-getter. By working his way up the ladder at a bank, he went from clerk to teller, and finally he was promoted to auditor within a period of eight or ten months. Everything seemed to be going well for him. He had a loving wife, two lovely children, and they were in the process of moving to a newer home in a nice subdivision. One day, while he was balancing the books, he noticed a teller had failed to record a $6,000 deposit. This was the amount the fellow I'm talking about needed to complete a down payment on his new home. On the spur of the moment a decision was made to take the money. I don't think I have to tell you what happened next. The bank noticed the shortage after the customer called. This young auditor came under suspicion, and I remember him sitting right where you are, telling me how sorry he was for taking the money.

The reason you remind me of him is that, just like him, you have a lot going for you. You are intelligent, ambitious, and basically very honest. I think what happened to you is that on the spur of the moment you decided to do this to help pay bills for food or maybe clothes for your family. . . ."

The third-person theme should somewhat parallel the present suspect's circumstances or motivation. Although the story should have a "happy ending," such as the person deciding to tell the truth, the investigator should not imply leniency as a result of the other suspect's confession. For instance, it would be *improper* in the previous example had the investigator stated, "After this fellow told the truth and explained his side of the story, the bank agreed to make the $6,000 out as a loan and to give him a raise to help support his family."

Specific Themes That Can Be Used

Theme 1: Sympathize with the Suspect by Saying That Anyone Else Under Similar Conditions or Circumstances Might Have Done the Same Thing

A criminal offender, particularly one of the emotional type, derives considerable mental relief and comfort from the investigator's assurance that anyone else under similar conditions or circumstances might have done the same thing. The suspect is thereby able, at least in part, to justify or excuse in his own mind the offensive act or behavior. Yet the person still realizes that a wrong or mistake has injured or damaged another person or the public in general. Self-condonation, therefore, does not completely satisfy the offender's desire for relief from a troubled conscience. As a matter of fact, the comfort derived from the investigator's assurances that another person might have committed a similar offense merely offers an added incentive to obtain the greater degree of relief and comfort that would be provided by telling the truth. While the suspect is in such a frame of mind, the solicitations of a sympathetic investigator may allow the suspect to believe that if the investigator can understand the reasons for his or her crime, others may also be understanding. Case 11-1: Hit-and-Run Driver illustrates how this technique may be used very effectively.

In hit-and-run cases, it is helpful for the investigator to bear in mind the various factors that may account for a person's behavior. The published literature on hit-and-run cases lists a number of reasons a person may have fled the scene of an accident, including (1) panic or psychological numbness from shock, (2) having been under the influence of alcohol, (3) having been driving without a license, (4) fearing financial loss or public shame, (5) having had a passenger in the car whose presence would have caused the driver or passenger considerable embarrassment, (6) having had stolen goods or other evidence of a crime in the car, or (7) fearing exposure for some other criminal offense. Suggesting to the suspect any appropriate one of these reasons, along with the possibility that anyone under similar circumstances, including the investigator, probably would have done the same thing, will contribute greatly to the success of the interrogation.

Once again, investigators are cautioned that in utilizing the presently discussed theme, they should not make a promise of immunity from prosecution or a diminution of punishment as an inducement for a confession. There is, of course, no legal objection to extending sympathy and understanding in order to feed into the suspect's own justifications for his criminal behavior, as described here, in an effort to elicit the truth.

Case 11-1: Hit-and-Run Driver

A hit-and-run driver was told that anyone else under similar conditions of panic might also have fled the scene. He was, therefore, afforded an opportunity to "square himself" with his own conscience. Meanwhile, his realization that the investigator did not perceive his leaving the scene as savage-like rendered his task of telling the truth much easier than would have otherwise been the case.

The following line of conversation illustrates how this central theme concept was presented to the hit-and-run suspect:

> *I'm sure in my own mind that a man like you wouldn't deliberately do a thing like this. I think I know what happened: Your car hit something. You were not sure what it was, but you had some doubts; so you got excited and drove away. Now you realize you did wrong. You are no different than anyone else and, under the same circumstances, I probably would have done what you yourself did. Now the shock is over and you, as a good citizen, should tell the truth as to what happened. You certainly did not do this deliberately!*

Theme 2: Reduce the Suspect's Feeling of Guilt by Minimizing the Moral Seriousness of the Offense

It is very common for guilty suspects to experience mental relief by believing that what they did could have been much worse and that many other people have committed similar crimes. This is particularly true in sex crimes. In such cases, it is desirable for the investigator to pursue a practice of having a male suspect believe that his particular sexual irregularity is not an unusual one, but rather one that occurs quite frequently, even among so-called normal and respectable persons. In this connection, it has been found effective to comment as follows:

> *We humans are accustomed to thinking of ourselves as far removed from animals, but we're only kidding ourselves. In matters of sex, we're very close to most animals, so don't think you're the only human being—or that you're one of very few—who ever did anything like this. There are plenty others, and these things happen every day and to many persons, and they will continue to happen for many, many years to come.*

In sex crimes, it is also very helpful for the investigator to state that he has heard many persons tell about sexual activities far worse than any the suspect himself may relate. This will serve to encourage the suspect to admit a particularly "shameful" kind of sexual act. His embarrassment will be minimized.

Whenever referring to the particular sexual act about which the suspect is being questioned, the investigator should not use vulgar terms unless, of course, the suspect is incapable of understanding more acceptable terminology. If, in connection with the offense under investigation, homosexuality on the part of the person being questioned becomes an issue, it should never be discussed or referred to as "abnormal" behavior. To the contrary, the investigator should convey the impression (irrespective of his own values) that homosexuality of a consensual nature is within the bounds of normality.

As earlier stated, the investigator must avoid any expressed or specific statement to the effect that because of the minimized seriousness of the offense leniency will be afforded. Through wishful thinking a suspect, of course, might surmise in his own mind that because his crime could have been much worse that he is due some leniency in court. An investigator cannot be held accountable for a guilty suspect's wishful thinking. But at no time should the investigator state, or imply, that the suspect will receive such leniency.

Theme 3: Suggest a Less Revolting and More Morally Acceptable Motivation or Reason for the Offense than That Which Is Known or Presumed

The true reason people steal is because they are basically dishonest. The true reason a man sexually molests a child is because he has a sexual perversion. The true reason a gang member kills a rival gang member in a drive-by shooting is because he has not developed the social consciousness to respect life. Yet, even within the deepest core of these people's minds, few of them accept the actual motive behind their crime. Rather, the thief believes that he steals because he is desperate, the child molester believes that his conduct represents an act of affection, and the gang member believes it is necessary to kill as a matter of his own survival. Whenever a person lies about a criminal act he committed, it can be safely assumed that, in his own mind, he has also distorted the true motive behind his crime. Because of this, the investigator should always consider theme concepts that describe the motive of the crime in a morally acceptable manner.

A good example of the utilization of this theme is in cases of sex-motivated arsonists, especially where deaths result from the fire. Upon reflection, an arsonist may find his conduct highly reprehensible, and his conscience can become greatly troubled. The investigator may diminish that feeling by starting off with a theme centered around starting the fire to get even with parents (where the fire was started in a parent's home) or to get a day off from school (where the fire was set inside a school). It is far easier to admit starting the fire for these reasons than for the deliberate act of sexual gratification. Once again, the objective is to have the suspect acknowledge intentionally starting the fire.

Intoxication is a guilt-diminishing factor that can be used for suspects who are interrogated regarding crimes that are, to say the least, embarrassing to the suspect. For example, consider the case of a respected citizen who is guilty of taking indecent liberties with a neighborhood child. The suggestion that alcohol affected his judgment permits the suspect an opportunity to "save face" by blaming alcohol for his conduct. This approach affords the suspect some comfort with regard to the reaction from relatives, friends, and other persons when they hear about his confession, particularly when a child victim is involved.[3]

A suspect's use of drugs may be approached in the same way as alcohol consumption. It, too, will serve to render a crime less reprehensible in the offender's mind. Moreover, drug addiction can also be presented as the actual motivation for a crime such as robbery or burglary—namely, the impelling need for money to support the drug habit.[4] In other words, the suspect had to rob, burglarize, or commit some other money-objective crime to survive. The investigator may also point out that when an addict is without drugs, his perceptions and judgments are clouded, causing the suspect to do things that he otherwise would not have done.

When using a theme that blames alcohol or drug intoxication, it is important that the investigator describe a situation in which the suspect's intoxicated state affected his judgment or impulse control. At no time during this theme, or any other, should the investigator suggest or state that the suspect's use of alcohol or drugs caused him to "black out" and forget that he committed the crime.

In a robbery-killing case, the investigator might suggest that the suspect had not intended, or had not planned, the killing, and that the only motive was to get some needed money; nevertheless, the shooting was necessary when the victim resisted the robbery attempt. Another effective theme for shootings that occur during the course of a robbery is to blame the suspect's emotional state at the time of the robbery. In essence, the investigator explains that the suspect is not a hard-core criminal and, because of that, was scared and may have been literally shaking when he pulled out the gun. Because of this nervous condition, the gun went off even though the suspect didn't specifically intend to pull the trigger.

In the interrogation of a suspected embezzler, the suggestion may be offered that there was only the intent to "borrow" the money rather than to steal it, and that had it not been for the untimely discovery of the shortage, he would have replaced the money somehow. Another approach with an embezzler, or any other suspect who has stolen money, is to suggest that the money was taken for the benefit of a spouse, child, or another person. This is particularly effective when the investigator knows that another person had been in need of financial aid and had actually received aid from some source. For instance, in one case, a suspected bank teller was known to be financing his son's attendance at a theological seminary, which the teller could not have afforded on his bank salary. The investigator suggested that the teller's desire to assist his son was the motive for the embezzlement, although the investigator knew that the embezzled funds far exceeded the money needed for tuition. The face-saving motive, however, served the purpose of securing the initial admission, after which the suspect eventually disclosed the real reason for the theft—his gambling activities.

Theme 4: Sympathize with the Suspect by Condemning Others

This theme is three-pronged: (1) condemn the victim, (2) condemn the accomplice, or (3) condemn anyone else upon whom some degree of moral responsibility might conceivably be placed for the commission of the crime under investigation. The psychological basis for these approaches can be appreciated quite readily by anyone who has committed noncriminal wrongdoings and has had to own up to them. There is a natural inclination to preface an admission with a condemnation of the victimized person or thing, or with a statement purporting to place part or even all of the moral blame upon someone or something else. The same mental forces are in operation in matters involving criminal offenses—and to an even greater degree because of their more serious nature.

In view of the fact that self-condonation of this type so frequently accompanies a confession of guilt—with the offender seeking by this means to more or less justify or excuse the offense in his own mind—it seems only reasonable to presume that an investigator's condemnation of the offender's victim, accomplice, or others would prove to be effective in persuading a suspect to tell the truth. Moreover, actual experience has demonstrated this to be so.

The following descriptions of several case situations illustrate the manner in which this technique can be applied.

Condemning the Victim The interrogation technique of condemning the victim can be used advantageously in sex crimes (for example, a forcible rape) by suggesting to the suspect that the victim was to blame for dressing or behaving in such a way as to have unduly excited a man's passions. The discussion might go somewhat as follows:

> *Joe, no woman should be on the street alone at night looking as sexy as she did. Even here today, she's got on a low-cut dress that makes visible damn near all of her breasts. That's wrong! It's too much of a temptation for any normal man. If she hadn't gone around dressed like that you wouldn't be in this room now.*

Degrading the character of the victim can also be used in cases such as one in which the suspect is being interrogated about the killing of a fellow criminal or even a police officer. The victim can be pictured as "no good" and as one who has always been involved in crooked deals and shakedowns.

In assault cases, the victim may be referred to as someone who had always "pushed other people around" and who perhaps finally got what was coming to him. Furthermore, the victim may be blamed for having initiated an argument or perhaps even for having threatened physical harm.

The main objective of the investigator in many instances is to have the suspect place himself at the crime scene or in some sort of contact with the victim. Once that is accomplished, the investigator will later be able to have the suspect relate the complete facts of what occurred. For instance, in an assault case, once the suspect admits having been involved in the incident, the exercise of a little patience will ultimately result in the disclosure of a guilty person's full responsibility for the occurrence.

In a robbery case, the victim may be blamed for having previously cheated the suspect or perhaps for stealing some property from him, and it may be brought out that the suspect's intent had been merely to settle the account. In a case where the victim was an assumed stranger, the victim can be blamed for "flashing money" or putting the suspect down in front of friends and the robbery described as merely an effort to teach the victim a lesson.

In theft cases involving employees, particularly first offenders and those whose motives arose from an actual need for money rather than from some other circumstances, the employer should be condemned for having paid inadequate and insufficient salaries or for some unethical or careless practice that may have created a temptation to steal.

Example of Blaming Victim Strategy to Elicit Confession

In interrogating a bank teller, the suspect might be asked, "How much money do you make, Joe?" after which the investigator could mention a purposely overstated amount. Then when the suspect states the actual salary figure, the investigator may say:

> *Ye gods, man, how in the world can anybody with a family the size of yours get along on that kind of money in this day and age? Look at the temptations you face every day! You handle thousands upon thousands of dollars for a salary like that! And you're not only supposed to live on it, but be a first-rate dresser as well. That's something common laborers don't have to do. They can go around in old, dirty clothes, and they make twice as much money a day as you do.*
>
> *I know how financially pressed you were. You were so hemmed in you could see no way out except to do what you did. Anyone else confronted with a similar situation probably would have done the same thing, Joe. Your company is at fault. You work hard but can't get by on your small salary; so you arranged for a loan and of course you had a hard time paying it back and you missed some payments. Then you probably tried to get another loan someplace else to pay off the previous one. So you're forced to do something like this to pay your bills and now you're being questioned about it. I can tell you this—if you received a decent salary in the first place, you wouldn't be here and I wouldn't be talking to you.*

Condemning the Accomplice For much the same reason that a youngster with a baseball bat in hand alleges to an irate homeowner near the playing field that "we" (he and his teammates) broke the window rather than stating "I" did it (meaning the boy who struck the ball its damaging blow), the criminal offender is naturally inclined to have someone else share the blame or even be blamed altogether for the commission of the crime in question. Any line of interrogation, therefore, that tends to lift from him some of the burden of guilt for the criminal act will make the suspect that much less reluctant to confess.

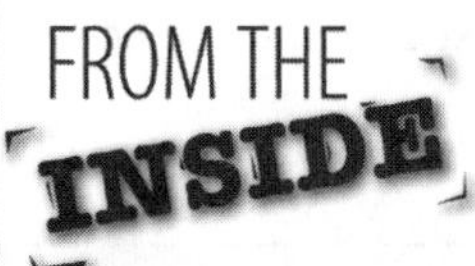

Example of Condemning the Accomplice Strategy

A suspect had invested heavily in a real estate project that, as it neared completion, seemed doomed to be a financial failure. In charge of the property in question was a handyman whose mental capacity was somewhat deficient. After a fire of suspicious origin, in which a large and heavily insured building was destroyed, the handyman, upon being questioned by investigators, confessed that he had set the fire at the request of the owner. On the basis of this confession and evidence that the fire was of incendiary origin, the owner was arrested. At first he denied his guilt, and he continued to do so even when confronted with the testimony of his employee. Then, the investigator proceeded to apply the suggested technique of condemning the accomplice. The investigator's expressions in this respect were somewhat as follows:

> *We all know—and you know—that there's considerable truth to what your employee says about the fire. We also know that a man of your type may not have done such a thing had it not been suggested or hinted at by someone else. It looks to me as if this fellow you have working for you may be the one who conceived the idea. He knew you were having a tough time financially, and he probably wanted to be sure his pay would go on, or perhaps he was looking for even more than that. For all I know, he might have done this just for the purpose of getting you in trouble. Maybe he wanted to get even with you for something he thought you had done to him. That I don't know, and we won't know the true explanation unless you tell us. We know this much: The place was set on fire. Your employee did it. He says you told him to do it. We also know you haven't told the whole truth.*

The suspect admitted that he had known the property was to be set afire and had approved of the burning. At first he insisted, as the investigator had indicated as a possibility, that it was the employee's idea. This version, of course, was false. Nevertheless, for a few minutes the investigator permitted the suspect to bask in the sunshine of this partial admission and reflected guilt and to derive therefrom the attending mental comfort and relief. Soon thereafter, the investigator began to point out the lack of logic and reasonableness in the suspect's fixation of primary blame upon his employee. The suspect was told that he still did not look as relieved as a man should look after telling the truth. Then the investigator proceeded to explain sympathetically that by coming out first with only part of the truth, he had done what all human beings would do under similar circumstances. Finally, as a climax to such comments, the investigator urged him to tell the whole truth. The suspect then admitted that the idea of burning the building was his own. For the purpose of inducing him to begin his confession, however, it was necessary and effective for the investigator to start off by first blaming the accomplice.

In applying this technique of condemning the accomplice, the investigator must proceed cautiously and must refrain from making any comments to the effect that the blame cast on an accomplice thereby relieves the suspect of legal responsibility for his part in the commission of the offense. Related to this concept is our strong recommendation to avoid any mention of a plea bargain in exchange for testifying against the accomplice. Any discussion of a possible reduced sentence or other favorable treatment should be instigated by the prosecutor, not the investigator. To reiterate, by suggesting this technique, the authors merely recommend a moral condemnation in the form of expressions of sympathy for the suspect's "unfortunate" experience in having been influenced by a "criminally minded associate."

Avoid any mention of a plea bargain in exchange for the suspect testifying against the accomplice.

Condemning Anyone Else Upon Whom Some Degree of Moral Responsibility Might Conceivably Be Placed In addition to victims and accomplices, there are others who may be condemned to good advantage. Sometimes, the investigator may find it effective to place blame on government and society for permitting the existence of social and economic conditions that are conducive to the commission of crimes such as that of which the offender is accused. On other occasions, even the offender's parents may be alleged worthy of blame for the offender's conduct. Numerous other possible recipients of the investigator's condemnation might also be mentioned, but Case 11-2: The Wife Killer and Case 11-3: The Arsonist will illustrate the application and effectiveness of this technique.

Case 11-2: The Wife-Killer

In the interrogation of an accused wife-killer, the investigator proceeded to condemn the wife's relatives, who were known to have meddled in the offender's marital affairs. They were blamed for having deliberately set out to render the suspect's married life unhappy. At one point, the investigator remarked that probably the relatives themselves deserved to be shot. During the discussion, the investigator did not spare the wife, of course, nor wives in general. The suspect's wife was alleged to be a provocative, unreasonable, and unbearable creature and was portrayed as a woman who would either drive a man insane or else to the commission of an act such as the present one in which she herself was the victim. In this respect, however, the investigator stated that the suspect's wife was just like most other women. He also said many married men avoid similar difficulties by becoming drunkards, cheats, and deserters, but unfortunately the suspect tried to do what was right by "sticking it out," and it got the better of him in the end. All of this, of course, rendered the offense less reprehensible in the suspect's own mind, thereby overcoming his desire to avoid an exposure of guilt.

Case 11-3: The Arsonist

In an arson case, an ambitious young man, who had worked hard to accumulate a sizable amount of money, was anxious to become successful in merchandising a new product. Some promoters led him to believe it was a "sure thing," and he was so convinced by them that he purchased a substantial amount of the product, rented a store, and rented a sizable unused warehouse on a long-term lease. But the merchandise soon proved worthless. The young man attempted to cancel his lease, but the landlord refused. A friend of the young man suggested he soak the premises with gasoline and set fire to it to terminate the lease. He followed this advice, but when he set the warehouse on fire, an explosion blew him out of a first-floor window. By quickly removing his clothing, he survived with only a few wounds. He left town until his wounds had healed.

Upon his return, he was interrogated about the occurrence. The investigator proceeded to place the blame on the landlord for not releasing the young man from the lease, whereas the suspect was lauded for his ambition and his honest desire to become successful. He was told that he should be grateful for still being alive and in good health. The suspect then disclosed the facts about setting the fire. He also stated that his anger toward the landlord was a factor in his use of an excessive amount of gasoline, which resulted in his being blown out the window.

When the offense is theft or embezzlement, a spendthrift wife or the financial burden of a child may be blamed for the suspect's thievery. He may be told something like the following:

> *Your wife [or daughter, or son, if such is the case] had been pressuring you for more money than you were earning. You cared enough for her that you wanted her to have all she asked for—even*

though you didn't have it to give, Joe. What you did here was for her, not for your own selfish interests. She shouldn't have asked for all she got from you. Now she will probably understand, and she should stick by you in your present difficulty. It's time now, Joe, for you to tell the truth.

A person who has taken indecent sexual liberties with a young girl may be told that her parents are to blame for letting her roam around by herself as they did. When the suspect had lured the child into his car or elsewhere by offering candy or something else in the way of a gift, the parents may be blamed for not providing such things themselves. Along with fixing blame on the parents, the investigator may blame the child herself, as was suggested in the discussion of the earlier technique of condemning the victim. A moral coward of this type finds it very comforting to have his conduct understood on the basis of one or more of these considerations.

In an arson case, blame may be placed on the insurance company for permitting the accused and others to take out excessive insurance and to insure property far in excess of its actual value. The point to be made by the investigator is that by this excessive insurance practice, the insurance company presented too much of a temptation to set property afire to resist, particularly in those cases where the owner was hard pressed financially.

When a suspect's home or neighborhood environment seems to be a factor accounting for his criminal conduct (as is so often the case), the investigator should point out that fact. The application of this technique is illustrated later in this chapter when examples of theme development with youthful (juvenile) suspects are described. In a burglary or robbery case, a theme may be developed on the basis that the suspect's life circumstances (e.g., unemployment for many months with a family to support) are to blame for driving the person to do what he did out of frustration and desperation.

Theme 5: Appeal to the Suspect's Pride by Well-Selected Flattery

It is a basic human trait to seek and enjoy the approval of other persons. Whether in professional activities or in ordinary, everyday living, most individuals receive a satisfying amount of approving remarks or compliments. However, those who engage in criminal activities, particularly those who operate alone, may seldom receive approving remarks and compliments; moreover, the need for such attention and status is just as great or even greater than it is with everyone else. When interrogating a criminal suspect, therefore, the establishment of effective rapport between investigator and suspect may be aided considerably through praise and flattery.

Consider the case of a juvenile or even an adult who is being interrogated as the suspected driver of a getaway car in the robbery-murder of a gas station attendant. Assume a police patrol car had given chase but was outdistanced by the fleeing vehicle because the officers could not run the risk of injuring innocent pedestrians or motorists. The driver of the fleeing vehicle, of course, had no such consideration, and his reckless driving made the escape possible. In such cases, there is much to be gained by speaking to the subsequently apprehended suspect somewhat as follows: "Joe, the officers who were chasing that car tell me that in all their years on the force, they have never seen a car maneuvered like that one was. It really took the corners on two wheels."

The investigator's complimenting the suspect serves to defuse the natural adversarial relationship that exists between the two. As any salesperson will tell you, it is difficult to dislike someone who offers a sincere compliment. This serves to reduce the guilty suspect's natural tendency to perceive the investigator as his enemy. Psychologically, it is much easier to justify lies told to someone who we resent than a person who we respect, admire and feel emotional attachment to.

This does not mean, of course, that (ordinarily) a confession will be immediately forthcoming because of flattering remarks; however, along with everything else the investigator says and does, it can be very helpful in obtaining a confession of guilt. Even if a confession is not obtained soon, or perhaps at all, if the suspect gives clear indications of lying, the investigator nevertheless will have achieved a considerable measure of success because other investigative efforts can be concentrated on that particular suspect.

In one case involving a robbery suspect, the suspect was told, with good effect:

> *I've been in investigative work a long time and I've talked to a lot of people who have done things like what you did, but I've never seen or talked to anyone who had as much guts as you do. I don't know how you could be as calm as you were under those circumstances. Moreover, this was the best planned job I've ever come across for a guy working alone. It's amazing how you found out where those materials [the stolen articles] were kept. And then when you got into action, you made John Dillinger look like a piker. [The reference here is to a notorious gunman in the early 1930s, but there are other, more current names the investigator may select.] He had all kinds of help from others, but you worked alone. Joe, how did you feel before you pulled off that job? I guess your nerves of steel didn't have any room for nervousness.*

In another case involving a jail chaplain accused of taking indecent liberties with a child, the investigator commented upon the chaplain's "dedication to God" and all the sacrifices he had made as "a man of God." It was then suggested that basically, he had the same human frailties as everyone else and that on this unusual occasion, he just could not sufficiently suppress his feelings. He was then advised to go into the chapel of the jail where the interrogation was being conducted and there, while alone "with God," to write out an account of what had happened. Within an hour, he presented the investigator with a fully detailed confession. (A result of this type is exceedingly rare, regardless of whether or not the suspect is a clergyman. It does illustrate, nevertheless, the potential of flattery, as well as of one of the previously discussed themes.)

Flattery is especially effective when it is in reference to a person's youthful appearance, attire, family background, good reputation, unselfishness, and so forth. Also, the uneducated and underprivileged are more vulnerable to flattery than the educated person or the person in favorable financial or social circumstances. With the latter types, flattery should be used sparingly and very discreetly.

Theme 6: Point out the Possibility of Exaggeration on the Part of the Accuser or Victim, or Exaggerate the Nature and Seriousness of the Event Itself

It is exceedingly common for guilty suspects to perceive themselves as victims of an unjust system. The guilty suspect is quick to point out any error, however slight, in a victim's account (e.g., "She said the guy who did this had brown eyes—mine are closer to black!"). It is common for guilty suspects to claim they were "set up" or "framed" for the crime they committed. They perceive the police and court system as corrupt and actively seek loopholes from which to escape the pending consequences for their crime. This "victim mentality" also accounts for the ease with which they place blame on others.

It is human nature to find fault in another person's apparent "unfounded accusations." This instinct is so strong that, in an effort to prove the other person wrong, the person defending his position may make very incriminating admissions. To illustrate this, one of the author's sons was sent home from school with a missing assignment notification that had to be signed by a parent. The son strongly maintained that he had turned in the referenced assignment and that the teacher was old and forgetful and should retire. To fortify his position, he boldly asserted that the assignment he actually missed was for the day before.

Similarly, when a suspect who is guilty of a crime is presented with false allegations concerning some elements of that crime or other possible crimes he committed, his victim mentality makes him vulnerable to confessing what he did do in an effort to disprove the erroneous allegations. Perhaps the reason for this is that he is willing to accept the possibility of receiving punishment for what he did do in order to maintain his self-esteem (e.g., "I beat the system by not copping to something I didn't do"). The motivation here is no different than when negotiating the "best" price for a new car. As long as the salesperson reduces the original asking price, the customer feels that he has won some sort of moral victory, even though inevitably the final cost for the car is more expensive than what was expected. Whenever circumstances permit credible exaggeration of the crime, the investigator should consider a theme centered around that concept.

In some instances in which an offender is accused by the victim, or by a witness to the crime, the investigator should tell the suspect that even though there must be a basis for the accusation, there is the ever-present possibility of exaggeration, and that the truth can only be determined by first obtaining the suspect's own version of the occurrence.

Pointing out the possibility of exaggeration on the part of the accuser is not only helpful in obtaining confessions from the guilty, but may also serve the purpose of exonerating the innocent. A good illustration of this point is Case 11-4: The Lieutenant's Daughter.

The exaggeration theme also may be utilized by exaggerating the intent of the suspect with respect to the offense. For instance, a suspected burglar may be told that a rapist has been terrorizing residents in their homes in the same neighborhood, and that the investigator is concerned over the possibility that the burglary suspect may be a rapist as well as a housebreaker. Another example of exaggeration

Suggesting the Accuser has Exaggerated

In a rape accusation case in which the suspect denies not only the rape but even the act of intercourse itself, it is effective to talk to the suspect in the following terms:

> *Something you need to realize is that right now all she is saying is that you had normal vaginal intercourse with her, just like a husband would have with his wife. What I don't want to see happen is for her to start claiming things that aren't true to make you look a lot worse. What happens sometimes with these women is that they start looking for sympathy and try to beef up their case by claiming that the man engaged in all sorts of perverted sex acts with them, and made them do things that are totally reprehensible. The problem you're in right now is that people will believe whatever she says. If you don't get your side in now, down the road she may make you sound like some sort of sex pervert from a different planet and people might believe her. I don't want her to get away with lies because that's not fair to you. If this was just normal vaginal intercourse that got a little rough, let's establish that now so if she makes further claims in the future I can stop her and say, hey, that's not true!*

of intent is to suggest that the burglary suspect may have been the person who attempted to set fire to one of the burglarized houses. **In general, the psychological principle to employ is to minimize in the suspect's mind the act he committed when compared with more offensive behavior possibilities.** Stated another way, the idea to be conveyed is that the suspect is not so bad a person after all.

Theme 7: Point Out to the Suspect the Grave Consequences and Futility of Continuation of Criminal Behavior

During the course of their criminal careers, many offenders experience a fleeting desire or intention to reform. This is particularly true with youthful offenders and with adults who are first offenders or in the early stages of their criminal career. Such a mood at times is manifested during an offender's period of failure, that is, when he is accused or under arrest and thus brought face to face with the stark realities on the debit side of such activities. During this time, the suspect can become quite vulnerable to comments regarding the future consequences and futility of continued criminal behavior, especially when the offense is not of the most serious sort and when the offender is not too well seasoned by a long

Case 11-4: The Lieutenant's Daughter

The 35-year-old daughter of a police lieutenant accused a cab driver of rape. The investigator was satisfied that the accused was telling the truth when he denied the rape, but he surmised that the cab driver was lying when he denied having the accuser as a passenger. The investigator then talked to him as follows:

> *Joe, you're not telling the whole truth. We also know that this woman is at least telling part of the truth. It may well be that she's grossly exaggerating what happened. But she was in your cab, and she may have had intercourse with you voluntarily. Then when she left, she may have feared a pregnancy, or a sexually transmitted disease, or she may have had some other reason for coming up with this rape story. But unless you tell us the truth as you know it, we'll just have to take what she says at its face value. My advice to you, Joe, is to tell the truth.*

To this the suspect responded, "All right. Now that you put it up to me that way, I'll tell you what actually happened." He then related that the woman had hailed his cab from in front of a tavern; that she had been intoxicated; that as he approached the address she had given him, she directed him to go into an alley in back of her family home and told him to stop at a particular place and to turn the lights out; and that she invited him to have sexual intercourse with her, which he did.

Following this disclosure, the investigator confronted the woman with the driver's statement, whereupon she admitted that he had told the truth. She explained her false accusation by saying that after the affair she had been concerned that a member of her family might have seen her get out of the cab in the alley, and that her ruffled clothing might have provoked suspicion. Furthermore, she had not thought police would find the cab driver because she had only hailed a passing cab and was not in one sent to the pickup location by the cab company, which probably would have had a record of the driver who was sent out on the call. Once she started with her lie, however, it had been difficult for her to retract her accusation. In this case, therefore, had it not been for the utilization of the exaggeration technique, the accused may have been prosecuted for a crime he did not commit.

series of offenses and police experience. Under these circumstances, the individual might be convinced (momentarily, anyway) that for his own sake, it is a good thing to have been caught early in the game because this experience may serve to avoid much more trouble later.

Suggesting Confession as a Way of Cutting Short a Crime Career

In a larceny case, the investigator might say the following:

> *You know what will happen to you if you keep this up, don't you? This time you've taken a relatively small amount of money; next time it will be more, and then you'll do it more often. You'll finally decide it's easier and more exciting to get what you're looking for at the point of a gun. Then someday you'll get excited and pull the trigger when the muzzle's resting against somebody's belly. You'll run away and try to hide out from the police. You'll get caught. There'll be a trial, and when it's all over, despite the efforts of your parents and relatives, who in the meantime have probably spent their last dime trying to save your neck, you'll probably have to spend the rest of your life in the penitentiary.*
>
> *Now's the time to put the brakes on—before it's too late. And remember this too, Joe: Do you know what the average amount of money that's taken in robberies is? About $18. So for a lousy $18, a guy puts his life on the line. It's downright crazy. Joe, there are better ways to live.*

It is advisable, whenever possible, to point out the relative insignificance of the offense in terms of how much worse it could have been.

Youthful offenders or adults who are not confirmed criminals, or who have not committed serious crimes, may be told:

> *Everyone makes mistakes, and we can all profit by such mistakes. A person with any brains at all can look upon them as lessons regarding his future conduct. And, after all, that's really what the judicial system is all about—to teach a fellow a lesson, in the hopes that he'll straighten himself out.*
>
> *Joe, if you don't own up to your present mistake and you think you've gotten away with something, you're bound to get yourself in worse trouble later on, and maybe then you won't have a chance to straighten yourself out. The police may do it for you when they catch you in a burglary or robbery: You may end up straightened out on a marble slab in the morgue. What a heartbreak that would be for your mother to go to the morgue and identify your body with a tag on your big toe and nothing else but the bullet in your head.*

Downplaying the Severity of the Crime

In a burglary case, for example, the investigator might say to the suspect:

> *Joe, all that happened the other night was the taking of money. But if you keep this up, some night you'll crawl in a window thinking that no one is home, but someone is home, and he comes at you with a gun or a knife. To save your own life, you grab the gun or the knife and you have to use it on him; or, if you don't kill someone yourself, eventually someone may kill or cripple you for life. One of your intended victims, or perhaps a policeman, may do this to you.*
>
> *Let me give you an actual example of this. [Here the investigator may incorporate a third-person theme relating to a past suspect or perhaps a personal experience.] When I was a kid, there were two young fellows in my neighborhood who were always doing flashy things. They were well dressed and dated the best-looking girls around. Yet neither one of them worked, and neither of their families had money to support their style of living. Well, the mystery was solved one night when a tavern owner who had been robbed twice decided to be prepared for the next attempt. When the two young men I told you about entered the tavern, the owner, who suspected what they were up to, ducked behind a partition where he had a pistol, and as the two fellows drew their guns and forced the cashier to hand over money, he shot and killed both of them. Had they been caught when they were new at the stealing game, their young lives would have been saved.*
>
> *Joe, you may not fully realize it now, but getting caught early like this may prevent something like that from happening to you. Put the brakes on now before it's too late.*

Interrogations that are handled in the manner of these examples tend to make an offender feel that he is indeed rather fortunate in having escaped more serious difficulty. Once in that frame of mind, the suspect may become less reluctant to tell the truth about his present criminal activity.

The basic validity and effectiveness of the present technique may be explained by the fact that many offenders do have some awareness of the ultimate consequences of their continued criminal behavior. Moreover, when an offender vows that he will go straight, he usually means it at the time. Perhaps that is the reason for the appealing effect of pointing out the grave consequences and futility of continuing with a criminal career.

Procedures for Nonemotional Offenders

As previously stated, the nonemotional offender attempts to avoid becoming emotionally involved in the interrogation; in effect, he insulates himself from the investigator's words and actions. This form of defensiveness often renders the previously discussed sympathetic themes ineffective alone.

Psychologically, the nonemotional offender perceives the interrogation as a contest of endurance, pitting his own willpower against the investigator's persistence. To this type of offender, the consequences of lost pride or embarrassment weigh somewhat as heavily as would the consideration of losing a job or going to prison. Regardless of the investigator's sincerity or credibility, the nonemotional offender tends to be suspicious of anyone offering assistance or seeking his trust. For these reasons, the use of sympathy, exaggerations of the crime, or condemning other persons for the crime are themes that, by themselves, are unlikely to persuade the suspect to tell the truth.

Tactic 1: Seek Admission of Lying About Some Incidental Aspect of the Occurrence

A suspect who has been caught in a lie about some incidental aspect of the occurrence under investigation loses a great deal of ground; thereafter, as the suspect tries to convince the investigator that he is telling the truth, he can always be reminded that he was not telling the truth just a short while ago. Under no circumstances, however, should the suspect be told "You lied to me once, and you'll lie to me again." The reminder of lying should be expressed in polite fashion, not in the form of a reprimand. To state it otherwise may result in a defiant attitude.

Suppose a male suspect had been accused of indecent liberties with a child, but denied to the investigators that he had even seen the child. In such an instance, the investigator should try to get the suspect to admit having seen and talked to the child. The investigator may say:

> *Joe, there's no question but that you were in this kid's presence and that you talked to her, and there's nothing wrong with that! There's also nothing wrong with giving her candy, or even patting her on the head. Joe, what did she say to you?*

If Joe is guilty, he may think he can avoid any further suspicion by acknowledging the conversation with the child. Thereafter, the investigator can proceed to utilize other appropriate techniques, such as blaming the child. (Here, of course, is a reversion to earlier discussed techniques.)

In the application of this technique, the investigator should bear in mind that there are times and circumstances when a person may lie about some incidental aspect of the offense without being guilty of its commission (see Case 11-5: Lying for Unrelated Reasons).

Whenever a suspect seems to be telling the truth regarding the issue under investigation but is reluctant to tell where he was at the time of its occurrence, the investigator may say something like the following:

Case 11-5: Lying for Unrelated Reasons

An investigation of the murder of a married woman disclosed that the suspect, who was also married, had been having an affair with her. When questioned by investigators about his whereabouts at the time of the murder, the suspect gave an alibi that was quickly established to be a falsehood. This so convinced the investigators that he was the murderer that one of them subjected him to physical abuse in an effort to obtain a confession. He did not confess. Subsequently, however, a professionally skilled and ethical investigator, seeking to ascertain the reason for the false alibi, was able to elicit from the suspect the fact that at the time of the murder, he had been in bed with another married woman. This was the reason for his having lied when he gave his previous alibi; in other words, he lied to avoid exposure of his latest indiscretion. The second alibi proved to be the truthful one!

> *Joe, if what you were doing at the time has nothing to do with this case, I give you my word I'll treat whatever you tell me as confidential. I'm not interested in your personal affairs. So tell me where you were at the time.*

Whatever an innocent person says in response should, of course, be kept confidential!

Tactic 2: Have the Suspect Place Himself at the Scene of the Crime or in Contact with the Victim or Occurrence

When a guilty suspect places himself far from the scene of the crime or denies any contact with the victim, it becomes much more difficult for him to eventually tell the truth about commission of the crime—he faces not only the consequences of committing the crime, but also the embarrassment of having to acknowledge his other related lies. Consequently, it is always to the investigator's advantage to have the suspect place himself in close proximity to the crime scene or victim. The initial attempt at doing this should be during the nonaccusatory interview, as presented in Chapter 6 of this text.

The technique's basic validity is illustrated in the questioning of a child regarding mischievous conduct or the taking of something that did not belong to him. If the child admits to having been present when the act occurred or to having seen the missing object earlier, acceptance of full responsibility is not remote. For instance, if a boy is thought to have taken some money or some object from his parents' bedroom, he may first be asked, "Johnny, did you see a dollar bill on the dresser in my room a while ago?" An admission that he had seen the money, and especially one that he picked up the dollar bill to look at it, warrants his being questioned further. His admission of seeing the money and touching it will constitute a substantial step toward a disclosure of the truth. Cases 11-6 and 11-7 (Initial Confession Leads to Full Confession, Versions 1 and 2) provide further illustration.

Tactic 3: Point Out the Futility of Resisting Telling the Truth

With all offenders, in particular the nonemotional type, the suspect operates from a belief that if he says nothing he will avoid suffering any consequences associated with his crime. As discussed under Step 1 of the interrogation process, the investigator must portray high confidence in the suspect's guilt. On occasion, though, merely expressing certainty in the suspect's guilt will not overcome the guilty suspect's resistance to telling the truth, and it will become necessary to further bolster this confidence by direct statements designed to allow the suspect to realize the futility of resistance to telling the truth. **The authors wish to make clear, however, that at no time should an investigator attempt to convince a suspect who claims not to recall whether or not he committed the crime that the suspect must have committed it.** However, an innocent suspect, even one who is uncertain of his possible involvement in a crime, is not apt to confess to a crime merely because the investigator expresses high confidence in his guilt and even points out logical statements explaining why continued denials will not necessarily prevent a guilty person from suffering the consequences of his crime.

Case 11-6: Initial Confession Leads to Full Confession

In a homicide interrogation in which the suspect was accused of stabbing to death a 12-year-old girl who was babysitting for friends, standard themes were unproductive in capturing the suspect's attention. The suspect maintained that, at the time of the killing, he was several miles away attending a party, and that he did not know the victim. The following theme, which resulted in the suspect's acknowledgment of being inside the victim's home on the night of the killing, was crucial in eventually eliciting a full confession from the suspect:

> *Joe, for a minute I will entertain the thought that you did not do this. However, it is very clear that you have not told the complete truth about seeing this girl that evening. A neighbor has identified you as the person who stopped by her house earlier that evening. [This statement was only partially true. A neighbor did see a man fitting the general description of the suspect earlier in the evening.] If you were there for some other purpose, such as to ask directions, or maybe you thought you knew someone who lived in the house and you went there to ask for that person, that would explain a lot. But there's no question that you were there. How long were you at that house that evening—hours or just a short while?*

Case 11-7: Initial Confession Leads to Full Confession – Version 2

An employee forged her manager's signature on a cash drop slip that the employee had stolen. The investigator decided to try to get her to acknowledge forging the manager's signature and used the same evidence that had been successfully used in an earlier bait question:

> *Julie, when I stepped out of the room following our earlier interview I had a fax waiting for me from the crime lab. The report I received from the document examiner indicated that indeed it was your handwriting on that drop slip—not your manager's. There's no question that you signed his name on that drop slip. As far as I know, it may have been a situation where he wasn't around and you were in a hurry and couldn't wait for him so you wrote his name down before dropping the deposit. If that's what happened, it would be important as an explanation for that report I received. Have you written his signature many times or was this unusual when it happened?*

Once the employee acknowledged forging her manager's signature, her game plan of denying all involvement quickly fell apart, and she admitted the theft shortly thereafter.

A central component of this theme is for the investigator to "argue against self-interest." That is, the investigator should not appear anxious to get the suspect to confess or portray to the suspect that a confession is necessary in order to resolve the case. Quite to the contrary, the investigator wants to present the interrogation as an opportunity for the suspect to explain his side of the story or to offer the reasons for his commission of the crime. Most of us have encountered high-pressured salespeople who are obviously interested only in obtaining a sales commission. We tend to despise such people. A *skilled* salesperson speaks favorably of his competition: He offers subtle reasons to buy his own product while clearly leaving the perceived choice of making a purchase up to the customer. By removing himself from any personal benefit resulting from the customer's decision to buy the product, he tremendously increases, in the customer's mind, whatever benefits his product offers. A forthcoming sale is likely.

The investigator should not appear anxious to get the suspect to confess or portray to the suspect that a confession is necessary in order to resolve the case.

One approach may be to reveal several of the various pieces of incriminating information or evidence already in the investigator's possession and then to ask the suspect, "Joe, if you yourself had this information or evidence against some other person, you'd believe he was the one who did it, wouldn't you?" Without waiting for a response, the investigator should continue: "Whether or not you acknowledge your involvement makes no difference to me; the evidence will speak for itself! My only reason for spending this time with you is to give you the opportunity to explain why this thing happened." The investigator may then suggest various "acceptable reasons" that may have led to the suspect's commission of the act.

In some situations it may be helpful to appeal to the suspect's logic by making the following statement:

> *Jim, I don't need someone to tell me that they did something for me to know that they did. Go down to the state penitentiary and talk to the inmates. Ninety-nine percent of them will tell you they're innocent. Do you think that 99 percent of the felons in this state were wrongly convicted by a jury of their peers? Every day defendants are found guilty based strictly on evidence presented to twelve members of a jury. A jury doesn't need to have someone tell them that they did it to vote guilty. The only reason I'm talking to you now is that I thought you deserved an opportunity to explain your side of the story.*

The investigator can then continue with a sympathetic theme.

Tactic 4: When Co-offenders are Being Interrogated and Previously Described Themes Have Been Ineffective, Play One Offender Against the Other

When two or more persons have collaborated in the commission of a criminal offense and are later apprehended for questioning, there is usually a constant fear on the part of each participant that one of them will "talk." Individually, each may feel confident of his own ability to evade detection and to avoid confessing, but neither of them seems to experience a comparable degree of confidence in the co-offender's ability or even willingness to do so. Uppermost in each of their minds is the possibility that one of them will confess in an effort to obtain special consideration.

This fear and mutual distrust among co-offenders can be made the basis for the very effective interrogation technique of playing one against the other. Because this theme largely involves a bluff on the part of the investigator, however, it should be reserved as a *last resort,* to be used only after other possible themes have failed to produce the desired result.

There are, in general, two principal methods that may be used in playing one offender against another. The investigator may merely intimate to one offender that the other has confessed, or the investigator may actually tell the offender so. In either event, there are two basic rules to follow, although they are, of course, subject to exceptions: (1) Keep the suspects out of sight and sound of each other, and (2) use, as the one to be led to believe the other has confessed, the less criminally hardened suspect. In other words, choose the follower rather than the leader, or the one who acted the lesser role in the crime: Target the one who is likely to be more vulnerable to the ploy. At times, however, the reverse procedure is warranted. Perhaps the leader may be the more vulnerable one because of concern that if he does not talk first, he may be left holding the bag after the weaker partner confesses first. The choice is a judgment call that the investigator must make on the basis of the particular case circumstances.

If the co-offenders both seem to be very naive—for example, young first offenders unfamiliar with the possibility of interrogation trickery—a simple form of intimation may consist of the practice of taking the second suspect into the interview room soon after the interrogation of the first, and then telling him something like the following:

> *This other fellow is trying to straighten himself out; how about you? Or do you want to let this thing stand as it is? I'm not going to tell you what I now know about your part in this job. I don't want to put the words in your mouth and then have you nod your head in agreement. I want to see if you have in you what it takes to tell the truth. I want to hear your story—straight from you own lips.*

Many are the occasions when this admonition has triggered a confession.

Whenever the more direct bluff is attempted—that is, when the suspect is actually told that his co-offender has confessed—the investigator must be careful not to make any statement purporting to have come from the co-offender. The person to whom it is related could recognize it as an inaccuracy and, therefore, as a wild guess and a falsehood on the part of the investigator. Once the investigator makes such a mistake, the entire bluff is exposed and it then becomes useless to continue with the act of playing one against the other. Moreover, the investigator is then exposed as a trickster and thereafter can do very little to regain the suspect's confidence. Therefore, unless the investigator is quite certain of the accuracy of any detail of the offense that he intends to offer to one suspect as representing a statement made by the co-offender, it is better to confine statements to generalities only.

An exception to the forgoing precautionary measure is to be made in a case in which one of the offenders is definitely known to have played a secondary role in the commission of the offense. In such a case, one suspect may be told that the other suspect has put the blame on him for the planning of the offense, or for the shooting, or so forth. At the same time, the investigator may add, "I don't think this is so, but that's what he says. If it's not the truth, then you let us have the truth." In this way, the investigator can avoid any danger to his bluff because he concedes the possibility of the statement being a falsehood. It can also be useful here to emphasize to an offender that he performed the less offensive role in the commission of the crime, as illustrated in the previous discussion of condemning the accomplice.

Before discussing the remaining steps, the authors wish to reiterate the statement made earlier that an investigator need not utilize the steps in the exact order in which they appear in this text. In fact, it would be impossible to do so in any given situation, since various developments in the early stages of an interrogation may require a shifting in the sequence of the remaining recommended steps. Moreover, there may be times when two or more steps will have to be intermingled so that they may seem to represent only a single step; consequently, the themes comprising Step 2 will have to be reused from time to time during the course of an interrogation. In other words, it is impossible in a text of this nature to compartmentalize or categorize the various tactics and techniques as though each one was self-supportive and exclusive of the others—they are all interrelated. Unavoidably, however, they must be discussed individually; otherwise, any discussion of them would be rambling and confusing. It is, therefore, essential for the investigator to exercise his own ingenuity when embarking upon an interrogation. This text must be used only as a set of principles rather than as a set of fixed, inflexible rules.

KEY POINTS

- After the direct, positive confrontation, an investigator should begin developing a theme that offers a moral excuse for the suspect's commission of the offense or minimizes the moral implications of the suspect's conduct.
- The investigator must be sure not to give any indication that the minimization of moral blame will relieve the suspect of criminal responsibility.
- Generally, the investigator should avoid going into too much detail about the evidence in hand.
- A third-person theme, in which the investigator talks about some person or situation that is removed from, but similar to, the suspect's present case can provide a foundation for the eventual presentation of a theme related to the suspect's crime.

Specific Themes That Can Be Used

- Sympathize with the suspect by saying that anyone else under similar conditions or circumstances might have done the same thing.
- Reduce the suspect's feeling of guilt by minimizing the moral seriousness of the offense.
- Suggest a less revolting and more morally acceptable motivation or reason for the offense than that which is known or presumed.
- Sympathize with the suspect by condemning others, such as the victim, an accomplice, or anyone else upon whom responsibility might be placed.
- Appeal to the suspect's pride by well-selected flattery.
- Point out the possibility of exaggeration on the part of the accuser or victim, or exaggerate the nature and seriousness of the event itself.
- Point out to the suspect the grave consequences and futility of the continuation of criminal behavior.

Additional Tactics Needed for Nonemotional Offenders

- Seek admission of lying about some incidental aspect of the occurrence.
- Have the suspect place himself at the scene of the crime or in contact with the victim or occurrence.
- Point out the futility of resisting telling the truth.
- When co-offenders are being interrogated and previously described themes have been ineffective, play one offender against the other.

KEY TERMS

theme A monologue presented by the interrogator in which reasons and excuses are offered that will serve to psychologically justify or minimize the moral seriousness of the suspect's criminal behavior.

third-person theme A real or fictitious event about the interrogator, friend, or other case depicting a similar type of crime and the extenuating circumstances that led to that act.

ENDNOTES

1. Psychologists refer to this internal process as techniques of neutralization. Those classifications are remarkably similar to what we refer to as themes. For example, "denial of responsibility"; "denial of injury"; "denial of victim" and "condemnation of the condemners." See Lillyquist, M., *Understanding and Changing Criminal Behavior,* Upper Saddle River, New Jersey: Prentice-Hall, Inc., 1980, 153–160.
2. For an in depth discussion of this argument see Jayne, B. & Buckley J. "Interrogation Techniques on Trial," *The Prosecutor* 1990, Fall.
3. In suggesting that intoxication may have been a factor underlying a suspect's criminal offense, a reference could be made to a 1979 study by the United States Department of Justice, which showed that nearly one-third of state prison inmates drank very heavily just before committing the crimes that led to their imprisonment. The study is entitled *Prisoners and Alcohol* (U.S. Dept. of Justice, Bureau of Justice Statistics, published Jan. 1983).
4. A study conducted by the U.S. Department of Justice, published in October 1983, contains statistics that reveal a high correlation between criminal offenses and the use of drugs by the offenders at the time of their crimes. See particularly p. 39 of the *Report to the Nation on Crime and Justice: The Data*, Document # U.S.J.-87068.

12

Step 3: Handling Denials

Chapter Objectives

Upon completion of this chapter you will be able to:

- Discuss indications of upcoming denials
- Explain the importance of and methods for deflecting denials
- Describe the ways in which a transition statement is made
- Describe considerations when evaluating denials

Principles

Confessions usually are not easily obtained. Indeed, it is a rare occurrence when a guilty person, after being presented with a direct confrontation of guilt, says: "OK, you've got me; I did it." Almost always, the suspect, whether innocent or guilty, will initially make a denial. It may be "No, I didn't do it" or a similar expression, or perhaps a meaningful gesture to that same effect. A denial is basically a response that an allegation is false. It is an indicated refusal to believe, recognize, or acknowledge the validity of a claim. This denial phase of an interrogation is one of the most critical stages for the investigator. Unless it is handled with expertise, the investigator's subsequent efforts may be exercises in futility.

denial a statement or action that contradicts or refuses to accept the truthfulness of an allegation.

One of the primary goals of Step 3 is to **discourage the suspect from engaging in unnecessary denials, which distract from the investigator's theme and subsequent efforts to persuade the suspect to tell the truth.** Furthermore, it is important for an investigator to appreciate a fundamental principle of interrogation: The more often a guilty suspect denies involvement in a crime, the less likely it is that he will tell the truth. This tenet of human nature applies not only during the interrogation process, but also prior to it. A guilty suspect who has already denied involvement in the crime to his spouse, parents, and friends is much less likely to eventually tell the truth than one who has not offered such preliminary denials. Simply stated, if the investigator allows the guilty suspect to voice multiple denials during an interrogation, it will be much more difficult for the suspect to eventually tell the truth.

Step 3 of the interrogation process is important for another reason. Depending on the nature and persistence of the suspect's denials, the investigator may become convinced of the suspect's actual innocence and bring the interrogation session to a close. In some instances, the suspect's denials may indicate secondary involvement in the offense under investigation, such as guilty knowledge or perhaps involvement in a similar, but unrelated, act as the one under investigation. In short, the nature and extent of a suspect's denials (or lack thereof) form an important basis for how the investigator will proceed with the interrogation.

During testimony, a defense lawyer may attempt to describe this stage of the interrogation as one in which an innocent defendant was prevented from telling the truth because of the investigator's efforts to stop the suspect's denials. It must be made clear that the suspect was not physically restrained from offering denials, but rather, that procedures were used to socially discourage the suspect from offering denials.

Procedures

Denials Following the Direct, Positive Confrontation

A weak denial following the direct, positive confrontation should be ignored by the investigator; it represents nothing more than the suspect following through with the mental game plan of "If I am accused of doing this, I will deny it." Without giving any heed to the offered denial, the investigator should immediately embark upon the transition statement to establish the purpose for the interrogation (e.g., to find out why the suspect committed the crime).

However, when the suspect offers a stronger denial to the direct, positive confrontation, the investigator should reassert his confidence in the suspect's guilt as the transition statement is introduced. The dialogue in Ignoring the Initial Denial illustrates this process.

The reason for ignoring a weak denial and responding to a more forceful one is that in the first instance, the investigator implies that he expected the denial and will not even waste his breath by responding to it. This nondefensive response has the effect of inhibiting further denials from such a suspect. With a more forceful denial, however, the investigator cannot be certain if it is coming from an innocent or guilty suspect, and a restatement of the investigator's confidence in the suspect's guilt has two desirable effects: (1) If the suspect is innocent, there will be no mistake about the investigator's position, and the innocent suspect will be highly motivated to prove the investigator wrong; (2) if the sus-

Ignoring the Initial Denial

I: "Joe, I have in this folder the results of our entire investigation. There is no doubt that you are the person who started that fire. I'd like to sit down with you this morning so we can get this clarified, OK?"

S: "That's crazy. I didn't start that fire!"

I: "As I said, Joe, the results of our investigation clearly indicate that you did start the fire, but the most important thing to establish right now are the circumstances that led up to this. A while back I was talking to a man who was under investigation for starting a fire in his home . . . " [continue on with a third-person theme].

pect is deceptive, the investigator's response indicates high confidence in the suspect's guilt, which is required for any successful interrogation.

Denials Made During the Theme

In the initial accusatory confrontation (Step 1) and throughout the development of the theme (Step 2), the investigator should have conveyed to the suspect the attitude and position that the investigation into the case has clearly indicated his guilt and, consequently, that the only reasons for the investigator to be talking to the suspect at all are to determine the circumstances of the crime and to obtain an explanation for its commission (or whatever the investigator's transition statement may have been).

Once the theme has been introduced and the investigator starts to develop it, there are three primary objectives with respect to handling denials:

1. Anticipate denials before they are voiced.
2. Discourage weak denials from being voiced.
3. Evaluate denials that are voiced.

Because these goals represent the essence of Step 3, each of them will be discussed separately, with specific recommended procedures offered at each stage.

Anticipating Denials Before They Are Voiced

It is significant to note that truthful and deceptive suspects frequently differ in their behavior just before a denial is offered. As a general statement, truthful suspects offer their denial in an outright fashion and display appropriate nonverbal cues reflecting the confidence of their verbal statement. However, deceptive denials are often preceded with verbal or nonverbal cues that allow the investigator to anticipate when the suspect is about to deny involvement in the offense under investigation.

interruption gesture universally recognized social signal often employed by deceptive suspects to let a speaker know, "Hey, it's my turn to talk. I have something to say!"

Nonverbal Indications of an Upcoming Denial

On the nonverbal level, deceptive suspects often employ **interruption gestures** before voicing a denial. These are so named because they are universally recognized social signals to let a speaker know, "Hey, it's my turn to talk. I have something to say!" Truthful suspects rarely engage in such nonverbal behaviors before expressing a denial—their denials are truthful and they don't feel a need to be polite or socially proper when voicing them.

To help visualize interruption gestures, picture yourself involved in a conversation with a co-worker. The co-worker is dominating the conversation, seeming to go on endlessly with accounts about his vacation or son's accomplishments in sports. You want to say something, but do not want to appear offensive in interrupting your friend. You will likely accomplish this by sending nonverbal signals to the co-worker that essentially express a desire to talk. One such nonverbal behavior is to extend a hand between the two of you as an illustrator preceding the spoken word.

In the interrogation situation, sometimes this hand gesture is expressed by placing a forefinger of one hand on the finger of the other hand, in anticipation of expressing specific points of dissension. A forward lean in the chair often precedes a denial. The suspect first prepares himself mentally to express the verbal denial and in doing so may lean slightly forward in the chair. The suspect may make an effort to catch the speaker's eye. During normal conversation, the lis-

Figure 12-1 Interruption gestures preceding a denial.

tener focuses his gaze on the speaker's mouth. When that gaze is elevated to the speaker's eyes, a clear message is being sent: "I am no longer listening to you; I have something to say." Finally, the suspect may open his mouth and take a breath, waiting for a pause in the investigator's theme to get a statement out.

These nonverbal symptoms—an extended hand, a forward lean, an effort to catch the speaker's eye, and the open mouth—each indicate that the suspect desires to interrupt the theme. Deceptive suspects will not interrupt the investigator to confess. They interrupt the investigator to offer a denial. **Figure 12-1** depicts a suspect using interruption gestures.

Verbal Indications of an Upcoming Denial

Innocent suspects disclose very little warning during the theme development stage that they are about to verbally deny involvement in the crime. They may give some general nonverbal signs that they are about to speak, such as shaking the head or leaning forward in the chair while making some hand gesture or arm movement, but they will usually give no verbal clues that a denial is forthcoming. Instead, they simply voice the statement "I did not do it," without any prefatory remark.

On the other hand, a guilty suspect may preface the denial with a permission phrase. The suspect knows that his upcoming denial is a lie and so introduces it by asking permission to speak. The following represent common permission phrases:

"May I say one thing?"

"Could I just explain something to you?"

"Would you please let me tell you something?"

Other verbal statements that often precede a deceptive denial might be described as pleading phrases, such as "But honestly," "Please," or "I understand what you're saying, but . . ."

permission phrase phrase used to ask permission to speak that may preface a denial.

pleading phrase other verbal statement that often precedes a deceptive denial such as "But honestly," "Please," or "I understand what you're saying, but . . ."

Discouraging Weak Denials from Being Voiced

Following the permission phrase or pleading phrase, a guilty suspect will be impelled to add "I didn't do it"; however, the investigator should seek to discourage this from occurring. It is incumbent upon the investigator, therefore, to recognize the significance of the permission phrase and then, upon hearing it, to interject a comment that will get the suspect's attention and discourage the completion of the denial statement. This type of comment should begin with an accentuated reference to the suspect's first name (e.g., "Joe!"), followed by something like "Before you say anything else, let me explain how important this is" or "Listen, I want you to understand this."

To emphasize the investigator's confidence in his position, the just-mentioned verbal assertion should be accompanied by the investigator engaging in appropriate nonverbal gestures. First, he should turn his head away from the suspect, denying him eye contact. This social gesture expresses disinterest in what the suspect is about to say and has the effect of discouraging completion of the statement. At the same time, the investigator should hold up his hand to make

Figure 12-2 Investigator's nonverbal response to discourage denials.

the well-recognized "stop" gesture. This will further assert the investigator's confidence. Finally, the investigator may move his chair slightly toward the suspect when continuing with his theme. Another way to maintain control over the situation is for the investigator to change his tone of voice by either speaking louder or, in some instances, by speaking more softly. Alternatively, he may change the rate of speech to underscore the significance of the statement. **Figure 12-2** illustrates an investigator's nonverbal response while saying to the suspect, "Dan! Hear me out. What I'm saying is important."

The statement "Joe, before you say anything else, let me explain how important this is" will often stop a guilty suspect from completing a denial statement. Following this remark of "importance," and the subsequent silence of the suspect, the investigator should immediately return to the development of his theme. As the investigator proceeds with theme development, often the suspect will attempt to reenter the conversation with a denial. Once again, as the guilty suspect attempts to introduce a denial with a permission phrase (e.g., "Can I just say something?"), the investigator should immediately interject a statement advising the suspect to "just give me a minute" because of the importance of what the investigator is saying. A guilty person is always interested in hearing the whole story or in finding out exactly what may be known about him so that an assessment may be made of the situation. As a result, most guilty suspects become quiet when told, in essence, that more incriminating information is coming.

As stated earlier, an innocent suspect will generally make a very direct, sincere, and spontaneous denial after the investigator's first positive confrontation. Nevertheless, to minimize the risk of an erroneous diagnosis, the investigator should continue a short while with the assumption that the suspect may be guilty. Again, the focus here is on suspects against whom there is reasonable evidence or certainty of guilt. In other words, before the investigator ever accuses a person of committing a crime, there should at least be a reasonable basis for believing that the person actually committed it.

An innocent suspect usually will not let the investigator continue for long before forcefully interjecting a denial into the conversation. Unlike guilty suspects, the innocent ones, as previously mentioned, will not preface their denials with permission phrases; rather, they will unequivocally state something to the effect of "You're wrong; I did not do it!" Nevertheless, the investigator should attempt to discourage denials in much the same way as was done with the denials of persons displaying symptoms of guilt.

In the majority of instances, innocent suspects will not allow the investigator to stop their denials; in fact, the intensity and frequency of denials from the innocent will increase as the interrogation continues. An innocent suspect will become angry and unyielding and often will attempt to take control of the interrogation by not allowing the investigator to talk until the suspect has made very clear the point that he did not commit the crime under investigation.

Evaluating Denials

The previously discussed procedures to thwart a suspect's attempts to deny guilt will not always be successful, of course. This will be true of all innocent denials, but many guilty suspects also persist in their efforts to voice their denial.

The final goal of Step 3 is to **evaluate** denials and respond to them effectively. To do this, the investigator must carefully evaluate exactly what the denial is actually saying. In this regard, a denial may offer significant insight as to how the investigator should proceed with the interrogation. Beyond the broad category of innocent versus guilty denials, the investigator needs to assess the strength and content of the denial, inasmuch as this will assist in knowing how to best handle it.

Denials from the Innocent

By far the easiest denials to identify during an interrogation are those emanating from an innocent suspect. Such suspects will generally respond to the investigator's first accusation (Step 1) with a spontaneous, direct, and forceful denial of guilt. They will likely express or otherwise indicate anger and hostility over the accusation and may even insult the investigator because of it. While making the initial denial, the innocent suspect will look the investigator straight in the eye and may very well lean forward in the chair in a very assertive or even aggressive posture. The verbal content of the denial may be something like: "You're wrong. You've got to be crazy if you think I did something like that!"

As the investigator continues with his transition statement and eventual theme development, the symptoms of an innocent suspect's denials become even more obvious. Nonverbally, the suspect becomes more and more agitated and focused (clearly emotionally involved in the process), and his attempts to deny become more frequent and persistent. The suspect eventually engages in nonverbal gestures similar to those an investigator uses to put off a denial. That is, he leans forward, extends a hand, and may look away when the investigator tries to talk; a verbal battle is likely to ensue, and the innocent suspect will win. This is such a significant sign of the innocent denial that it needs to be emphasized: When an investigator attempts to discourage denials by using the previously mentioned tactics but the suspect wins the verbal battle and the investigator becomes the silent listener, strong consideration should be given to the probability that the suspect is innocent.

Innocent suspects often emphasize their denials by distinctly enunciating their words. Their denials often contain descriptive language such as, "I did not *murder* anyone!" or "I did not *steal* any money from work!" While making this statement, the innocent suspect's eyes may convey an injured or angry look similar to that of a person who has been deeply offended. Furthermore, innocent suspects will rarely move past this state of denial during an interrogation; they will remain adamant in their position and refuse to allow the investigator to continue with an unchallenged development of the interrogation theme.

Denials from the Guilty

Guilty denials range from being weak and apologetic to being persistent but lacking conviction. The content of a denial may also identify it as coming from a guilty person. Frequently, a suspect's guilt will be apparent from his initial reaction during Step 1, the positive confrontation. One category of common deceptive responses to the confrontation statement involves asking a question such as, "Why do you think I did that?" "Are you sure?" "How can that be?" or "It does?" A second category of common deceptive responses to the direct, positive confrontation involves qualified phrases. Examples of these include "Honestly, I don't remember being with her that night!" or "I pretty much told you everything I know."

Upon being confronted with their crime, some guilty suspects will take a defensive stance and make a statement such as "I knew this would happen" or "You're just out to get me. I'm being framed!" Perhaps the most revealing example of this defensive strategy was exhibited by a suspect confronted with falsifying a deposition in a sexual harassment investigation. Upon being told by the investigator that he clearly lied during his deposition, the suspect, with a smile on his face, got out of his chair, shook the investigator's hand, and in a very civil manner stated, "Well, I figured you wouldn't believe me. It's been nice talking to you but I have an attorney to see." As quickly as he could, he exited the interview room.

Denials offered by a guilty suspect during theme development may be recognized by the suspect's avoidance of descriptive language. For instance, "I didn't do *that!*" or "I didn't *take* that money!" The deceptive denial may be preceded with a statement indicating theme acceptance, such as, "I understand what you're saying, but honestly I wasn't even there." The mere fact that the suspect acknowledges relating to the theme concepts serves as an indication of guilt. Innocent suspects are much more likely to challenge theme concepts: "What difference does it make if I was behind on bills? I never robbed anyone in my life!" Similarly, a deceptive denial may incorporate an apology, such as, "I'm really sorry to have caused you this trouble, but honestly, I didn't do this."

In conjunction with the guilty suspect's offering verbal denials, he will usually engage in such nonverbal actions as avoiding eye contact with the investigator, slouching in the chair, moving the chair itself back, or shifting posture, including crossing and uncrossing arms and legs. Evaluating a suspect's paralinguistic behavior during a denial will often reveal the deceptive nature of the denial. In this regard, deceptive denials can be described as weak or pleading. The statement "Oh really, you've got to believe me," said in a pleading fashion, is typical of the guilty. The denial that is said softly or passively also lacks the strength and conviction typically heard from an innocent person.

Responding Effectively to Denials

The following procedures for responding to denials should be considered as general guidelines offering suggested approaches that have frequently been found to be effective. Ultimately, a number of factors enter into the investigator's approach to handling a suspect's voiced denial, including the level of rapport established with the suspect, the strength of evidence against a suspect, and the investigator's personality.

Denials from a Probably Innocent Suspect

When the investigator senses that the suspect may be innocent, he should begin to diminish the tone and nature of the accusatory statements. Rather than concentrate on the fact that the suspect committed the act in question, the investigator should soften the accusation to the point of indicating that the suspect may not have actually committed the act but was only involved in it in some way, or perhaps merely has some knowledge about it, or else harbors a suspicion as to the perpetrator. This process of stepping down the intensity of the accusation is a very deliberate one; the investigator should continue with the evaluation of the suspect's verbal and nonverbal behaviors. Moreover, he should look for indications of something the suspect may have done of a less relevant nature that evoked the suspicion about the suspect's commission of the principal act. For example, in a $5,000 embezzlement case, the investigator should explore the possibility that the suspect stole a smaller amount of money, unrelated to the larger amount, and that this could account for the behavior symptoms displayed during the initial phases of the interview regarding the $5,000.

The investigator may find it advisable to expand the interrogation into such areas as the possibility that the suspect gave a false alibi for some personal reason unrelated to the crime under investigation. Perhaps the alibi that was offered, which proved to be false, may be accounted for by an impelling need to prevent the disclosure of an indiscretion, such as having been in the company of an individual other than the suspect's spouse at the time the crime was committed. The possibility of the suspect's commission of some other crime similar to, but unrelated to, the one under investigation might also be explored.

Whenever the verbal and nonverbal behavior exhibited by the suspect during an interrogation seems sincere and indicates that the suspect was not involved in the offense under investigation, no statement should be made immediately that he is clear of any subsequent investigation. The suspect should merely be told that as a result of cooperating with the investigator, other leads will be pursued in an attempt to substantiate the suspect's claim of innocence. Similarly, if the investigator is convinced of a suspect's guilt but is unable to move him past the denial phase of the interrogation, the suspect should be advised that the investigation will continue in an effort to establish the suspect's true status.

Weak, Qualified, or Apologetic Denials from the Guilty

An investigator has a number of options from which to choose when responding to weak denials. All of them involve a statement that there is absolutely no doubt as the suspect's guilt. The investigator then attempts to redirect the suspect's attention away from his guilt or innocence and back to the stated purpose for the interrogation (e.g., to find out what kind of person the suspect is).

Redirect the Suspect's Attention Back to the Stated Purpose of the Interrogation

S: "But honestly, I don't know anything about this."
I: "Joe, there's absolutely no doubt that you did this. That's in the past. You can't change that, and I can't change that. The only reason I'm talking to you now is to find out what kind of person you are. I don't think you have a criminal mind, where you carefully planned this thing out for months in advance, and calculated it down to the second. I think you are basically an honest person who acted out of character. That's what we need to establish." [Return to theme.]

Some suspects will not be content simply being told that there is no doubt as to their involvement—they want to know what the evidence against them is before deciding to tell the truth. The vast majority of cases involving criminal interrogation involve no overwhelming evidence of a suspect's guilt: That is precisely why the interrogation is being conducted—to obtain such evidence. Many guilty suspects, however, must be convinced that the truth is already known or will be established shortly before they decide to tell the truth. In this situation, the investigator must make a decision as to whether to introduce evidence during the interrogation.

One motivation for guilty suspects to offer denials during an interrogation is to evaluate the strength of the investigator's case. Consequently, once the investigator brings up evidence, he is playing into the suspect's hand because the suspect now knows precisely how strong the case is against him and he has something tangible to attack and argue. For this reason, mentioning specific evidence against a suspect during an interrogation should be a carefully considered tactic to overcome persistent denials. The foregoing statement assumes, of course, that the investigator does *not* have clear and convincing evidence of the suspect's guilt; if the investigator actually has prima facie evidence of the suspect's involvement in a crime, some of that evidence could be presented with good effect at this stage to overcome the suspect's persistent denials.

As previously mentioned, most interrogations do not include physical evidence that clearly indicates the perpetrator of the crime. Therefore, the investigator may have only circumstantial evidence to present as "proof" of the suspect's involvement. In many cases, the best indication of a suspect's guilt may be the investigator's analysis of the suspect's behavior during the interview. Consequently, when a suspect responds, "Hey man, I swear on my mother's grave, I don't know nothing about this," the investigator would be unlikely to persuade the suspect to tell the truth by explaining that his alibi appears a little weak and that the suspect's nonverbal behavior is consistent with others who have withheld information.

If an investigator chooses to present evidence during an interrogation, the first attempt should be through implication. The dialogue in Case 12-1: Hotel Safe Heist, from an actual interrogation, nicely illustrates this technique.

Case 12-1: Hotel Safe Heist

The issue under investigation was the theft of $600 from a hotel safety deposit box. The investigator knew going into the interrogation that whoever stole the money used the manager's key to open the box, and that the thief left the key by a bell stand. Further, it was known that the envelope that had contained the money was left in a trash can near the safety deposit boxes. The suspect's denials were weak but persistent at this stage of the interrogation.

> S: "But honestly, I didn't even see that money. I don't know why you think I did this."
>
> I: "Listen, Sam, we know that you used Margie's key to open that safety deposit box and we know you left the key by the bell stand after you took the money. We already know that. We also know that after you took the money from the deposit box, you removed it from the envelope and threw the envelope away in a trash can down the hall from there—we know all that. What we don't know is how you got the key and that's important . . ." [Return to theme.]

The suspect's denials stopped at this point and, within 15 minutes, he offered a full confession of the theft. The investigator never presented any evidence against the suspect; he only ambiguously stated that he knew certain things. It was never stated how the investigator knew them, only that he did.

In any crime, an investigator can be certain of specific things the guilty person must have done. The technique of implication simply involves telling the suspect that the investigator already knows he did those things without explaining how or why the investigator knows.

Some guilty suspects will not be satisfied with the investigator's statement that "We know you handled that knife in her apartment." They will demand to know specifics about the evidence. In this situation the investigator has two choices. The first is to evade the issue of documented evidence entirely (covered in the next section); the second is to fabricate a response. An outright lie about evidence implicating a suspect should be an investigator's last effort to persuade the suspect to tell the truth. It must be remembered that the guilty suspect knows exactly what he did and did not do during the commission of a crime. For example, if an investigator lies about finding the suspect's fingerprints at a crime scene where the suspect knows he wore gloves, the investigator's credibility is lost and, under that circumstance, a confession will be unlikely.

Although it is perfectly legal to verbally lie about evidence connecting a suspect to a crime, it is a risky technique to employ. Before presenting such evidence, careful consideration should be given to the level of rapport established with the suspect, the probable existence of the evidence, and the investigator's ability to "sell" the existence of the evidence. A miscalculation of any of these principles may cause the technique to backfire and fortify a guilty suspect's resistance to telling the truth.

Furthermore, fictitious evidence implicating the suspect in the crime should not be used when the suspect takes the position that he does not remember whether he committed the crime (because of being intoxicated, for example). Under that unusual circumstance, it may be argued in court by a defense lawyer that the introduction of evidence was used to convince the suspect of his guilt. For these reasons, introducing false evidence during an interrogation should be considered only when other attempts to stop the suspect's persistent, but weak, denials have failed.

Stronger, Persistent Denials from the Guilty

friendly/unfriendly act act played out by one or two investigators that accentuates sympathetic characteristics after the suspect is verbally attacked, in order to get the suspect to truthfully answer questions about the case.

When the various techniques of sympathy and understanding have proved to be ineffective in stopping the denials of a suspect whose guilt is definite or reasonably certain, the investigator may consider using a so-called **friendly/unfriendly act**. This act may involve two investigators or one investigator working alone.

The following procedure applies when two investigators are involved. Investigator A, after having employed a sympathetic, understanding approach throughout his interrogation, expresses regret over the suspect's continued lying. A then leaves the room. Interrogator B enters and proceeds to make uncomplimentary statements to the suspect, by pointing out his objectionable characteristics or behavior. (Or, B may enter while A is still in the room, and B can start his efforts by admonishing A for wasting his time on such an undesirable person; whereupon A will leave the room with pretended hurt feelings over the suspect's refusal to tell him the truth.)

After interrogator B (the unfriendly one) has been in the interview room for a short while, interrogator A (the friendly one) reenters and scolds B for his unfriendly conduct. A asks B to leave, and B exits with a pretended feeling of disgust toward both the suspect and A. A then resumes his friendly, sympathetic approach.

This technique has been effectively applied by using a detective as the friendly investigator and a police captain as the unfriendly one. As the captain leaves the room after playing his unfriendly role, the detective may say, "Joe, I'm glad you didn't tell him a damn thing. He treats everybody that way—individuals like yourself as well as people within the department. I'd like to show him up by having you tell me the truth. It's time he learns a lesson or two about decent human behavior."

The psychological reason for the effectiveness of the friendly/unfriendly act is that the contrast between the two methods serves to accentuate the friendly, sympathetic attitude of the first investigator and thereby renders that approach more effective. Investigators must bear in mind, of course, that in the employment of the friendly/unfriendly act, the second (unfriendly) investigator should resort only to *verbal* condemnation of the suspect; **under no circumstances should physical abuse or threats of abuse or other mistreatment ever be employed.**

Although the friendly/unfriendly act is usually performed by two persons, one investigator can play both roles. In fact, the authors are of the opinion that this is the more effective way to apply the technique.

Solo Performance of the Friendly/ Unfriendly Act

When a single investigator acts out both parts, he feigns impatience and unfriendliness by getting up from his chair and addressing the suspect somewhat as follows: "Joe, I thought that there was something basically decent and honorable in you, but apparently there isn't. The hell with it. If that's the way you want to leave it, I don't give a damn." The investigator sits down on the chair again and after a brief pause, with no conversation at all, may say, "Joe you'd tax the patience of a saint the way you've been acting. But I guess there is something worthwhile in you anyway." The investigator may even apologize for his loss of patience by saying, "I'm sorry. That's the first time I've lost my head like that."

The investigator then starts all over with the reapplication of the sympathetic approach that formed the basis for his efforts prior to the outburst of impatience. By reason of the contrast with which he has been presented, the suspect finds the investigator's sympathetic, understanding attitude to be much more appealing. This places the suspect in a more vulnerable position for a disclosure of the truth.

Under no circumstances should physical abuse or threats of abuse or other mistreatment ever be employed.

The friendly/unfriendly act is particularly appropriate in the interrogation of a suspect who is politely apathetic—the person who just nods his head, as though in agreement with the investigator, but who says nothing in response other than a denial of guilt. With a suspect of this type, a change in the investigator's attitude from friendly to unfriendly and back to friendly again will at times produce a change of attitude. The suspect may then become more responsive to the investigator's efforts to seek the truth.

Responding to a Suspect's Attempt to Leave the Interrogation Room

A suspect who is not in custody, of course, is free to walk out of the interview room at any time he chooses. Furthermore, the investigator cannot physically restrain the suspect from doing so. This behavior is much more often observed in guilty suspects than in ones who are innocent. The guilty suspect wants to leave the interview room to reduce anxiety from having to further lie to the investigator.

Once the suspect gets out of the chair and approaches the interview room door, the investigator should continue to address the now-empty chair. Initially, he should not even acknowledge that the suspect has gotten up out of the chair; the investigator should certainly not get out of his own chair. To do so forces the suspect to make the next move, which is often to open the door and leave.

Figure 12-3 When a suspect gets out of his chair, the investigator should remain seated.

After talking to the empty chair for 30 or 60 seconds, the investigator should turn to the suspect and politely ask him to have a seat so that the matter can be straightened out. In many cases, by following this procedure, the suspect will sit back down and eventually confess. **Figure 12-3** illustrates the procedure to use when the suspect stands during an interrogation.

KEY POINTS

- The suspect must be discouraged from engaging in unnecessary denials, which distract from the investigator's theme and subsequent efforts to persuade the suspect to tell the truth.
- An investigator's nondefensive response to a weak denial has the effect of inhibiting further denials from a guilty suspect.
- If a suspect offers a stronger denial to the direct, positive confrontation, the investigator should reassert his confidence in the suspect's guilt as the transition statement is introduced.
- Once the theme has been introduced and the investigator starts to develop it, there are three primary objectives with respect to handling denials: (1) Anticipate denials before they are voiced, (2) discourage weak denials from being voiced, and (3) evaluate denials that are voiced.
- As the guilty suspect attempts to introduce a denial with a permission phrase, the investigator should immediately interject a statement advising the suspect to "just give me a minute" because of the importance of what the investigator is saying.
- Recognize the characteristics of the denials that may be suggestive of an innocent person: spontaneous, direct, and forceful denials; angry and hostile over the accusation; may insult the investigator. If the investigator becomes convinced of the suspect's innocence, the tone of the interrogation should shift from accusatory to a question and answer format.
- When the various techniques of sympathy and understanding have proved to be ineffective in stopping the denials of a suspect whose guilt is definite or reasonably certain, the investigator may consider introducing either real or fictitious evidence.

KEY TERMS

denial A statement or action that contradicts or refuses to accept the truthfulness of an allegation.

friendly/unfriendly act Act played out by one or two investigators that accentuates sympathetic characteristics after the suspect is verbally attacked, in order to get the suspect to truthfully answer questions about the case.

interruption gesture Universally recognized social signal often employed by deceptive suspects to let a speaker know, "Hey, it's my turn to talk. I have something to say!"

permission phrase Phrase used to ask permission to speak that may preface a denial.

pleading phrase Other verbal statement that often precedes a deceptive denial such as "But honestly," "Please," or "I understand what you're saying, but . . ."

13 Step 4: Overcoming Objections

Chapter Objectives

Upon completion of this chapter you will be able to:

- Recognize and understand the motivation behind objections
- Explain how to treat objections
- Explain the importance of turning the objection around

Principles

The guilty suspect who realizes the futility of uttering a simple denial may resort to a change in tactics in order to achieve some control over the situation and dissuade the investigator's confidence in his guilt. This change will ordinarily take the form of a reason as to why the accusation is wrong. It will fall far short, however, of presenting evidence of innocence, but the guilty suspect offers it in the hope that it will lend support to his denial and to engage the investigator in an argument and thus distract from the focus of the theme. Statements of this type may be termed **objections**. For instance, in an armed robbery case, the objection may be: "I couldn't have done that; I don't own a gun!" In offering this objection, the guilty suspect hopes that the investigator will argue the point and thus allow the suspect to reduce anxiety by engaging in verbal comments.

objection a statement that is proposed by the suspect as an excuse or reason why the accusation is false.

A denial is a natural defensive strategy that both innocent and guilty suspects use. **Objections, however, represent an offensive strategy and are heard, almost**

exclusively, from guilty suspects. Step 4 of the interrogation process involves turning the objection around to use it as a reason why the suspect should tell the truth.

With respect to the manner in which the investigator handles objections, a defense attorney may claim that the investigator used his client's own words against the client. There is nothing illegal about using logic and rationale statements during persuasion, and the investigator should openly acknowledge that he recognized the defendant's statement as an excuse and not a denial, and therefore he incorporated the defendant's excuse within his theme.

Procedures

During interrogation there is a tendency by investigators to view objections in the same way as denials, and to deal with them in the same manner—that is, to attempt to stop the suspect from voicing them and, if they do surface, to refute the suspect's statements. It must be recognized that the objection signifies a different frame of mind than that of a suspect simply denying commission of the crime; consequently, instead of stopping the suspect, the investigator should indulge the voicing of an objection. The reason for this is that it will provide the investigator with helpful information for the development of interrogation themes. Instead of discouraging objections, the investigator should let the suspect voice an objection and then seek to overcome it.

There are three objectives at this stage of the interrogation. The first is to recognize the suspect's statement as an objection and to draw it out if it is not fully voiced. Second, the investigator should reward the objection. Finally, the investigator should turn the objection around by incorporating it within the interrogation theme. Each of these stages is presented separately in this chapter.

Recognizing the Objection

Some objections will be stated outright; for example, during an interrogation in a theft case, the suspect may come right out and say, "But I've got money in the bank!" or "I can get money from my parents any time I want." On other occasions, the suspect may offer an **introductory phrase** as a prelude to voicing the objection. These may take the form of such expressions as "I couldn't have done it," "I wouldn't do a thing like that," "That's impossible," "That's ridiculous," or "How could I ever do something like that?"

introductory phrase phrase used as a prelude to the voicing of an objection.

emotional objection a type of objection. Examples include "I'd be too scared [nervous, shy, etc.] to do something like that," "I loved her," or "I like my job."

factual objection a type of objection. Examples include "I don't even own a gun," "I wasn't even there that day," or "I could never hurt someone."

moral objection a type of objection. Examples include "I wasn't brought up that way" and "A person who would do something like this is really sick."

Because of the significantly different way in which the investigator handles a suspect's attempt to deny as opposed to handling objections, the investigator must listen closely to the suspect's statements. As previously stated, the investigator wants to discourage the denial, but to encourage and draw out the objection.

Upon hearing such introductory phrases, the investigator should seek an elaboration by asking the suspect such questions as "Why couldn't you have done this?" or "Why would it be ridiculous?" The importance of doing this is similar to the reason the automobile salesperson allows a prospective customer to express his objections to committing to the purchase of a car: The salesperson or investigator may thereby ascertain the specific nature of the objection.

The majority of objection statements that suspects offer can be categorized into three general groups: **emotional objections**, **factual objections**, and **moral objections** (**Table 13-1**).

Table 13-1 Types of Objections

Emotional objections:

"I'd be too scared [nervous, shy, etc.] to do something like that."

"I loved her."

"I like my job."

"I could never hurt someone."

"I have too much to lose by doing something like this."

Factual objections:

"I don't even own a gun."

"I wasn't even there that day."

"I don't even know him."

"It's impossible because the security is too good."

"I wouldn't even know how to do something like that."

"I don't need money; I have $5,000 in my account."

"I don't even have the combination to the safe."

Moral objections:

"I'm a good Catholic [Protestant, Jew, etc.], and that kind of thing is against our religion."

"I wasn't brought up that way."

"A person who would do something like this is really sick."

Rewarding the Objection

Statements of the type given in Table 13-1 are feeble explanations, even in those instances in which they may be partially true. In any event, the investigator should not argue with the suspect over the statement, nor should there be any indication of surprise or irritation. The investigator should act as though the statements were expected. Such a reaction will have a discouraging effect upon the suspect, who will perceive that he made the wrong statement, or at least an ineffective one.

Following is an illustration (again using the armed robbery suspect situation) of the inappropriateness and ineffectiveness of arguing with the suspect over his statement objecting to the accusation:

I: "You said it's ridiculous. Why, Joe?"

S: "Because I don't even own a gun."

I: "Sure you do, and you used it that night!"

S: "Hey, I just said I don't own a gun; I've never bought or owned one. You think I own a gun? Prove it!"

I: "Look, fellow, you used your damn gun that night. Quit being a wise guy!"

S: "I don't own a gun, damn it!"

This type of exchange allows the suspect to gain control of the interrogation, while at the same time allowing the suspect to relieve pent-up anxiety through talking. It puts the investigator on the defensive and causes a great deal of unnecessary hostility and frustration for the investigator to overcome.

In contrast to the foregoing expressions of the investigator, the appropriate response would have been a statement of agreement or understanding, such as the following: "I hope that's true," "I'm glad you mentioned that," "I was hoping you'd say that," "I certainly understand what you're saying," or "I know that may be true."

Turning the Objection Around

Immediately after rewarding the suspect's stated objection, the investigator should attempt to reverse the significance of the suspect's objection and return to the interrogation theme without delay. **Table 13-2** shows an example and analysis of the dialogue that should occur between the investigator and the suspect in a hypothetical case involving the armed robbery of a liquor store.

Table 13-2 Elements of Dialogue in Step 4

Dialogue	Analysis
I: Joe, I don't think this was your idea or something you planned well in advance. I think that you and some of your buddies when into that liquor store, saw that there weren't any customers around, and one of your buddies told you to go up there and get the money. You just didn't know how to stop it. Then this whole thing happened with the gun and everything else.	Theme development
S: But that's ridiculous.	
I: Why is it ridiculous, Joe?	Follow-through
S: Because I don't even own a gun.	Objection
I: I'm glad you mentioned that, Joe, because it tells me that it wasn't your idea to do this—that one of your buddies talked you into this, handed you the gun, and then the whole thing happened. You see, Joe, if you *did* own a gun and carried it in that night, ready to use it, to kill somebody if they got in your way, that's one thing. But if the other guy stuck it in your hand, to use it just to scare everybody, that's something else again. . . .	Overcoming objection by agreement and understanding, and by pointing out negative aspects of the situation if the objection were untruthful
[Continuation of dialogue]	Continuation of theme development

absolute declaration a vehicle by which the investigator sidesteps the objection. It actually does not mean anything, but it creates the impression that the investigator is encouraged by the suspect's statement, which is the opposite effect from that which the suspect anticipated when he offered the objection.

On occasion, the investigator may be confronted with an objection that is very difficult to deal with or to transpose into material for development of the theme. For example, in a child molesting case, it would be inappropriate for the investigator to accept, or to agree with, a suspect's objection that "I'd never do something like that because whoever did that is a pervert." The investigator's response should be one of a general nature, perhaps describable as an **absolute declaration**, such as, "Exactly, Joe. Don't you see, that's why we should get this thing cleared up." In effect, this declaration is merely a vehicle by which the investigator sidesteps the objection. It actually does not mean anything, but it creates the impression that the investigator is encouraged by the suspect's statement, which is the opposite effect from that which the suspect anticipated when he offered the objection. The guilty suspect is usually not perceptive enough to question the investigation's statement at this point. The investigator can then resume the interrogation theme.

A second method of sidestepping difficult objections is to use a response such as, "That's possible I suppose, Joe, but let me tell you this . . ." or "That may be true, Joe, but the important thing is this . . ." An example of sidestepping and then properly overcoming a difficult objection is illustrated in the following interrogation in a child molesting case:

> I: "Many times I've seen people, including myself, do things under the influence of alcohol that we would never do on our own."
>
> S: "But I'd never do anything like that because whoever did that is a pervert."
>
> I: "Exactly, Joe. Don't you see? That's why we should get this thing cleared up, because I don't want anyone to think that about you. I know that you would never do something like this when you're sober. The people who might do that when sober have a real problem. But all of us do things when we're drinking that are totally out of character, like this thing you did. This isn't like you normally; I know that. This thing happened because you weren't yourself . . ."

At this stage of the interrogation, when a guilty suspect's objections have been properly handled and even used as a reason for why the suspect should tell the truth, the suspect may become very uncertain about the situation and may become withdrawn. This development requires the utilization of procedures in Step 5 of the interrogation process.

KEY POINTS

- Objections take the form of reasons as to why the accusation is wrong. An objection will fall far short of presenting evidence of innocence, but the guilty suspect offers it in the hope that it will lend support to his denial and to engage the investigator in an argument and thus distract from the focus of the theme. Objections are heard, almost exclusively, from guilty suspects.
- The investigator should discourage the denial, but encourage and draw out the objection.
- The investigator should act as though the statements were expected. Such a reaction will have a discouraging effect upon the suspect, who will perceive that he made the wrong statement, or at least an ineffective one.
- Immediately after rewarding the suspect's stated objection, the investigator should attempt to reverse the significance of the suspect's objection and return to the interrogation theme without delay.

KEY TERMS

absolute declaration A vehicle by which the investigator sidesteps the objection. It actually does not mean anything, but it creates the impression that the investigator is encouraged by the suspect's statement, which is the opposite effect from that which the suspect anticipated when he offered the objection.

emotional objection A type of objection. Examples include "I'd be too scared [nervous, shy, etc.] to do something like that," "I loved her," or "I like my job."

factual objection A type of objection. Examples include "I don't even own a gun," "I wasn't even there that day," or "I could never hurt someone."

introductory phrase Phrase used as a prelude to the voicing of an objection.

moral objection A type of objection. Examples include "I wasn't brought up that way" and "A person who would do something like this is really sick."

objection A statement that is proposed by the suspect as an excuse or reason why the accusation is false.

14 Step 5: Procurement and Retention of the Suspect's Attention

Chapter Objectives

Upon completion of this chapter you will be able to:

- Explain the importance of recognizing the symptoms of psychological withdrawal
- Describe techniques to employ in keeping the suspect's attention on the theme

Principles

As previously noted, most guilty suspects will not initially sit back and allow the investigator to dominate the conversation during presentation of the interrogation theme. The suspect may deny involvement in the offense (Step 3) or offer objections (Step 4). If the investigator successfully discourages the suspect's denials and turns around the suspect's objections, there is one primary strategy left for the suspect who does not want to tell the truth (other than to invoke his *Miranda* rights or leave the room)—to psychologically withdraw from the interrogation and ignore the investigator's theme.

We can all relate to situations where we have psychologically tuned out a speaker. Perhaps as students when we were not interested in the subject matter being taught, we would allow our mind to drift off in class. Even during a face-to-face social interaction when the other person is dominating the conversation with tiresome rhetoric, we may find ourselves "zoning out" and thinking about something else in an effort to escape the boredom.

A guilty suspect who has abandoned verbal efforts to dissuade the investigator's confidence can remain emotionally detached for hours, if necessary, in an effort to resist telling the truth. Because of this, it is important for the investigator to **recognize symptoms of psychological withdrawal** and to employ specific techniques to keep the suspect's attention on the theme.[1]

psychological withdrawal emotional detachment from a situation, including the tendency to abandon verbal efforts and avoid eye contact.

It is important to note that innocent suspects who have been accused of committing a crime will not psychologically withdraw. This response goes against every basic instinct for someone who realizes that he may be wrongly facing severe consequences. Provided that the investigator has not threatened the innocent suspect or offered promises of leniency, an innocent suspect will remain at the denial stage during an interrogation or, out of frustration and anger, terminate the interrogation by leaving the room or invoking his rights under *Miranda*.

Procedures

Recognizing Psychological Withdrawal

The suspect who has psychologically turned off the investigator's theme is generally quiet. His thoughts are turned inward and he is no longer interacting with the investigator—verbally or mentally. He does not have the confidence or persistence to argue his position further. In essence, he is quite content to sit back and allow the investigator to continue with his monologue. The suspect's thoughts during this withdrawal may be centered on the consequences of his crime or, more likely, may be unfocused, where the investigator's words are like background music that is present, but not specifically listened to.

Because eye contact signals a mental connection with another person, during withdrawal the suspect will generally not establish eye contact with the investigator. Typically, the suspect will look up or to the side (not downward), and his eyes will appear vacant and expressionless. Facial expressions will also be noticeably flat or absent. The suspect's eyebrows, forehead, and mouth are fixed and set—they fail to register any changes of emotion or thoughts.

A suspect may assume a number of different postures during withdrawal. Most common is one that is nonfrontally aligned, that is, turned to one side or the other, away from the investigator. Frequently the suspect will have crossed legs, but there will be minimal foot bouncing. Occasionally the suspect may have crossed arms. More likely, one arm will be involved in a supporting posture, where the hand comes in stationary contact with the head. In summary, the suspect who has withdrawn is immobile verbally, mentally, and nonverbally, as illustrated in **Figure 14-1**.

Chair Proximity

Once the investigator recognizes that the suspect is psychologically withdrawing from the interrogation, one effective technique to get the suspect's attention is for the investigator to move his chair closer to the suspect's. It is a recognized fact that the closer a person is to someone physically, the closer he becomes to

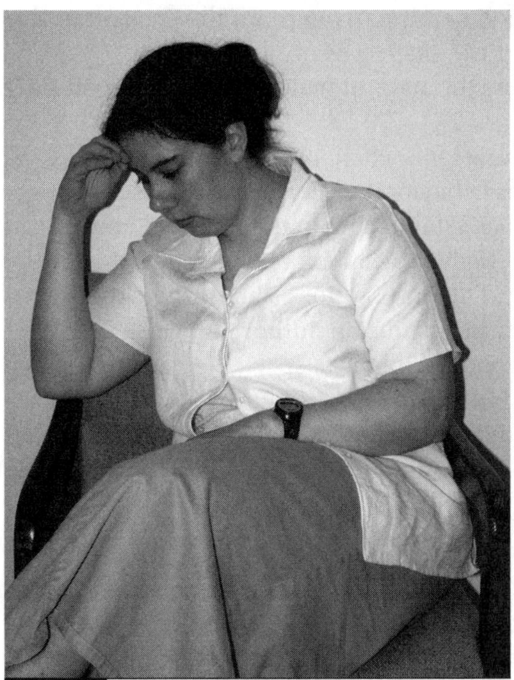

Figure 14-1 Posture of suspect who has withdrawn.

that person psychologically. In essence, it is more difficult for the suspect to turn off the investigator's theme when it is being presented in this closer, more intimate, spatial layout.

At the outset of the interrogation, the investigator should be seated approximately four feet from the suspect. Once signs of withdrawal are apparent, the investigator should slowly move his chair in closer to the suspect's. The investigator's physical action of moving closer to the suspect should be a gradual, unobtrusive process, and should seem to be the natural result of the investigator's interest and sympathy. It would be inappropriate and unnecessarily distracting for the investigator to all of a sudden pick up the chair and place it directly in front of the suspect, as though for a nose-to-nose confrontation. The investigator instead should first move his body to the front edge of the chair and lean forward. This posture change immediately reduces the distance between the investigator and suspect. From that point on, movements by the investigator should consist of pulling the chair forward in small increments.

As the forward movements are made, the investigator should not focus attention on them by pausing in his conversation. The investigator should continue to talk and to maintain eye contact with the suspect, without looking down at the chair as it is moved. A guilty suspect will usually be aware of an increased feeling of uneasiness as the investigator moves closer but often will not consciously recognize that the cause for it is the physical proximity of the investigator. The suspect simply senses or perceives that lying is becoming more uncomfortable.

Before the investigator contemplates moving closer to a suspect, the situation must be carefully evaluated. Any premature action may destroy the atmosphere created to this point. In general, moving in on the suspect in this fashion should take place only when the suspect is not looking directly at the investigator, when he is quiet and past the stage of making denials and offering objections.

As the investigator gradually moves his chair closer to the suspect's, he should carefully monitor the suspect's behavioral response to the closer arrangement. Any defensive behaviors, such as establishing tighter barriers, movement of the suspect's chair backward, or a defiant facial expression, should alert the investigator to maintain his distance. The purpose for establishing closer proximity is not to intimidate the suspect or assume an authoritative position over him. If either of these motives are perceived by the suspect, he may engage in a natural fight-or-flight response and return to denials (fight) or terminate the interrogation (flight). Again, the investigator's intent in establishing a closer proximity is to maintain the suspect's attention and to become more emotionally close to the suspect.

Establishing Eye Contact

Eye contact is one of the most reliable social signals of attention—either the want or avoidance of it. As participants in a training class, most people can relate to the experience where the instructor asks a question of the class. Participants who do not want to be called upon immediately look down as if searching through their notes for the correct response—their purposeful break of gaze with the instructor is sending the clear message "I don't want to interact with you, please don't call on me." On the other hand, participants who want to respond to the instructor's question engage in quite different behavior. They make efforts to catch the instructor's eye and may even raise their hands in an effort to bring further attention to themselves. They are clearly communicating a desire to interact with the instructor.

From this common personal experience, the following principle of interrogation should be evident: If a suspect is not looking at the investigator, the suspect is not relating to him. While it is inappropriate and ineffective to verbally challenge a suspect to "look the investigator in the eye" at this stage of the interrogation, other, more subtle efforts can be made in an effort to make this nonverbal connection.

As the investigator gradually moves his chair closer to the suspect's, he should also direct his own body to a position where he moves into the suspect's line of vision. Often this will be to one side or another. In essence, the investigator should attempt to direct his interrogation theme while looking at the suspect's eyes. If the suspect switches posture, allowing his gaze to focus away from the investigator, the investigator should again gradually switch posture so as to establish mutual gaze with the suspect.

The same precautionary measures relating to moving closer to the suspect apply when making attempts to establish eye contact. If the suspect responds in a negative fashion to this attempt, the investigator should immediately cease further efforts to establish eye contact and continue with his theme. Later, after some of the theme concepts have registered with the suspect, the investigator may again attempt to establish eye contact.

The Use of Visual Aids

One technique that may be effective in maintaining the suspect's attention and may also be beneficial in establishing eye contact is for the investigator to use visual aids at this stage of the interrogation. Ordinarily, these aids should not be in the form of photographs. For example, an investigator should not show the suspect crime scene photographs, which might reveal information only the guilty person would know. Also, showing the suspect gruesome autopsy pictures may negate the sympathetic and understanding demeanor the investigator has worked so hard to develop.

visual aid item referenced or produced in order to attract the suspect's visual attention toward the investigator's statements.

However, the investigator may produce, and make reference to, physical evidence such as a weapon, plaster cast of a footprint, or spent shell casings recovered at the scene of the crime. The purpose in doing so is not to reinforce the investigator's confidence in the suspect's guilt (this will have been done during Step 3), but rather to attract the suspect's visual attention toward the investigator's statements.

The following visual aid has been used to good advantage on many occasions (particularly in sex or embezzlement cases). The suspect is advised that by telling the truth, he can perform somewhat of a mental operation on himself—an operation equally as important and necessary as the removal or destruction of injurious tissue in a cancer patient. In this respect, it may be helpful to draw a circle on a piece of paper, mark off a small area on the rim of it, and tell the suspect that, in effect, the marked-off portion represents a piece of infected tissue in his mind or soul that if untreated or not removed will continue to spread and produce other and more serious offenses than the present one. The suspect should then be told that there is only one way that the necessary mental operation may be performed, and only he can do it—and that is by telling the truth.

In a homicide or rape case where it is known that the suspect was under the influence of alcohol at the time of the offense, the investigator may draw two equal circles on a piece of paper, representing the normal balance between behavior and emotions. The investigator emphasizes that under normal conditions our emotions will not overpower our behavior. A second diagram is then drawn, depicting the emotional circle much larger than the circle representing behavior. It is explained to the suspect that when a person is under the influence of alcohol his emotional drives become greatly exaggerated to the extent that they overpower and control behaviors.

Asking Rhetorical Questions

The interrogation theme, as described in Step 2, is intended to be a monologue transmitted by the investigator. However, when the suspect is turning off this monologue by psychologically withdrawing, an effective technique is to ask rhetorical questions. The principle in using rhetorical questions is that we are all conditioned to respond to questions. From our earliest childhood memories, we each recall answering questions from parents, from teachers, and on written examinations. To ask a question begs an answer at some level. The rhetorical questions used at this stage of the interrogation encourage the suspect to make internal decisions that either agree or disagree with the stated principle.

rhetorical question question posed that does not require a response, but is used to encourage the suspect to make internal decisions that either agree or disagree with the stated principle.

Rhetorical Questions to Maintain a Suspect's Attention

(Rhetorical questions are italicized.)
"Brian, I realize how difficult it is to tell the truth sometimes, *but we all make mistakes, right?* I don't think you've ever done anything like this before in your life. In that respect, you're kind of like a young student in grade school. *Back when you were in grade school, the teachers had you use a pencil when you took tests, right?* The reason for that is that pencils have erasers on them so the learning students could correct their mistakes. *Well, even as adults, we still make mistakes, right?* I know I'm not perfect, and I can't judge someone harshly because they've made a mistake as long as that person has the willingness to correct it. *The first step in correcting a mistake is to admit the mistake. Wouldn't you agree, Brian?"*

As the example in Rhetorical Questions to Maintain a Suspect's Attention illustrates, the investigator does not necessarily want to elicit a verbal acknowledgment from the suspect through the use of rhetorical questions. In fact, forcing a verbal agreement from the suspect at this stage of the interrogation is likely to result in a denial. Rather, the rhetorical questions are thrown out as food for thought. The investigator should look for subtle signs of acknowledgment, such as a nodding of the head or a change in eye contact.

The rhetorical questions asked of a suspect should address positive personal traits or real-life expectations. For psychological reasons, the investigator should not inquire as to possible real consequences the suspect may want to avoid. Examples of rhetorical questions that address real consequences and should be avoided are "Do you really think you're going to beat this thing in court?" "Do you want a criminal record for the rest of your life?" or "How long do you think a young man like yourself will last in prison?" By mentioning these real consequences, the investigator is simply reminding the suspect of what faces him if the suspect decides to tell the truth.

KEY POINTS

- It is important for the investigator to recognize symptoms of psychological withdrawal and to employ specific techniques to keep the suspect's attention on the theme.
- Once signs of withdrawal are apparent, the investigator should slowly move his chair in closer to the suspect's.
- The investigator should also direct his own body to a position that is in the suspect's line of vision.
- Using a visual aid may serve to recapture the subject's attention.
- The investigator might have success in regaining the suspect's attention by asking a rhetorical question.

KEY TERMS

psychological withdrawal Emotional detachment from a situation, including the tendency to abandon verbal efforts and avoid eye contact.

rhetorical question Question posed that does not require a response, but is used to encourage the suspect to make internal decisions that either agree or disagree with the stated principle.

visual aid Item referenced or produced in order to attract the suspect's visual attention toward the investigator's statements.

ENDNOTES

1. Some guilty subjects psychologically withdraw at the outset of an interrogation, immediately following the direct, positive confrontation. These individuals have developed this response to any threatening situation because it has been effective in the past for avoiding punishment from parents, teachers, or law enforcement.

15

Step 6: Handling the Suspect's Passive Mood

Chapter Objectives

Upon completion of this chapter you will be able to:

- Recognize when and why the suspect has become passive
- Explain how to recapture a suspect's attention to the theme

Principles

At the conclusion of Step 5, the investigator should have achieved a desirable rapport with the suspect. As a consequence, the suspect, if guilty, will have become very reticent and quiet. He becomes more willing to listen, attributable in part to an increasing awareness that the deception does not possess its anticipated effectiveness. The suspect may begin to assume a defeatist posture—slumped head and shoulders, limp legs, and glassy eyes. In general, the guilty suspect will seem downcast and depressed. At this stage, the investigator should begin to concentrate on the central core of the selected theme while preparing the groundwork for the possible alternative question that will be presented in Step 7.

Procedures

Content of Statements

Whereas earlier the investigator merely suggested possible reasons why the suspect committed the offense and coupled them with embellished statements designed to offer psychological escapes, the investigator should now start to distill those reasons from the general framework of the theme and concentrate his verbal statements on the specific basic reason implicit in the theme. The following example of this procedure is useful because of its factual simplicity, although the same principle may be utilized in more serious cases, such as a robbery-murder.

A suspect is being interrogated about a theft of money from his employer. The investigator may have developed a theme along the following lines:

> *Joe, I know how tough it is in today's economy to make ends meet. Every paycheck you get has to stretch further and further to cover the costs of the basic things we all need: food, home, car, and other necessities. And what has happened over the last few years is that as prices have gone up, more money is needed just to buy the same things we bought earlier. And it seems like employers, the people we work for, forget this. Instead of getting the pay raises we need just to keep up with things, we are stuck with the same pay month after month. Pretty soon an honest person like you finds himself in a position where his pay just doesn't cover the necessities, and he begins to wonder how he'll ever make ends meet.*
>
> *Then one day, when someone leaves work in a hurry and money is accidentally left out, you begin to give in to the temptation that you've been able to fight off up until that time. The pressure becomes unbearable, and in one split second, you give in and make a mistake in judgment and do something like this. We all face these pressures and have to scramble these days to make ends meet.*

The investigator should continue with the development of this specific theme as long as the suspect maintains interest, even though he may have actually committed the theft in order to purchase alcohol or drugs, or to gamble, or to provide entertainment for himself that he could not afford with his legitimate income. Throughout it all, the investigator must, of course, fend off the suspect's denials and objections in the manner previously described.

As the suspect drifts into a passive mood, the investigator should move closer to the suspect (if this has not occurred thus far) to recapture attention to the theme. Then, when the suspect begins to display the indications of being about to give up, the investigator must focus more intently on his statements about the possible central reason for the theft, as in the following example:

> *Joe, I'm sure you were just over your head in bills at home, and this money appeared to solve your problem; it seemed to be the only way out, or maybe someone in the family was sick and needed an operation or some medical attention that you couldn't take care of but*

yet couldn't ignore. And so this money was there and this seemed to be the solution to an impossible situation.

The various motives the investigator offers for the theft are designed to prepare the suspect for the alternative question (Step 7), which is discussed in Chapter 16. As each reason is presented, the investigator must closely observe the suspect's behavior for signs of acceptance or rejection, to determine whether or not the offered reason presents an acceptable possibility for the commission of the act.

At this time, it is very important for the investigator to **continue displaying understanding and sympathy** in urging the suspect to tell the truth. As the investigator repeats and reiterates reasons for the commission of the offense, it may be appropriate to interject statements that if the suspect were the investigator's own brother (or father, sister, etc.), he would still advise telling the truth. The investigator may also urge the suspect to tell the truth for the sake of his own conscience, mental relief, or moral well-being, as well as "for the sake of everybody concerned."

During a noncustodial interrogation, it is often effective, at this stage, to remind the suspect of the voluntariness of his presence. This not only serves as an impetus to tell the truth, but also can be beneficial later in court when the investigator can testify that shortly before the suspect confessed, he was reminded that he was free to leave.

Example of a Statement Reminding the Suspect of the Voluntariness of His Presence

"Mark, no one forced you to come in today to talk to me. You know that door is unlocked and you can leave at any time. The fact that you did choose to come in to talk to me about this tells me you are sorry about what happened and want to get it straightened out. If you were a hard-core criminal you never would have even agreed to see me. The fact that you are here now tells me that you want to tell the truth."

In urging or advising an offender to tell the truth, **the investigator must avoid expressions that are objectionable on the grounds that they constitute illegal promises or threats.** However, by speaking in generalities, such as "for the sake of your own conscience" or "for the sake of everybody concerned," the investigator can remain within permissible bounds.

Investigator's Demeanor

While making the statements just described, at this stage of the interrogation, the investigator's tone of voice should be at its peak of sincerity. The investigator should talk slowly and perhaps more quietly than before in an effort to sell the suspect on his genuine interest in having the matter resolved. The investigator's tone of voice should also be emotional, sometimes to the extent of seeming to stammer or stutter in an effort to relay the importance of what he is saying. The well-known actor Jimmy Stewart comes to mind. During a particularly emotional scene, he would engage in similar paralinguistic behaviors to convey his sincere and genuine feelings.

The investigator's eye contact with the suspect should be soft and warm. At times, it will be appropriate for the investigator to look down at the floor while speaking, again in an express effort to appeal to the suspect's emotions. The clergyman who offers comfort to the bereaved family after a recent death often will speak in softened tones with his hands clasped in front of him while looking down. He represents the epitome of sincerity.

At this stage of the interrogation, the investigator should already have moved his chair to within a foot or so of the suspect's. In conjunction with the recommendations just given, it is beneficial for the investigator to assume a head and body slump. Often the suspect will mirror the investigator's posture and follow his lead.

Recognizing the Signs of Resignation

resignation point at which the suspect is mentally debating whether or not to tell the truth.

The investigator should continue with the procedures described in this chapter until the suspect shows some physical sign of **resignation**, at which time Step 7, presenting the alternative question, should immediately be employed. The change in the suspect's behavior from withdrawal in Step 5 to the signs of resignation indicate that the suspect is mentally debating whether or not to tell the truth. If the investigator misses these signs and continues on with the theme, the opportunity to develop the first admission of guilt by asking an alternative question may be lost.

The following physical signs of resignation may occur in isolation from each other, or several may occur simultaneously.

Changes in Arm and Leg Position

One symptom of resignation is the suspect who drops leg or arm barriers, essentially uncrossing the legs or dropping the arms to the side. This less defensive posture indicates that the suspect is mentally prepared to "open up" to the investigator. During withdrawal, it is not uncommon for suspects to engage in a supporting posture, where the hand rests on the chin or even covers the mouth. A movement of the hand, perhaps to the side of the face or especially away from the face, also signifies a desire to "open up."

Nonverbal Agreement

A suspect who begins to nod his head in silent agreement with the investigator's theme concepts is sending the message that he has internalized the investigator's statements and thus is psychologically in a desirable state of mind for the alternative question.

Change in Posture

A suspect who changes posture in an attempt to establish frontal alignment with the investigator is showing a clear sign that he is mentally prepared to tell the truth. This may be a turning of the body toward the investigator, or a gentle lean forward, toward the investigator. The classic posture of resignation is the head and body slump, illustrated in **Figure 15-1**.

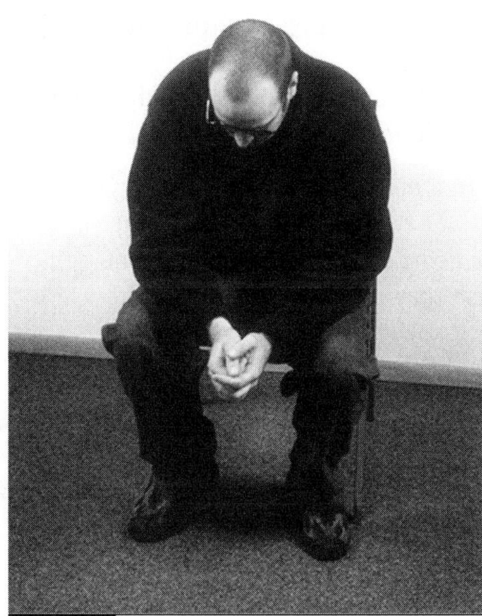

Figure 15-1 Classic posture of surrender.

Change in Eye Contact

One of the most reliable indications that a suspect is considering telling the truth will be observed in the suspect's facial expression, especially eye contact. A suspect who has been looking up to the ceiling or to the side and suddenly drops his gaze to the floor is signaling resignation. This change of eye contact downward indicates that the suspect is in a "feeling" mode and is experiencing significant emotions.

Tearing or Crying

Another sign to carefully watch for at this stage of the interrogation is tearing or watery eyes. The signal may be the suspect's movement of a hand to the eyes to cover or wipe away tears. Occasionally, a sob or sniff may also signify that the suspect is on the verge of crying.

When a suspect starts to cry outwardly, the investigator should not leave the room and give the suspect a chance to "cry it out"; the suspect who is given that opportunity may fortify himself and return to the denial stage. When a suspect begins to cry, the investigator should commiserate with the suspect and offer encouragement by attempting to relieve his embarrassment. Crying is an emotional outlet that releases tension. It is also a very good indication that the suspect has given up and is ready to confess. The suspect's emotional outburst is evidence of remorse and is often perceived by the suspect as exposing his inner feelings of guilt. A positive attitude on the part of the investigator will cause the suspect to feel that a confession is expected at that time.

Sometimes female suspects cry as a ploy or as a final, yet insincere, effort to gain sympathy. This **manipulative crying** will most likely be seen much earlier

manipulative crying
crying as a ploy or as a final, yet insincere, effort to gain sympathy.

during an interrogation, typically during the denial stage. In essence, the tearful denial is nothing more than the previously mentioned pleading denial often heard from the guilty suspect or, in some instances, represents the histrionic behaviors of an adult tantrum.

When a male suspect cries, which is usually tantamount to an admission, it is suggested that the investigator proceed as follows:

> *You know, Joe, the problem today is that men are too ashamed to cry and everything is bottled up inside. They are afraid to let it out. That's why men have so many more heart attacks than women. I'm glad to see those tears, Joe, because they show me that you care about this and that you want to get it straightened out.*

Of course, quite the opposite effect will be realized if the investigator criticizes the male suspect who cries. For example, an investigator who admonishes the behavior, "Come on, Joe, don't be a baby about this. You didn't cry when you killed her, did you?" is likely to alienate the suspect beyond the point of wanting to tell the truth.

KEY POINTS

- The suspect, if guilty, will have become very reticent and quiet by this point in the interrogation. At this stage, the investigator should begin to concentrate on the central core of the selected theme.
- As each reason for the commission of the crime is presented, the investigator must closely observe the suspect's behavior for signs of acceptance or rejection, to determine whether the offered reason presents an acceptable possibility to the suspect.
- It is very important for the investigator to continue displaying understanding and sympathy in urging the suspect to tell the truth.
- During a noncustodial interrogation, it is often effective, at this stage, to remind the suspect of the voluntariness of his or her presence.
- In urging or advising an offender to tell the truth, the investigator must avoid expressions that are objectionable on the grounds that they constitute illegal promises or threats.
- The investigator should continue presenting reasons and urging the suspect to tell the truth until the suspect shows some physical sign of resignation, at which time Step 7, presenting the alternative question, should immediately be employed.
- Physical signs of resignation include dropping of arm and leg barriers, nodding of the head, slumping of the head and body, changes in eye contact, and tearing or crying.

KEY TERMS

manipulative crying Crying as a ploy or as a final, yet insincere, effort to gain sympathy.

resignation Point at which the suspect is mentally debating whether or not to tell the truth.

16

Step 7: Presenting an Alternative Question

Chapter Objectives

Upon completion of this chapter you will be able to:

- Explain the concept of an alternative question
- Understand how to select an appropriate alternative question
- Explain how to present positive and negative supporting statements

Principles

Servers in some restaurants are very skilled at encouraging customers to order dessert. It is, of course, to their advantage when dessert is ordered because the tip will be larger. An unskilled server may ask the customer a question such as, "Can I interest you in dessert today?" If he is really unskilled, this request will be followed up with the question, "Or are you full?" Obviously, this technique is unlikely to produce many dessert orders. A skilled server describes the dessert options and, after closely watching the customer's behavior, will focus the next question upon the two most likely offerings. He will then ask the customer, "What shall it be today, the pie or the cake?" This strategy is much more likely to result in an order.

It may be a bit unfair to draw a comparison between ordering dessert and confessing to a crime, but a similar principle is involved: People are more likely to make a decision once they have committed themselves, in a small way, toward

alternative question a question which offers the suspect two incrimination choices concerning some aspect of the crime.

that decision. This is precisely what the **alternative question** accomplishes during an interrogation. It offers the guilty suspect the opportunity to start telling the truth by making a single admission.

The alternative question presents the suspect with a choice between two explanations for possible commission of the crime. It is a face-saving device that renders easier the burden of the suspect's start toward telling the truth. For example, in an issue involving theft, the suspect may be asked, "Did you blow that money on booze, drugs, and women and party with it, or did you need it to help out your family?" The investigator, of course, encourages the suspect to accept the latter explanation. If the suspect agrees that the money was taken to help out his family, he understands that the acknowledgment is tantamount to a confession and that he will still face consequences for the crime. However, the alternative question has allowed him the opportunity to tell the truth while saving face.

A defense attorney may criticize the use of an alternative question, arguing that the investigator offered his client only two choices and that his client was forced to incriminate himself. The investigator should explain that the defendant had three possible choices. He could have accepted either one of the alternatives presented or, as happens frequently, rejected both of them. Further, the investigator certainly does not force a suspect to accept one of the alternative questions. Tactics are used to encourage the suspect to accept one or the other, but **no force whatsoever is involved in the suspect's agreeing that one alternative is true.** When questioned on the stand about the use of the alternative question, it may also be beneficial for the investigator to explain that the purpose for asking an alternative question is merely to elicit an initial admission of guilt. From that point on, through the questioning process, the defendant offered details about the crime that eventually constituted the full confession.

Procedures

Selecting the Alternative Question

An investigator should always be mindful of the fact that when a criminal offender is asked to confess a crime, a great deal is being expected of the suspect. First of all, it is not easy for anyone to own up to wrongdoing of any kind. Furthermore, in a criminal case, the suspect may be well aware of the specific serious consequences of telling the truth—the penitentiary or even a death sentence. Therefore, the task of confessing should be made as easy as possible for the suspect.

Toward that end, the investigator should avoid a general admission of guilt question, such as "You did kill him, didn't you?" or "You did rape her, didn't you?" "You did hit him with your car, didn't you?" or "Tell us all about it." Any such question will recall to the suspect's mind a revolting picture of the crime itself—the scream of the victim, the blood spurting from a wound, or the pedestrian's body being thrown over the hood of an automobile or dragged along the street. No person should be expected to blurt out a full confession of guilt; the investigator must ease the ordeal. As the great Austrian criminal investigator Hans Gross stated in his 1907 book, *Criminal Investigation,* "It is merciless, or rather psychologically wrong, to expect anyone boldly and directly to confess his crime. . . . We must smooth the way, render the task easy" (p. 120).

The following suggestions are offered in selecting the appropriate alternative question for a given suspect.

- **A properly formulated alternative question must not mention legal charges, offer a promise of leniency to the suspect, or threaten the suspect with inevitable consequences.** This is a threefold guideline.

  (1) The alternative question should not make any mention of legal charges. An alternative question that violates this guideline, and is therefore *improper,* is, "Did you plan on killing her, in which case it will mean first-degree murder and life in prison, or did this just happen in the heat of passion, which would just be manslaughter?" This suspect is essentially being told that he will face reduced charges if he confesses to manslaughter rather than first-degree murder. A *proper* alternative question to ask in this case is, "Did you plan on doing this since the day you got married, or did it pretty much happen on the spur of the moment because of the fight you had?" With this latter question, no mention whatsoever of a possible consequence is made, and the suspect cannot later argue, with legitimacy, that he confessed to obtain a reduced sentence.

  (2) The alternative question should not threaten inevitable consequences. A suspect must be able to reject both sides of an alternative question without fear of facing adverse real consequences because of that decision. During an interrogation, these negative consequences are often presented as a threat of inevitable consequences (e.g., confess to me or suffer this negative consequence). An *improper* alternative question that threatens inevitable consequences in a noncustodial interrogation is, "Do you want to cooperate with me and confess or do you want me to lock you in jail where you can sit for the next two or three days?" The choice this suspect faces is to either confess or lose his freedom; he is not being offered the choice of rejecting both sides of the alternative question without facing a real negative consequence. A *proper* alternative question to consider in this case may be, "Are you sorry this happened or don't you care?"

  Another example of an improper alternative question that threatens an inevitable consequence is, "If you don't tell me about the sexual contact you had with your daughter, your kids will be taken away and you will never see them again." One of the guidelines governing confession admissibility is that the confession must be essentially the product of the suspect's free will. When the impetus for confessing is to avoid a jail cell or to be able to see one's children, the statement is clearly the result of compulsion. A good rule to follow in this regard is to use alternative choices that address some aspect of the crime, for example, "Did you force your daughter to touch your bare penis or did she do it on her own?"

  (3) The alternative question should not offer a promise of leniency. Courts have consistently ruled that confessions obtained in conjunction with a promise of leniency were improperly obtained. Therefore, the following alternative question is *improper:* "If you've done this dozens of times before, that's one thing. But, if this was just the first time it happened, I can explain that to the prosecutor and work out a deal for you." Not only

is it psychologically improper to bring up legal terminology during an interrogation (possible charges, the judge, the prosecutor), but also the mere mention of legal issues may invite a claim of an actual or perceived promise of leniency. A *proper* way to ask the previous alternative question is, "If you've done this dozens of times before, that's one thing. But if this was just the first time it happened, that would be important to establish."

- **An alternative question must be based on the assumption that the suspect actually committed the crime under investigation.** In other words, if the suspect accepts the alternative question, it must represent an admission of guilt. It would, therefore, be *improper* to ask a suspect who was being interrogated concerning the fondling of a young girl, "Did you touch her vagina intentionally or did the contact occur accidentally?" This suspect may very well affirm that the contact was inadvertent and maintain that position. Under this circumstance, the investigator has not developed any incriminating statement that can be legally used against the suspect.
- **In selecting the alternative question, primary consideration should be given to the theme that the investigator has been using.** The alternative should be a natural extension of the theme. It puts into focus, in one question, the central core of the theme that was emphasized by the investigator, especially in Step 6. For example, while questioning a suspected embezzler, the investigator may have used the theme that the suspect had originally intended to merely borrow the money for a short period of time. The alternative question may then be, "Mary, did you plan to keep that money all along, or did you only borrow it with the plan of paying it back?"

  When interrogating a burglary suspect, where the primary theme has placed blame on an accomplice, the alternative question that naturally grows out of this theme is, "Was this whole thing your idea, where you were the master mind and you planned everything out, or did someone talk you into it?" A child molester may be interrogated with a primary theme minimizing the number of victims he has molested. In this event, the alternative question should be: "Larry, are we looking at hundreds of kids here, where you have done this to almost every child you've ever had contact with, or would the total be a lot less? It's not over 500, is it?"
- **The alternative question usually focuses on the reason why the suspect committed the act, but it does not necessarily have to be limited to just this element of the offense.** The alternative question may focus on some detail of the offense, preferably something preceding or following the occurrence itself. A detail question is based on the *where, when,* or *how* of an act or event pertinent to the crime under investigation, but yet is removed in point of time or place from the main occurrence itself. In an armed robbery case, for instance, the question may be: "Did you bring the gun yourself, or did one of your buddies give it to you?" In a rape case, where the suspect has denied ever seeing the victim, an appropriate question would be: "Were you with her for a long time before this happened or for just a few minutes?" In an arson case, the question may be: "Did you use a match or a lighter?"

detail question a question that is based on the where, when, or how of an act or event pertinent to the crime under investigation, but yet is removed in point of time or place from the main occurrence itself.

- **Depending upon the nature of the crime and the suspect's demeanor during the interrogation, occasionally it becomes advisable to use a**

one-sided alternative question. An example is, "You are sorry about this, aren't you, Joe?" The negative possibility—the absence of any feeling of remorse—is not stated, but the implication of its presence is readily apparent to the suspect.

Presenting the Alternative Question

In using the alternative question, the investigator must bear in mind the need to phrase it in terms of a clear contrast between two opposite choices; for instance, "Joe, is this the first time you did something like this, or has it happened many times before?" In other words, the question must not be phrased in such a manner as to expect the suspect to offer a full confession, as would occur if the suspect is merely asked, "You did do it, didn't you?"

In phrasing the alternative question, the investigator should **avoid any emotionally charged words** that would recreate a revolting recollection of the event. For example, in a rape case, there should be an avoidance of expressions like the following: "Is this the first time you raped a girl, or have you raped a lot of girls before?" Instead, the question should be phrased: "Is this the first time something like this has happened, or has it happened a lot of times before?" The suspect will know, of course, what the investigator means when reference is made to the event as "this."

Harsh or descriptive language may be utilized, in some cases, when speaking of the "negative" side of the alternative question. For instance, the investigator may ask, "Did you rob that guy because you enjoy that sort of thing; where you get a kick out of scaring people, or did this thing happen just because you were desperate for money?" By using the contrasting words "rob" and "this thing," the suspect is further encouraged to accept the more understanding "positive" side of the alternative question—committing the robbery out of desperation.

When the alternative question is first presented, the suspect may not make any comment, in which event the question should be repeated in basically the same form, unless the suspect's behavioral responses are suggestive of a total rejection. If that occurs, a different alternative question should be introduced and developed.

When the investigator presents the alternative question to the suspect, it is not enough to simply ask the question and then wait for the suspect to answer. The investigator must encourage the suspect to select one of the two options. This is accomplished through the use of positive and negative supporting statements.

A **positive supporting statement** is one in which the investigator reinforces his belief that the correct choice is the one that seems to be morally excusable or at least one that represents a less socially revolting reason for committing the act. The investigator should state that if the positive alternative is true, that it is something he can understand.

On the other hand, the **negative supporting statement** paints a disturbing picture of the suspect if the negative alternative is true. The investigator may effectively state (in reference to the negative alternative), "If that's why you did this I don't even want to talk to you further because it means I've really misread you today!"

positive supporting statement a statement discussing the desirable side of the alternative question designed to encourage the suspect to select that side.

negative supporting statement statement that paints a disturbing picture of the suspect if the negative alternative is true.

leading question a question phrased in such a way as to expect agreement.

The supporting statements close with a leading question that calls for a one-word answer or a nod of the head in acceptance of the less offensive of the two options. In appropriate instances, the supporting statement should be coupled with a gesture of understanding and sympathy, such as a pat on the shoulder. This indication of sincerity, coupled with the timing of the supporting statement, can be the key to success in this particular procedure.

Generally speaking, at least several minutes must be spent on developing both positive and negative supporting statements. However, the technique culminates in asking the positive or negative alternative in a leading manner.

Positive and Negative Supporting Statements

Alternative question: "Joe, was this money used to take care of some bills at home, or was it used to gamble?"

Negative supporting statement: "You don't seem to be the kind of person who would do something like this in order to use it for gambling. If you were that kind of person, I wouldn't want to waste my time with you, but I don't think you're like that."

Positive supporting statement: "I'm sure this money was for your family, for some bills at home. That's something even an honest person might do, if he was thinking of his family."

Presenting a leading question: "It was for your family's sake, wasn't it, Joe?"

An important part of the supporting statement is to develop a concern in the suspect's mind that if he does not accept the understandable alternative, others may believe the reprehensible one. As an example, the investigator may state, "If you want your family and friends to believe that you are dishonest and can never be trusted, my advice to you is to say nothing!" This implication represents the incentive for a guilty suspect to accept the positive alternative. In other words, a guilty suspect understands full well that accepting either side of the alternative question represents an admission of guilt and, with it, the subsequent consequences for committing the crime. However, even the most hard-core criminal will take positive action to preserve his dignity or reputation, even at the cost of a confession that may well result in an incarceration.

The effect of contrasting the clearly disapproving connotations of the negative alternative with the more understanding circumstances of the positive alternative should be transmitted at all three levels of communication. While presenting the negative alternative, therefore, the investigator should use descriptive language, use a demeaning tone of voice, and use judgmental nonverbal behavior. The opposite behaviors should be used when discussing the more understandable, positive side of the alternative question. An attempt is made to illustrate this interaction in the transcript in Case 16-1: Negative Alternative Contrasted with a More Positive Interpretation, from a teenage boy being interrogated concerning the stabbing death of his neighbor. The nonverbal elements are denoted by brackets.

Case 16-1: Negative Alternative Contrasted with a More Positive Interpretation

"Mark, I think that she simply misinterpreted some of your behaviors and overreacted to the situation. [compassionate, gentle] But I could be wrong. If you went over to her house that day fully intending to kill her, I think that's despicable and I'm probably wasting your time and mine trying to get this clarified. [louder voice, strong language, harsh facial expressions, chopping hand motion] But I don't think that is the case. I think this happened on the spur of the moment and you're sorry about it. [compassionate, soft, warm eyes] Either you're sorry or you're not. I think you're sorry you did this, aren't you?" [compassionate]

At this point, the suspect said, "Yeah."

Step 7 is frequently the key to a successful interrogation. Just as there are salespeople who are very good at selling the benefits of a product but unable to close the sale, many investigators simply do not know what to do at this stage of the interrogation in order to trigger an admission. In many unsuccessful interrogations, the use of an alternative question along with its supportive statements would probably have produced a favorable result.

The alternative question represents the culmination of theme development. Through Step 6 of the interrogation, the investigator attempts to maintain a sympathetic monologue wherein he essentially suggests morally acceptable reasons that may account for the suspect's commission of the crime (the theme). This control over the interrogation is essential to convince the suspect of the investigator's confidence in his guilt and to respond effectively to any resistance offered. **Not to be overlooked during the first three steps of the interrogation process is the investigator's awareness of the behavior offered by an innocent suspect.**

Once the suspect exhibits symptoms of resignation in Step 6, the investigator condenses the theme down to central elements and introduces the alternative question. The alternative question contrasts two possible aspects of the crime, one of which is presented as clearly less understandable and more reprehensible than the other. The suspect is encouraged to accept the more understandable alternative.

It is important to note that even the most experienced and skilled investigators achieve a confession rate of only about 80%. Of the approximately 20% of suspects who do not confess after being offered an alternative question, it might be argued that a small percentage of them could have been innocent. However, the vast majority of suspects who have exhibited the previously described behaviors indicative of deception throughout the course of the interrogation are, in fact, guilty of the offense. The investigator must accept that not every guilty person will confess during a legally permissible interrogation.

KEY POINTS

- Once the suspect exhibits symptoms of resignation in Step 6, the investigator condenses the theme down to central elements and introduces the alternative question.
- The alternative question offers the guilty suspect the opportunity to start telling the truth by making a single admission.
- An investigator should always be mindful of the fact that when a criminal offender is asked to confess a crime, a great deal is being expected of the suspect. Thus, the task of confessing should be made as easy as possible for the suspect.
- A suspect must be able to reject both sides of an alternative question without fear of facing adverse real consequences because of that decision.
- One of the guidelines governing confession admissibility is that the confession must be essentially the product of the suspect's free will.
- A good rule to follow when formulating alternative questions is to use choices that address some aspect of the crime.
- Among the issues courts evaluate when determining confession admissibility is whether or not the confession was obtained without offering any promises of leniency or threatening the suspect with physical harm or inevitable consequences.
- The alternative question should be a natural extension of the theme the investigator has been using.
- The alternative question usually focuses on the reason why the suspect committed the act, but it does not necessarily have to be limited to just this element of the offense.
- The investigator must phrase the alternative question in terms of a clear contrast between two opposite choices.
- In phrasing the alternative question, the investigator should avoid any emotionally charged words that would recreate a revolting recollection of the event.
- Supporting statements close with a leading question that calls for a one-word answer or a nod of the head in acceptance of the less offensive of the two options.
- An important part of the supporting statement is to develop a concern in the suspect's mind that if he does not accept the understandable alternative, others may believe the reprehensible one.

KEY TERMS

alternative question A question which offers the suspect two incrimination choices concerning some aspect of the crime.

detail question A question that is based on the where, when, or how of an act or event pertinent to the crime under investigation, but yet is removed in point of time or place from the main occurrence itself.

leading question A question phrased in such a way as to expect agreement.

negative supporting statement Statement that paints a disturbing picture of the suspect if the negative alternative is true.

positive supporting statement A statement discussing the desirable side of the alternative question designed to encourage the suspect to select that side.

17

Step 8: Having the Suspect Relate Details of the Offense

Chapter Objectives

Upon completion of this chapter you will be able to:

- Discuss the importance of reinforcing the suspect's admission
- Identify ways of asking initial questions seeking more details
- Explain how to draw out a full admission of guilt from the suspect, including corroborative information
- Describe having a confession witnessed

Principles

In movie portrayals of criminal interrogations, once the suspect cracks the investigator sits back and says, "Okay, tell me all about it." The suspect then proceeds to offer a fully detailed and elaborate confession, often in the presence of a number of investigators. This is pure fiction.

During an actual interrogation, out of necessity the investigator has dominated the conversation to the extent that the suspect is quite content to sit back and listen. At the point of accepting an alternative question, the suspect has merely offered an admission of guilt. **The investigator now needs to draw the suspect into the conversation to develop a full confession.** Because of the psychological impact of accepting full responsibility for his crime, the suspect will be very reluctant to provide details necessary to constitute a confession. Therefore, the investigator must employ a great deal of patience and allow the suspect to relate the details of the crime at his own pace. This is a gradual effort done in stages. Once a full confession has been elicited, it is generally advisable to have the suspect's confession witnessed by a second party.

Procedures

The Statement of Reinforcement

When the suspect accepts one of the choices presented in the alternative question, he has, in effect, made an admission of guilt. The objective of Step 8, then, is to develop this admission (which only tends toward proving the suspect's guilt) into a legally acceptable and substantiated confession that discloses the circumstances and details of the act.

As stated in the discussion of Step 7, the alternative question and its supporting statements should be phrased so that the suspect needs only a nod of the head or a one-word response to indicate acceptance of one or the other of the alternative choices. At the precise moment when the suspect accepts an alternative, it is critical that the investigator immediately proceed to having the suspect further commit himself to a discussion of the details of the crime. If the investigator gives the impression of being uncertain or hesitates after the suspect accepts one of the alternative choices, the suspect will then have an opportunity to retract his statement. The investigator should encourage the suspect to continue beyond the acceptance of an alternative by making a **statement of reinforcement**, such as, "Good, that's what I thought is was all along" or, "I was hoping that was the case."

statement of reinforcement statement that encourages the suspect to continue beyond the acceptance of an alternative and commit himself to a discussion of the details of the crime.

As the investigator makes a statement of reinforcement, he should appear to share the suspect's relief and should, while still looking directly at the suspect, ask a question calling for some additional detail regarding the suspect's act, such as, "Do you have any of the money left?" "Have you ever done anything like this before?" or "Have you told anyone else about this?" These types of initial questions should not delve into sensitive areas of the crime that are difficult to talk about, such as the true motivation, the extent of planning involved, or the names of accomplices. Furthermore, the suspect should be able to answer them with a short verbal answer. The purpose here is simply to further commit the suspect to his admission of involvement in the offense.

Developing the General Acknowledgment of Guilt

Once the suspect is fully committed to the admission, the investigator should begin to develop the confession by asking questions that call for somewhat longer responses. These questions should avoid emotionally charged terminology, such as *stab, rape, rob,* or *sexually molest.* As examples of possible questions, the investigator may ask, "Then what happened?" or "What happened next?" Once the suspect starts talking about the crime, the investigator's questions should attempt to develop a general description of the criminal act. **The questions presented to the suspect during this initial phase of the confession should be brief, clear, and, to the extent possible, call for a short narrative response** as opposed to simply agreeing with the investigator's statement. Case 17-1: Murderer Confesses Killing Family provides an illustration.

Case 17-1: Murderer Confesses Killing Family

The suspect, Jack, was suspected of having stabbed to death his wife and three children. When Jack mumbled the word "table" in response to the alternative question "Was the knife on the table or in the drawer?" the investigator followed with a statement of reinforcement: "Good, Jack, that's what I thought all along." The following dialogue ensued:

Investigator: "Then what happened?"

Jack [after a pause]: "I did it to her."

I: "What did you use?"

J: "The knife."

I: "How many times did you use the knife, Jack?"

J: "A couple of times."

I: "Where on her body did the knife cut her?"

J: "The chest."

I: "Did you cut her on the back at all, Jack?"

J: "No." [The investigator knew from the facts in the case that she was only stabbed in the front, but several times. The details of the number of times she was stabbed should be left to a later time when it will be much easier for the suspect to tell the number of times he estimates that she was stabbed. Also, the investigator should bear in mind that in the suspect's frenzy, he may not know the exact number of times he stabbed his wife.]

I: "Then what happened?"

J: "The kids were crying."

I: "And what did you do?"

J: "I put them in the tub."

I: "What tub?"

J: "The bathtub."

I: "What did you do then?"

J: "I used it on them."

I: "What did you use on them, Jack?"

J: "The knife."

I: "What did you do then?"

J: "I thought about using it on myself, but I didn't have the guts, so I left."

I: "What did you do with the knife, Jack?"

J: "I left it in the bathroom."

I: "Where in the bathroom?"

J: "With them in the bathtub."

At this point, the investigator has the suspect, Jack, totally committed to the murders. The investigator should then pursue in detail the circumstances of the act, as well as what the suspect did before and after he committed the crime. The investigator would now use, for the first time, fully descriptive, incriminating words such as *stab* (or in other cases, *shoot, steal, rob, burglarize,* etc.) so that when these words are used in the formal written confession, the suspect will be accustomed to them. It is also at this point that Jack should be asked more details about the manner and number of times he stabbed his wife.

During the initial phase of eliciting the full confession, the suspect may not be psychologically prepared to talk about some aspects of his crime. When asked a question that is too difficult to discuss, the suspect may simply not respond or, more commonly, may state that he can't remember or doesn't know about the circumstance. The investigator should not pursue this sensitive area until later and should move on to another question, such as, "What is the next thing you remember doing?"

While developing the general acknowledgment of guilt, the investigator should refrain from taking any written notes. To do so may discourage the suspect from continuing with the confession.

Eliciting the Corroborated Confession

After a suspect has related a general acknowledgment of guilt, the investigator should return to the beginning of the crime and attempt to develop information that can be corroborated by further investigation, and should seek from the suspect full details of the crime and information about the suspect's subsequent activities. What should be sought particularly are facts that would be known only by the guilty person (e.g., information regarding the location of the murder weapon or the stolen goods, the means of entry into the building, the type of accelerant used to start the fire, or the type of clothing on the victim).

corroborative information facts that would be known only by the guilty person.

independent corroboration information about a crime learned from the suspect's confession that is verified as true after the confession.

When developing **corroborative information**, the investigator must be certain that the details were not somehow revealed to the suspect through the questioning process, news media, or the viewing of crime scene photographs. In this regard, it is suggested that early during an investigation, a decision be made by the lead investigator as to what evidence will be withheld from the public, as well as from all suspects. This information should be documented in writing in the case file so that all investigators are aware of what information will be withheld.

The best type of corroboration is in the form of new evidence that was not known before the confession but that can be later substantiated (**independent corroboration**). Prior to conducting the interrogation, the investigator should consider what types of independent corroborative information should be sought. Examples include the present location of a murder weapon or the suspect's bloody clothing, where stolen goods were fenced, or with whom the suspect has discussed the crime.

At this stage of the process, the investigator may return to the alternative question that was used to develop the first admission of guilt. **If it is believed that the alternative question does not represent the whole truth, an attempt should be made, at this point, to obtain a correction from the suspect because of his present penitent frame of mind**, whereas previously it would have been inadvisable to do so. Most suspects will now usually answer any questions as truthfully as they can. In other words, once a suspect begins to confess, he will typically continue to do so unless the investigator becomes abrasive, offends the suspect by an impertinent attitude, or violates the suspect's privacy by bringing into the interview room additional people or equipment to record the conversation. Of course, there are exceptions to this rule where a guilty suspect, for a number of reasons, will be reluctant to offer a full and complete disclosure of his crime.

Having the Oral Confession Witnessed

oral confession a confession that is expressed verbally.

When initially eliciting an oral confession, it is important that the investigator be the only one in the room with the suspect. The presence of any other persons may discourage suspects from giving details about their actions. Later, however, when the investigator is satisfied that adequate details surrounding the commission of the crime have been obtained, he may decide that it would be appropriate to have another person witness the oral confession. In such cases, the suspect should be told that the investigator is going to step out of the room for a minute but will return shortly. The investigator should then locate someone to witness the suspect's acknowledgment of guilt. This should be done without delay; otherwise, the suspect will have time to reconsider what was said and may decide to retract his confession.

The purpose of having the suspect's oral confession witnessed is twofold: (1) After the suspect has told two persons, instead of just one, that she did commit the crime, she has so fully committed herself that she will be less likely to refuse to give and sign a written statement, and (2) in the event the suspect does refuse to give or sign a formal statement, there will be two persons available, the investigator and the witness, to testify at trial that the suspect did confess orally. This will be more effective than the testimony of the investigator alone.

Before the investigator returns to the interview room with the witness, the witness should be told what the suspect's statements were and what the witness should do after the investigator and the witness enter the room together. The witness should also be told not to say anything at the outset—that the investigator will initially do all the talking. Furthermore, the witness ought to be instructed to stand to the side, near the seated suspect, and to look directly at the investigator rather than at the suspect (**Figure 17-1**). Finally, the witness should be aware that the investigator will relate to the witness the fundamental points of the suspect's confession.

When the suspect's oral confession is witnessed, he should not be asked to repeat the details; to do so would create an added burden for the suspect, who may then reassess his situation and retract the confession. Therefore, upon entering the room with the witness, the investigator should say, "This is Officer Smith. He has been working with me on this case." Following this brief introduction, the investigator should then repeat to the witness (Officer Smith) the essential elements of the suspect's confession.

Figure 17-1 Position of investigator and witness during the verbal witnessing of a confession.

Having a Confession Witnessed

In the previously described wife-killing case, the investigator would state: "Jack said that he stabbed his wife last week, that the whole thing happened on the spur of the moment and without any previous planning; in fact, he said he went to her apartment to get some information for his lawyer about the divorce and that she started an argument with him. He also told me that he stabbed the children but only because they were crying and he didn't know what to do. He also said he intended to stab himself, but didn't do it and then left."

Following this statement by the investigator, the witness, pursuant to an earlier instruction to him, would ask a few confirmatory questions. The ensuing dialogue would be as follows:

> Witness: "Now Jack, is what [investigator's name] just told me the complete truth?"
>
> Jack: "Yes, it is."
>
> W: "Jack, did you plan on doing this before you went to the apartment?"
>
> J: "No, sir, it just happened. I can't even believe it happened."

witness's confirmatory questions questions posed by the witness to have the suspect actually verbalize to the witness what has already been told to the investigator.

W: "Was anybody with you when you stabbed your wife and kids?"

J: "No, I was alone."

The purpose of having the witness ask a few questions is to have the suspect actually verbalize to the witness what had already been told to the investigator. This will be more effective than a mere acknowledgment of the truth of what the investigator told the witness.

After the suspect has fully committed himself, the witness should leave the room and the investigator should proceed to obtain a full written confession (Step 9). The elements necessary in a written confession and the appropriate procedural considerations are discussed in Chapter 18.

KEY POINTS

- The objective of Step 8 is to develop an admission into a legally acceptable and substantiated confession that discloses the circumstances and details of the act.
- At the precise moment when the suspect accepts an alternative that has been presented to him in Step 7, it is critical that the investigator immediately proceed to having the suspect further commit himself to a discussion of the details of the crime.
- The investigator should encourage the suspect by making a statement of reinforcement.
- Next, the investigator should ask a question calling for some additional detail regarding the suspect's act, while avoiding sensitive areas of the crime that are difficult to talk about.
- Once the suspect is fully committed to his admission, the investigator should begin to develop the confession by asking questions that call for somewhat longer responses.
- The investigator should then pursue in detail the circumstances of the act, as well as what the suspect did before and after committing the crime.
- The investigator must employ a great deal of patience and allow the suspect to relate the details of the crime at his own pace.
- It is important to develop corroborating information from the suspect, such as details of the crime that only the guilty person would know.
- Once a full confession has been elicited, it is generally advisable to have the suspect's confession witnessed by a second party. The witness should ask a few questions to have the suspect verbalize what had already been told to the investigator.

KEY TERMS

corroborative information Facts that would be known only by the guilty person.

independent corroboration Information about a crime learned from the suspect's confession that is verified as true after the confession.

oral confession A confession that is expressed verbally.

statement of reinforcement Statement that encourages the suspect to continue beyond the acceptance of an alternative and commit himself to a discussion of the details of the crime.

witness's confirmatory questions Questions posed by the witness to have the suspect actually verbalize to the witness what has already been told to the investigator.

18

Step 9: Converting an Oral Confession into a Written Confession

Chapter Objectives

Upon completion of this chapter you will be able to:

- Describe how and when to warn a suspect of his or her constitutional rights
- Prepare a written confession for signing
- Describe how to get a suspect to sign a confession
- Understand how to safeguard the effectiveness of the confession

Principles

The interrogation, simply stated, represents an effort by an investigator to persuade a suspect to tell the truth about alleged involvement in a criminal offense. Once the suspect has told the truth, he may subsequently reflect on the possible consequences of deciding to do so. The suspect is then likely to retract the confession—if not shortly after making it, certainly by the time his court date approaches and the suspect's attorney points out how damaging the confession will be to his case.

The investigator, therefore, must attempt to preserve the confession as not only a court-admissible document, but also one that will stand up under the court's scrutiny and the challenges of a defense attorney. Step 9 of the interrogation involves the procedures and legal considerations of converting the oral confession into a written one.

Procedures

The Importance of Documentation

Most confessed criminal offenders will subsequently deny their guilt and allege that they either did not confess or that they were forced or induced to do so by physical abuse, threats, or promises of leniency. Occasionally, a defendant in a criminal case will even go so far as to say that he was compelled to sign a written confession without reading it or having had it read to him, or that he was forced to sign a blank sheet of paper and all that appears above it was inserted later.

In a community or jurisdiction where the police enjoy the respect and confidence of the public, false claims of this nature are rather easily overcome; the prosecution may even secure a conviction on the basis of an oral, unwritten, or unrecorded confession with very little corroborating evidence. In most cases, however, the problem is much more difficult, and a written or recorded confession is considered far preferable to an oral one. When the confession is in writing, the controversy between the prosecution and the defense becomes more than merely a matter of whether the court or jury is to believe the oral testimony of the police or of the accused; the written statement lends considerable support to the prosecution's contention that the accused did, in fact, confess.

It is essential that an oral confession be reduced to writing and be signed as soon as possible. The next morning, or even a few hours after the oral confession, may be too late, because the confessor, having reflected upon the legal consequences of his confession, may retract it. No time should be lost, therefore, in preparing for and obtaining a written, signed confession. If time and circumstances do not afford the opportunity for a stenographic transcription, or even for writing out a detailed confession, the investigator should write or type a brief statement of what the suspect orally related—even if only two or three sentences long—and present it to the confessor for signature. Once an offender has committed himself in writing, regardless of its brevity, there is a reduced probability that he will refuse later on to make and sign a more detailed version of the crime.

Warning of Constitutional Rights

During custodial interrogations, where the warnings required by *Miranda v. Arizona* have already been issued before the interrogation or interview began, it is advisable, nevertheless, to repeat the warnings at the beginning of the written confession, making reference, of course, to the fact that the suspect had received and waived them earlier. One reason for this reference is to establish further evidence that the warnings had been given at the required time, prior to any questioning, rather than only at the time of the taking of the formal confession. Then, too, because a suspect has a right at any time to revoke his waiver of rights, the incorporation of the warnings in the confession itself will thereby preserve evidence of the fact that the waiver was a continuing one up to the time of the signing of the confession. Moreover, at this stage, because the suspect has already confessed orally, the incorporation of the warnings into the written confession is not likely to deter him from signing the document. The psychological factors are now different, obviously, from those prevailing at the time when the investigator sought a waiver of *Miranda* rights before an interview or interrogation even began.

Printed forms are usually available for the typing or handwriting of a confession for submission to the confessor for his or her signature. It should start with a statement such as the following one.

> *Having been told, before being questioned about the following offense, of my right to remain silent, that anything I say could be used against me, and that I had a right to a lawyer, without cost if I could not afford one, I nevertheless was willing to talk and I also am now willing to give this written statement:*

In the event the confessor informs the investigator that he does not wish to make or to sign the statement, or that a lawyer is wanted, the investigator must cease any further questioning or recording. Nevertheless, the oral confession is still usable as evidence.

If the oral confession has been made to the police by a person not in custody when the interrogation began (and to whom, therefore, the warnings did not have to be issued initially), but the suspect is to be taken into custody following the writing and signing of the confession, it is advisable, as a precautionary measure, that the warnings be given now at the start of the written confession in the way and manner just described, including the statement of waiver.

On the other hand, if the suspect is to be released and presumably arrested later (after further investigation confirms his confession), no *Miranda* waiver is required. Furthermore, a private security officer does not have to issue the warnings to any suspect unless the security officer is empowered with full police authority, or is acting in conjunction with the police, and the suspect is in custody.

The Preparation and Form of the Written Confession

A written confession may be prepared in the form of questions (by the investigator) and answers (by the confessor), or in the form of a narration by the confessor. Such confessions may be written out by hand, typed by the investigator, or taken down by a stenographer and transcribed into typewritten form.

Most prosecutors prefer the question-and-answer format of confession; others prefer the narrative form. Perhaps the best procedure is to effect a compromise whereby the preliminary and concluding aspects of the offense are elicited by means of specific questions from the investigator, but the details of the actual occurrence are given by the confessor in narrative form. For instance, the suspect may be asked specific questions as to his name; whether or not he is known by any alias; his address, age, place of employment; whether (in some types of situations) he understands and reads the English language; the time he arrived at the scene of the crime; and the names of persons who were with him up to that time. Then, after the investigator's questions have brought the suspect right up to the time and place of the crime, he may be asked, "What happened then?" Thereafter, as long as the suspect confines himself to an orderly recitation of the occurrence, he should be permitted to continue to narrate what happened. If he hesitates or seems to be relating events out of sequence, the investigator can interpose a specific question in order to have the suspect continue in an orderly fashion. At the same time, however, some irrelevant talking should be permitted, because its very irrelevancy may be considered as evidence of the voluntariness of the confession.

After the main occurrence has been covered in the confession, the investigator may return to the use of specific questions, such as, "Where did you go then?" "What time did you get there?" and so forth. Specific questions may also be used, of course, to bring out previously revealed facts that were omitted from the suspect's narrative portion of the statement.

In addition to the previously mentioned advantages, a question-and-answer format of confession lends itself more readily to the deletion of certain parts, if the trial court should consider any deletion necessary before the confession is read to the jury. All of the investigator's questions should be short, very simply worded, and to the point. The use of lengthy, complicated questions and the kind of answers that are likely to follow will render the document much less impressive.

Under no circumstances should a confessor be put under oath by a notary public, justice of the peace, or by anyone else before the taking of a confession. Such a practice has been viewed by some courts as a coercive influence that nullifies the legal validity of the confession.

For the psychological effect on the jury when the written confession is read, it is advisable to ask the confessor, very early in the confession, a question that will call for an acknowledgment that he committed the crime. This can be done after initial questions about name, address, age, and so forth. (For example, "As regards the fire in the store at First and Main streets, do you know who started it?" Answer: "I started it.") Then, after the acknowledgment, the investigator can continue with further preliminary questions as he leads up to the main event and asks the suspect to narrate the details of what occurred.

Early acknowledgment of guilt in a confession will serve to arouse immediate interest in the document by the jury as it is read. It makes clear to the jury at the very outset that what is being read is a confession of guilt, and jury members will then follow more closely the details that are subsequently disclosed. An additional advantage of early acknowledgment of guilt is the effect it has on the confessor personally. The suspect who has thus committed himself is far less likely to balk at continuing with the details.

The details of a confession should not only contain the details of the offense itself, such as the date, time, place, motive, and manner of its commission, but also such things as the places where the confessor had been before and after the crime, and the names of individuals he saw and talked to before and after the event. In some instances, the confessor should also be asked to describe the clothing he wore at the time because this may be an important factor with respect to courtroom identification testimony by victims or witnesses.

During the taking of a confession, no one should be in the interview room other than the confessor, investigator, and stenographer. In addition to the previously discussed psychological reasons for such privacy, there is a persuasive legal factor. In some jurisdictions, each person present during the interrogation or the taking of a confession will have to be produced as a witness at the trial whenever the defendant contends that improper methods were used to obtain his confession. This obviously imposes a burden on the prosecution that can and should be avoided.

Even in those instances where the investigator himself writes or types the confession, there is no need to have a third person present to actually witness its preparation or signing. The confessor's subsequent acknowledgment to a witness or witnesses that the written confession and signature are his will be sufficient.

The person who types the confession should avoid placing a signature line at the end of it for two reasons: (1) The line connotes too much legalism and may discourage the confessor from affixing his signature to the document; (2) in the event that a confessor refuses to sign the confession, the document will look far better without the unused signature line on it. An unsigned confession has been held to be usable as evidence as long as the investigator can testify that it accurately represents what the defendant said. Moreover, a preceding oral confession will still be usable, even if a typed one is rejected.

The Language of the Confession

Readable and Understandable Language

Throughout the taking of the confession, the investigator must always be on guard to see that its contents will be readily understood and easily followed by a reader or subsequent listener who has no other independent knowledge as to what occurred. All too often, the investigator neglects to realize that although what is going into the confession is perfectly clear to him, its contents may be vague and indefinite to others, including the judge or jury who will hear the case. For instance, when a person has orally confessed to a rape, the investigator who takes the written confession knows full well what the confessor means when he admits he did "it," but "it" may be rather meaningless to someone else. Also, when a confessor says he set fire to "the place," and that it was on "that night," the person who does not have the benefit of other independent knowledge about "the place" or "that night" is at a loss to comprehend the confession. Moreover, when a confession is that vague and indefinite, a trial judge may refuse to let it be used at all.

The way to clarify indefinite words or phrases is to interrupt the confessor and ask a question that will explain away the uncertainty. In a rape case, if the confessor speaks in terms of "it," he may be asked, "What do you mean, 'it'?" or "By 'it,' you mean sexual intercourse [or the suspect's equivalent terminology]?" In an arson case, the suspect may be asked, "What do you mean by 'place'?" or "By 'the place,' you mean the house at the corner of First and Main Streets in this city?" and "What do you mean by 'that night'?" or "By 'that night,' you mean the night of July 10th of this year?"

Furthermore, the language of the statement should clearly identify the legal nature of the act. For example, in a theft case, the word *steal,* rather than *take,* should be used. In a rape case, the confession should indicate "forced sexual intercourse" rather than "had sex with."

Avoidance of Leading Questions

A confession in which the investigator does most of the talking, and which consists primarily of "yes" or "no" answers, is not nearly so convincing and effective as one in which the investigator plays the minor part and the confessor the leading role of both informer and confessor. It is highly important, therefore, that the investigator let the confessor supply the details of the occurrence; to this end, the investigator should avoid or at least minimize the use of leading questions.

To illustrate the point, suppose a person is in the process of confessing a murder in which it is a known fact that the gun involved in the crime was thrown away under a certain house. The confessor has been giving various details of the crime, and the investigator is about to inquire regarding the disposal of the gun. At this stage, some investigators may say, "Then you threw the gun under the house, didn't you?"—a question calling merely for a "yes" answer. Far more convincing to a court or jury is to have the gun details appear in answer to a nonleading question, such as, "Then what did you do with the gun?"—a question calling for detailed information from the confessor himself.

Confessor's Own Language

In the preparation of the written confession, no attempt should be made to improve the language used by the confessor himself. The statement represents that person's confession and should be in the confessor's original words. A judge or jury may be reluctant to believe that a defendant whose education may have ended at the third grade gave a confession that contained the language of a college graduate. Also, in a sex offense case, the confessor's own terminology should go into the written confession without any attempt being made by the investigator to "clean it up." For instance, the words *sexual intercourse, vagina,* or *anal penetration* should not be substituted for the crude language used by the confessor, provided that the crude language accurately describes the sexual behavior. Along the same lines, if the suspect is to write out a confession, the investigator should not assist in the spelling of any of the words even if asked to do so. The suspect should be told to do the best he can with the spelling.

Personal History Questions

personal history question question calling for answers known only to the offender.

At the trial, the offender may allege that the confession represents only what he had been told to say—that the investigator "put the words into my mouth." An excellent precautionary measure to effectively meet such a defense is the practice of incorporating into the confession a number of more or less irrelevant **personal history questions** calling for answers known only to the offender. For instance, the suspect may be asked the name of the grade school he attended, or the place or hospital in which he was born, or other similar information. Care must be exercised, however, to avoid questions that call for answers about which the confessor may not be sure (e.g., the name of his grade school principal). When accurate personal information is included in a confession, the prosecutor may point to it as evidence that the accused actually gave the information contained in the confession and was not merely accommodating the investigator by repeating what he was told to say.

On occasion, the confession should reflect the fact that the suspect had the opportunity to satisfy such physical needs as being able to use the washroom facilities or having something to eat or drink, particularly if the circumstances surrounding the interrogation involved several hours. For similar reasons, if the suspect requires regular medications (insulin, heart medications, etc.), it may be helpful to indicate in the confession that he was allowed to take his normal medications. It also may be important in some situations to clarify with the suspect whether or not any drugs or alcohol had been consumed within the previous 12 hours. This may become relevant in those cases in which the defendant later claims to have been under the influence of drugs or alcohol at the time of his alleged confession.

Final Details

Reading and Signing the Confession

It is advisable for the investigator to read aloud a carbon or photocopy of the confession as the confessor follows the original one word for word. The suspect should be requested to place an "OK," followed by his initials or signature, at the bottom of each page after the contents have been read by or to him. Then, at the end of the confession, it is well to have the offender write out, in his own hand, some such statement as the following: "I have read this ___ page statement of mine and it is the truth. I made it of my own free will, without any threats or promises having been made to me by anyone." After this should appear his signature.

When the time comes for the signing of a confession, the investigator should never say, "Sign here." It is much better, psychologically, to say, "Put your name here" or "Write your name here" while pointing out the place for the signature. The word *sign* connotes too much legalism.

Witnesses

In most instances in which the offender does not object to the oral confession being reduced to writing, he will readily sign it in the presence of one or more witnesses in addition to the investigator. As already stated, however, it is better to maintain the element of privacy throughout the taking of the confession. Moreover, there are some occasions when a hesitating and wavering confessor may balk at signing the confession if other persons, particularly uniformed police officers, enter the room for the obvious purpose of witnessing the signature.

A written confession does not need to be signed by any witnesses. All that is required is to have one person authenticate it—someone who can testify that he saw the defendant sign it and acknowledge its truthfulness. Indispensable, of course, will be the testimony of the investigator that the accused voluntarily made the confession and that the written document was read by or to him before it was signed.

Confining the Confession to One Crime

When a person confesses to having committed two or more crimes, separate confessions should be taken for each one, unless the crimes are so closely related in point of time, place, or other circumstances that the account of one crime cannot be related without referring to the others. For instance, if a suspect confesses several robberies, or several burglaries, or a robbery and a burglary, a separate confession should, as a rule, be taken of each offense. Exceptions are when several persons are robbed at the same time, or when the occupant of a burglarized home is also robbed by the burglar, or when a kidnapped person is also murdered. In such instances, the crimes are so closely related that it is practically impossible to describe one offense without referring to the other offense or offenses.

The situation is different, of course, as regards the robbery of John Jones on Monday night and the robbery of Frank Smith on Wednesday night. Either of such offenses can be described without reference to the other one. Moreover, the courts hold that it is improper, because of the inherent prejudicial effect, to offer evidence to a jury about a crime other than the one for which the defendant is on trial. There are certain exceptions where, at trial, evidence of another crime or crimes may be presented to establish motive, lack of accident, and so forth, but those situations are of no practical concern to the person taking a confession. Consequently, each offense should be treated separately when taking written or recorded confessions.

For similar reasons, a confession should never contain any reference to the fact that a suspect had previously been arrested or convicted, or that he has taken (or refused to take) a polygraph examination. Any such statement would have to be deleted from the confession before it could be accepted in evidence at the trial.

Safeguarding the Effectiveness of the Confession

Preservation of Notes

Although a confession written and signed as previously outlined will be difficult to attack in court, there may be occasions when it will become necessary to refute certain objections to it by calling as a witness the stenographer who prepared the typewritten copy from shorthand notes. The only way this can be done, of course, is to have the stenographer read to the court and jury the original shorthand notes. It is advisable, therefore, that these notes be preserved until the case has been finalized in court.

At the time of trial, usually several months after the confession, an investigator may be cross-examined at considerable length regarding the conditions and circumstances under which the confession was obtained. To meet such a contingency, he should never rely solely upon memory. It is desirable, therefore, to keep notes regarding such matters as the issuance of the *Miranda* warnings, the time when the interrogation was begun and ended, the time when the confession was signed, the names of persons who witnessed the confession, and information as to the general condition of the interview room, particularly with reference to its lighting arrangements and approximate temperature.

Photograph and Medical Examination of Confessor

In communities where defense counsel indulge in a rather routine practice of attempting to show that the police investigators employed "third-degree" methods to obtain confessions, much can be gained, if time and circumstances permit, by photographing the confessor after the confession. The photographs should include not only a front view but also both side views. However, the photographs should not be taken of the suspect in a posed position; it is much better to take them while he is talking to someone.

Moreover, whenever such defense tactics are anticipated in important cases, it may be well to have a physician examine the confessor so as to be able to establish at the trial the lack of bruises or other alleged evidence of the "third degree."

Confession Is Not the End of Investigation

Many investigators have the impression that once a confession has been obtained, the investigation is ended, but seldom, if ever, is this true.

A confession unsubstantiated by other evidence is far less effective at the trial than one that has been investigated and subjected to verification or supporting evidence. For instance, assume that a confessed murderer has revealed when and where he purchased the knife used in the killing; he also identified a gas station where he obtained a washroom key so he could wash his bloody hands; and he told of a chance meeting he had with an acquaintance as he left the gas station. There should then be an immediate investigation regarding the purchase of the knife. If the seller remembers the transaction, he should be asked to give a signed statement about it. This will serve to ensure his cooperation at the time of the trial; furthermore, it will minimize the risk of his possible appearance as a witness for the defense to deny any such transaction. For similar reasons, interviews should be conducted with, and written statements obtained from, the gas station attendant who gave the suspect the key and who may have observed blood on the suspect's hands. Perhaps the suspect may have even made a significant comment about the blood. Then, too, the suspect's acquaintance should be interviewed and a written statement sought from him also.

A confession thus supported and substantiated will be far more valuable than the bare document itself. Moreover, there will be many occasions when a thorough post-confession investigation will produce enough incriminating evidence to render unnecessary the use of the confession itself. In some instances, the investigator may find that the post-confession investigation contradicts minor information provided in the suspect's confession. This is not unusual, but the investigator should review with the prosecutor the best manner in which to handle the inconsistency at trial.

In murder and other serious cases in which a post-confession investigation has resulted in the discovery and procurement of overwhelming physical and circumstantial evidence of guilt, it is well for the prosecuting attorney of the jurisdiction to anticipate a possible plea of insanity. It is advisable, therefore, for him to arrange for the immediate taking of signed statements from the offender's relatives and friends in which they express themselves as to the offender's mental condition (e.g., whether he was normal, whether he had ever sustained a head injury). At this stage of the case, the truth will be more prevalent than at the time of trial.

Another matter that deserves a prosecutor's serious consideration is the advisability of trying the case without even using the confession. Many prosecutors are of the view that if there is sufficient other evidence of guilt, procured either before or after the confession, it is better to rely on such evidence and not to use the confession as part of the prosecution's case in chief. The confession will be available, of course, for rebuttal purposes or for the impeachment of the confessor if he takes the stand and testifies.

The principal reason for the practice of omitting the confession from the prosecution's proof of guilt is that an attack on the confession and on the investigator who obtained it—however unfounded the attack may be—might divert the jury's attention from the significance and weight of all the physical or circumstantial evidence presented by the prosecution. Each case, of course, will present its own separate problems; consequently, a prosecutor should not follow any set rule about the use or nonuse of a confession as evidence.

KEY POINTS

- A written or recorded confession is considered far preferable to an oral one. It is essential that an oral confession be reduced to writing and signed as soon as possible.
- During custodial interrogations, where the warnings required by *Miranda v. Arizona* have already been issued before the interrogation or interview began, it is advisable, nevertheless, to repeat the warnings at the beginning of the written confession, making reference, of course, to the fact that the suspect had received and waived them earlier.
- In the event the confessor informs the investigator that he does not wish to make or to sign the statement, or that a lawyer is wanted, the investigator must cease any further questioning or recording.
- It is advisable to ask the confessor, very early in the confession, a question that will call for an acknowledgment that he committed the crime.
- Throughout the taking of the confession, the investigator must always be on guard to see that its contents will be readily understood and easily followed by a reader or subsequent listener who has no other independent knowledge as to what occurred.
- The investigator should let the confessor supply the details of the occurrence; to this end, the investigator should avoid or at least minimize the use of leading questions.
- In the preparation of the written confession, no attempt should be made to improve the language used by the confessor.
- Incorporate in the confession a number of more or less irrelevant questions calling for answers known only to the offender.

KEY TERMS

personal history question Question calling for answers known only to the offender.

EXERCISES

A clerk at a supermarket is robbed of about $800 by a masked man with a gun. The clerk says she thought she recognized the robber's voice as a regular customer who lives nearby. Further investigation develops a possible suspect, Jim Smith, who lives two blocks from the store and does shop there regularly. Jim has a prior record for burglary and it is known that he has been unemployed for six months and is about to be evicted from his apartment. In addition, Jim has lost money gambling on sports events and there is talk on the street that he owes more than $5,000 to bookies.

1. Correct the following direct positive confrontation for the above suspect: "Jim, the results of my investigation clearly indicate that you robbed that store clerk!"

2. What are possible themes to develop during Jim's interrogation?

3. During theme development, Jim leans forward in the chair and says, "Could I just say one thing?" How should the investigator respond?

4. Jim now makes the statement, "I wouldn't even know how to pull off a robbery!" How should the investigator respond?

5. Jim becomes quiet, crosses his arms and legs, and looks up at the ceiling. How should the investigator respond?

6. Jim now uncrosses his arms and legs, leans forward in the chair, and his eyes drop to the floor. The investigator needs to ask an alternative question to elicit the first admission of guilt. What would be an appropriate alternative question for Jim, and how should it be asked?

7. What initial questions could Jim be asked after he accepts the alternative question?

A

False Confession Cases: The Issues

In the past several years a number of false confession cases have received extensive publicity. In several of these cases the convicted individual has been exonerated by DNA testing and the actual perpetrator, in turn, has been identified. In these cases it is important to examine in detail exactly what happened; what went wrong; what are the lessons to be learned, and what are potential safeguards that can be put into place to prevent future mistakes.

To be sure, in the experience of most professional interrogators the frequency of false confessions is rare. When we do learn of them, however, the interrogation tactics and techniques should be scrupulously examined, as well as the circumstances surrounding the interrogation. When this has been done, there are four factors that appear with some regularity in false confession cases:

- The suspect is a juvenile; and/or
- The suspect suffers some mental or psychological impairment; and/or
- The interrogation took place over an inordinate amount of time; and/or
- The interrogators engaged in illegal tactics and techniques

Juveniles/Mental Impairment

Every interrogator must exercise extreme caution and care when interviewing or interrogating a juvenile or a person who is mentally or psychologically impaired. Certainly these individuals can and do commit very serious crimes. But when a juvenile or person who is mentally or psychologically impaired confesses, the investigator should exercise extreme diligence in establishing the accuracy of such a statement through subsequent corroboration. In these situations it is imperative that interrogators do not reveal details of the crime so that they can use the disclosure of such information by the suspect as verification of the confession's authenticity.

When a juvenile younger than 15, who has not had any prior experience with the police, is advised of his *Miranda* rights, the investigator should carefully discuss and talk about those rights with the subject (not just recite them) to make sure that he understands them. If it is apparent that the suspect does not understand his rights, no interrogation should be conducted at that time. The same is true for a person who is mentally or psychologically impaired.

Threats/Promises

A review of the available information in false confession cases has revealed that in many of the interrogations the investigators engaged in the use of impermissible threats and promises. Interrogators in these cases have made such statements as:

"You're not leaving this room until you confess."

"If you tell me you did this you can go home and sleep in your own bed tonight (when such is not the case)."

"You will be sentenced to the maximum term unless you confess."

"With the evidence that we have, there's no doubt that you will be convicted of this. The only question is how long you are going to sit in jail."

"If you don't tell the truth I will get your children turned over to protective services and you'll never see them again."

"The other guys want to charge you with 1st degree murder but if you tell me it was just manslaughter nothing bad will happen to you."

It goes without saying that in the questioning of a criminal suspect no professional interrogator should engage in any illegal interrogation practices, including any threats, promises of leniency or the exercise of any physically abusive tactics. Furthermore, the rights of the suspect should be scrupulously respected.

Theme Development

It has been suggested by some that the interrogator's effort to develop a theme during the interrogation is not just offering the suspect a moral excuse for his criminal behavior, but is actually offering the suspect a promise of reduced punishment. As we have pointed out several times in this text:

- "During the presentation of any theme based upon the morality factor, caution must be taken to avoid any indication that the minimization of the moral blame will relieve the suspect of criminal responsibility." (p. 138)
- "As earlier stated, the interrogator must avoid any expressed or intentionally implied statement to the effect that because of the minimized seriousness of the offense, the suspect is to receive a lighter punishment." (p. 139)
- "In applying this technique of condemning the accomplice, the interrogator must proceed cautiously and must refrain from making any comments to the effect that the blame cast on an accomplice thereby relieves the suspect of legal responsibility for his part in the commission of the offense." (p. 146)

Alternative Questions

In The Reid Technique the alternative question should never threaten consequences or offer promises of leniency. The following are ***improper*** alternative question examples:

"Do you want to cooperate with me and tell me what happened, or spend the next five to seven years behind bars?" (improper)

"Do you want to be charged with first degree murder, which will mean life in prison, or was this just manslaughter?" (improper)

"Are you going to get this straightened out today, or do you want to spend a few days in jail to think about it?" (improper)

There has been the suggestion by some critics of police interrogation techniques that the alternative question—"Was this your idea or did your buddies talk you into it?" is potentially dangerous because it only offers a suspect (including an innocent one) only two choices, both of which amount to an admission of guilt. Obviously the third choice is for the suspect to deny any participation in the commission of the crime that is under investigation.

However, there is an additional issue raised by some critics about the alternative question—namely, that saying "Was this your idea or did your buddies talk you into it" is essentially the same as saying "If this was your idea you are going to spend time in jail, but if your buddies came up with the idea you won't have any problems." This theory is called "pragmatic implication" and was developed from a research study in which college students read various transcripts of interrogations and then speculated on the type of punishment the suspects would receive based on the interrogation process used. Specifically, the students theorized that when the interrogator suggested in a murder case interrogation that the victim may have done or said something to have provoked the suspect, that he would receive the same punishment as in those interrogations in which the suspect was directly offered a promise of leniency that if he confessed he would receive less punishment.

The courts have rejected the idea that a confession is inadmissible if a suspect confesses because he harbors some internal hope that his confession may lead to a lesser sentence.

State v. Nunn – ". . . even if a suspect . . . influenced perhaps by wishful thinking . . . assumed that he would get more lenient treatment . . . [this] would not, as a matter of law, make the confession inadmissible."

R. v. Rennie – "Very few confessions are inspired solely by remorse. Often the motives of the accused are mixed and include a hope that an early admission may lead to an early release or a lighter sentence."

R. v. Oickle – The Supreme Court of Canada indicated that the type of alternative question we suggest does not create an inadmissible confession, and offered a clear test of whether or not an implied threat or promise crosses the legal line: "The most important decision in all cases is to look for a *quid pro quo* offer by interrogators, regardless of whether it comes in the form of a threat or a promise."

Confession Corroboration

As we have stated earlier, it is imperative that interrogators do not reveal details of the crime so that they can use the disclosure of such information by the suspect as verification of the confession's authenticity. In each case there should be documented "hold back" information about the details of how the crime was committed; details from the crime scene; details about specific activities perpetrated by the offender; etc. The goal is match the suspect's confession against these details to establish the veracity of the statement. It should be remembered, however, that suspects do not always tell us everything that they did and they do not always remember all of the details themselves.

Nevertheless, when significant and substantial contradictions exist between the known facts about the crime and what the suspect describes in his confession, extreme care must be exercised in the assessment of the confession's validity.

Factors to Consider

With the above discussion in mind, the following represents some factors to consider in the assessment of the credibility of a suspect's confession. These issues are certainly not all inclusive, and each case must be evaluated on the "totality of circumstances" surrounding the interrogation and confession, but nevertheless, these are elements that should be given careful consideration:

1. The suspect's condition at the time of the interrogation
   a. Physical condition (including drug and/or alcohol intoxication)
   b. Mental capacity
   c. Psychological condition
2. The suspect's age
3. The suspect's prior experience with law enforcement
4. The suspect's understanding of the language
5. The length of the interrogation
6. The degree of detail provided by the suspect in his confession
7. The extent of corroboration between the confession and the crime
8. The presence of witnesses to the interrogation and confession
9. The suspect's behavior during the interrogation
10. The effort to address the suspect's physical needs
11. The presence of any improper interrogation techniques

The Testimony Data Sheet provided below will help to document information relevant to these considerations. For more information on these issues go to **Helpful Info** at **www.reid.com** and then click on the **Critics Corner**.

Testimony Data Sheet

Name: DOB:

Language:

People involved in the interrogation:____________________________

1. Was *Miranda* given? Y N time ________ place _______________
Witness _________

2. Behavior Analysis Interview start _________ end _________

How do you feel about being interviewed today? ____________________

____

Why have you agreed to talk to me about this matter? _______________

____

How would you describe your physical health right now? ____________

____

How much sleep did you get in the last 24 hours? __________________

When was your last full meal?__________________________________

Have you had any alcohol or drugs in the last 24 hours?______________

3. Interrogation start ___________ end ___________

Primary Theme: _____________________________________

Alternative Question: _____________________________________

First admission of guilt time __________

Suspect left interrogation room time __________

Did the suspect request an attorney ? Y N

Did the suspect say he no longer wanted to answer questions? Y N

Did the suspect attempt to leave the room ? Y N

4. Document any washroom breaks; beverages; food; cigarette breaks, etc:

____

____

5. Confession Witnessed by ____________________________

Why did you decide to tell the truth about this?_____________________

____

Do you have any complaints about the way you were treated today? _____

____

Completed by: ____________________________

Answers to Exercises

B

Chapter 1

Identify whether the following statements or behaviors would be associated with an interview, an interrogation or would apply to both interviewing and interrogation.

1. "John, if you are making up a story about being robbed, our investigation will clearly indicate that, so before we go any further let me ask you: Last Saturday night did someone steal $1500 from you?"

   Answer: Interview. This is a non-accusatory question and, therefore, a statement that would be made during an interview.

2. The only people present in the room are the suspect and the investigator.

   Answer: This would be appropriate for either an interview or an interrogation.

3. "Joe, did you plan this thing (robbery) out months in advance or did it just happen on the spur of the moment? It was the spur of the moment wasn't it?"

   Answer: Interrogation. This question assumes the suspect is guilty of the robbery and, therefore, would be appropriate for an interrogation.

4. The investigator makes a note following each verbal response the subject offers.

   Answer: Interview. During a formal interview, the investigator should take a written note following each response by the subject. During an interrogation there should be no note-taking until the suspect has offered a full confession.

5. The subject is advised of his *Miranda* rights prior to a conversation with the investigator.

   Answer: Interview or Interrogation. If the suspect is in custody, prior to an interview or interrogation he must be advised of his *Miranda* rights and voluntarily waive those rights.

6. The conversation between the investigator and subject occurs at the subject's home with the subject's wife and two children present.

   Answer: Interview. The uncontrolled environment described here would not be suitable for an interrogation. Therefore, this conversation would be an interview.

Chapter 2

Richard has worked as a teller for a bank for three years. On this particular day he was closing out his cash drawer and discovered a $1000 shortage. He spent about an hour after work trying to identify the cause of the shortage and even took apart his cash drawer to see if money may have gotten caught behind it. The shortage remained unresolved. Working on one side of Richard is Kathy. Kathy has been employed as a teller at the bank for about a year. While she has had some problems balancing her cash drawer on occasion, she has no known financial difficulties. Working on the other side of Richard is a part-time teller named Keith. Keith is 18 years old and has only worked at the bank for a month.

1. Who should be interviewed first during this investigation? Why?

   Answer: Richard. Because Richard reported the theft the investigator must make certain of the circumstances surrounding the shortage and also eliminate the possibility that Richard stole the money himself.

2. What questions should Richard be asked to help resolve this investigation?

   Answer:

   "Did you allow anyone to work out of your cash drawer on the day of the shortage?"

   "Did you leave your cash drawer unlocked or unattended at any time on the day of the shortage?"

   "Did you have any large transactions on the day of the shortage?"

   "Did you verify any money you received from the main vault on the day of the shortage?"

   "What do you think happened to cause the shortage?"

   "If the money was stolen, who do you suspect may have taken it?"

3. Which suspect is most likely guilty of the theft? Why?

   Answer: Keith stands out as the most likely suspect because he is part-time and has the shortest tenure.

Chapter 3

You must go out of town to conduct a series of interviews of caregivers of a young child who has been sexually abused. There is no suitable office space to use and you do not want to interview these people in their homes. Consequently, you end up renting a meeting room at a local hotel to conduct your interviews. The meeting room has a number of advantages in that it offers privacy and is a neutral setting with respect to reminders of authority. Even though the door does have a lock on it, the door can be opened from the inside. The problem is the size of the room and the existing furniture arrangement. The meeting room is 25 feet by 15 feet, with a large conference table in the center of the room surrounded by 12 chairs. How can you rearrange the furniture in this room to make it suitable for interviewing or interrogating?

Answer : The table should be placed against one wall, essentially cutting the area of the room down to 15-by-15 feet. Using a quarter of this space, two chairs should be positioned about 4 and a half feet apart facing each other. The investigator's chair should not be placed between the door and the subject's chair.

Chapter 4

Identify whether these descriptions of an investigator's behavior during an interview would be considered proper or improper:

1. An investigator starts an interview off with this statement, "Jim, I'm going to question you about a robbery in your neighborhood. I don't like to be lied to, so you better tell me the truth when I ask the questions."

   Answer: Improper. The investigator's tone is obviously threatening and intimidating. Many suspects will become defensive, guarded, and non-cooperative when an investigator assumes an authoritative demeanor.

2. At the outset of an interview of a woman who claims she was sexually assaulted, the investigator states, "Mary, I know this is uncomfortable for you and I can't imagine how anyone could do something like this to a nice girl like you but, unfortunately, I do have to ask a few questions just because it's part of my job."

   Answer: Improper. This investigator is approaching the interview as if the victim is telling the truth. While it is important for the investigator to be sensitive to a subject's emotional needs, it is also important to maintain a neutral position with respect to a subject's credibility.

3. A subject has denied ever seeing or handling a bag of cocaine found in his car during a traffic stop: "Bill, if we were to check that bag of cocaine for fingerprints, is there any reason we would find your fingerprints on it?"

   Answer: Proper. This is a proper question in that it is not accusatory but does allow the investigator to evaluate the suspect's confidence when he denies ever handling the bag of cocaine.

4. The subject of an interview is a ten-year-old girl who is claiming that her uncle forced her to engage in oral sex. "Jenny, before we talk about what you told your mom, I just want to go over some words with you just so that when you say something or I say something, we know that we are both talking about the same thing. I'm sure you know that boys and girls are different when they undress, right? What do you call the boy's thing? What do you call the girl's?

   Answer: Proper. When discussing sexual issues, especially with young children, it is important to establish common terms for the male and female sex organs, as well as for sexual intercourse.

5. An investigator catches a suspect in a lie concerning a question about being at home on a particular date and the investigator responds, "You liar! I know you weren't at home that day because I talked to your neighbors. If you continue to lie to me I'll show you what I do to liars, and you won't like it!"

   Answer: Improper. Once an investigator accuses a suspect of lying during an interview, often the suspect stops volunteering information and the purpose for the interview is defeated. In addition, this investigator is clearly making a veiled threat to the suspect's well being which is clearly improper.

Chapter 5

1. Last Friday someone entered a manager's office on the sixth floor of an office building and stole $80 in cash from a petty cash fund as well as an MP3 player from a desk drawer. Surveillance video indicates that a custodian by the name of Fred was on the sixth floor around 9:00 p.m. Friday, even though he was not assigned to clean that floor. In addition, the next day Fred was seen with an MP3 player that matches the description of the one stolen from the manager's office. What would be an effective technique to invite Fred to be interviewed concerning the theft?

   Answer: "Fred, I have been assigned to investigate an incident that occurred last Friday where some things were taken from an office on the sixth floor. I have reviewed the surveillance video outside of the elevator on the sixth floor and have identified a number of individuals who were on that floor after hours, including yourself. I am in the process of scheduling interviews of these people to see if they can help me out with the investigation, would you be able to come to my office around 4:00 this afternoon?"

2. What questions would you ask Fred at the beginning of the interview?

   Answer:

   Please spell your last name for me.

   What is your first name?

   What do most people call you?

   What is your present address?

   How long have you lived there?

   Who is your present employer?

   What are your duties with (employer)?

3. What would be an appropriate introductory statement to use during Fred's interview?

   Answer: "Fred, last Friday evening someone entered the manager's office on the sixth floor of this building and stole money and property. Because you were on the sixth floor last Friday night, I would like to ask you some questions about that. Some of the questions that I'll be asking you I already know the answer to, but the important thing is for you to be completely truthful with me before you leave this afternoon."

Chapter 6

1. Re-phrase each of the following interview questions so they are asked properly.

   A. "Where were you last Saturday at 3:15 in the afternoon?"

   Answer: "Tell me everything you did last Saturday between 1:00 and 5:00 in the afternoon."

   B. "Did you sell any marijuana at the ball game or did anyone approach you asking to buy drugs?"

   Answer: "Did you sell any marijuana at the ball game? Did anyone approach you during the ball game asking to buy some drugs from you?"

C. "Do you recall leaving the bar with anyone last night?"

Answer: "Did you leave the bar with anyone last night?"

2. Ask an appropriate follow-up question for the following dialogues:

Q: "Did you return to work last Friday night?"

A: "My wife had the car."

Follow up: "I understand your wife had the car, but I was wondering if you returned to work last Friday night?"

Q: "Did you handle a gun over the weekend?"

A: "To the best of my knowledge I didn't."

Follow up: "Is it possible you handled a gun over the weekend?"

Q: "Have you ever been questioned before concerning sexual contact with a minor?"

A: "When I was in high school there was an incident involving this girl I was dating. She was 16 and I was 18."

Follow up: "Other than that incident, have you been questioned before about sexual contact with a minor?"

Chapter 7

Determine whether these responses to the following interview questions are more typical of a truthful or deceptive suspect:

Q: "Did you steal a car from the Ford dealership?"

A: "Absolutely not!" [Direct eye contact, on time.]

Answer: Truthful.

Q: "Do you know who stole that car from the dealership?"

A: "I'm not even certain it was stolen (laugh)." [Slight delay, sitting back in chair.]

Answer : Deceptive.

Q: "Has anyone ever approached you, asking you to help them take a car from the dealership?"

A: "Has anyone ever approached me? No." [On time, hand to mouth, eyes to ceiling.]

Answer : Deceptive.

Q: "Have you ever just thought about taking a car from the dealership?"

A: "No way." [Forward lean, direct eye contact.]

Answer : Truthful.

Q: "Over the weekend were you inside a stolen car?"

A: "I would have to say no." [On time but drawn out.]

Answer : Deceptive.

Q: "How do you feel about being interviewed concerning this stolen car?"

A: "It doesn't bother me. I know you're just doing your job." [The subject crosses his legs and bounces his foot.]

Answer : Deceptive.

Q: "Once we complete our entire investigation, how will it come out on you?"

A: "It better show that I'm not the person who stole that car." [The subject had direct eye contact and extends his hand toward the investigator.]

Answer : Truthful.

Chapter 8

Identify a cause other than deception for the following behavior symptoms:

1. The subject exhibits very little eye contact throughout the course of the interview.

   Answer: Cultural differences, shy personality, youthful suspect.

2. The suspect appears defeated throughout the interview and many of his responses are delayed.

   Answer: Depression, general fatigue, medication, or illegal drug use.

3. When relaying what happened to him, the person exhibits very little eye contact, and talks slowly and at a low volume. The person also exhibits a collapsed posture throughout the interview.

   Answer: Traumatized victim.

Part II (end of Chapter 18)

A clerk at a supermarket is robbed of about $800 by a masked man with a gun. The clerk says she thought she recognized the robber's voice as a regular customer who lives nearby. Further investigation develops a possible suspect, Jim Smith, who lives two blocks from the store and does shop there regularly. Jim has a prior record for burglary and it is known that he has been unemployed for six months and is about to be evicted from his apartment. In addition, Jim has lost money gambling on sports events and there is talk on the street that he owes more than $5,000 to bookies.

1. Correct the following direct positive confrontation for the above suspect:

   "Jim, the results of my investigation clearly indicate that you robbed that store clerk!"

   Answer: "Jim, the results of *our* investigation clearly indicate that you *are the person who took the money* from that store clerk."

2. What are possible themes to develop during Jim's interrogation?

   Answer: He acted out of desperation because of his financial difficulty and because he was being pressured by people like his landlord and the bookies. The economy can be blamed for not providing adequate job opportunities to allow Jim to earn a decent living. His robbery can also be contrasted with a worse situation, such as his having shot and killed the clerk.

3. During theme development, Jim leans forward in the chair and says, "Could I just say one thing?" How should the investigator respond?

   Answer: "Jim, hear me out because this is important for you to know." [Discourage the denial from surfacing.]

4. Jim now makes the statement, "I wouldn't even know how to pull off a robbery!" How should the investigator respond?

   Answer: "Jim, that's exactly why I'm talking to you, and I think you're absolutely right. This whole thing was totally out of character for you and I'm sure it just happened on the spur of the moment. If you had had a long history of holding up places like this I wouldn't even bother coming in here and talking to you about this."

5. Jim becomes quiet, crosses his arms and legs and looks up at the ceiling. How should the investigator respond?

   Answer: The investigator should move his chair closer to Jim's chair and incorporate rhetorical questions within the theme. In addition, the theme should be directed toward Jim's eyes.

6. Jim now uncrosses his arms and legs, leans forward in the chair, and his eyes drop to the floor. The investigator needs to ask an alternative question to elicit the first admission of guilt. What would be an appropriate alternative question for Jim, and how should it be asked?

   Answer: "Jim, I don't think you had this thing planned out weeks or months in advance. I think it pretty much happened on the spur of the moment. You got frustrated and didn't know where else to turn for money and in a split second decision you decided to get some from the store. It's boiling down to this. Either you have been planning this thing out for a long time or it just happened on the spur of the moment. I can't see you planning something like this out. I think it just happened on the spur of the moment. It was the spur of the moment, wasn't it?"

7. What initial questions could Jim be asked after he accepts the alternative question?

   Answer:

   "Do you have any of the money left?"

   "Have you told anyone else about this?"

   "Was anyone with you when you did this?"

Index

Page numbers followed by *t* indicate tables.

A

Absolute declaration, 184–185
Adaptor behaviors, 96–98
Alternative questions, 203–204
  false confession cases, 237
  presenting, 207–210
  selecting, 204–207
Angry suspects, 107
Assumption of guilt, 39
Assumption of innocence, 39–40
Assumption of neutral position, 40
Attention of suspect, 187–188
  chair proximity and, 188–190
  eye contact, 190
  psychological withdrawal, 188
  rhetorical questions, use of, 191–192
  visual aids, use of, 191
Attitude of suspect, 82
  concerned *versus* unconcerned, 83
  cooperative *versus* uncooperative, 83–84
  helpful *versus* unhelpful, 83
  personality, distinguished, 82
  sincere *versus* insincere, 83
  spontaneous *versus* guarded, 82–83

B

Behavior analysis, 77–78
  and attitude of suspect, 82–84
  communication channels, 80–81
  nonverbal. *See* Nonverbal behavior
  paralinguistic behavior. *See* Paralinguistic behavior analysis
  principles of, 80–82
  research studies, 78–80
  testimony data sheet, 239
  verbal behavior. *See* Verbal behavior analysis
Behavior symptoms, 105
  analysis of. *See* Behavior analysis
  anger, 107
  children and, 112
  cultural differences, 113
  despair. *See* Despair and resignation
  emotional condition and, 112–113
  impertinence, 107
  intelligence and, 112
  versus investigative findings, 108–109
  maturity and, 112
  medications and, 109
  mental illness and, 109–111
  misinterpretation of, 108–113
  nervousness, 106–107
  normal range, 105–106
  resignation. *See* Despair and resignation
  reticence, 106
  social responsibility and, 112
Behavioral pause, 130–131

C

Case facts, 11
Chair/seating arrangement, 30, 41
  attention of suspect, 188–190
Challenging questions, 70
Channels of communication, 80–81
Children
  and behavior, 112
  juvenile false confession cases, 235–236
Clarifying questions, 66–67
Clipped words, 92
Communication channels, 80–81
Concerned suspect, 83
Condemnation of accomplice, 146–148
Condemnation of others, 144–150
Condemnation of victim, 145–146
Confessions, 213
  false. *See* False confession cases
  oral. *See* Oral confessions
  testimony data sheet, 239
  written. *See* Written confessions
Confrontation. *See* Direct, positive confrontation
Confrontation statement, 128–130
Consequences, reminders of, 27–28
Contact with occurrence or victim, 158–160
Controlled environment
  interrogations, 6
  interviews, 5
Co-offenders, playing one against the other, 161–163
Cooperative suspect, 83–84
Corroboration
  dependent, 12
  false confession cases, 238
  oral confessions, 216–217
Crime scene, placement at, 158–160
"Crutch," 137
Crying, 199–200
Cultural differences, 113
Custodial suspect, 48

D

Deceptive responses, 85, 86–90
Demeanor of investigator
  during an interview, 41–43
  passive mood of suspect, 197–198
Denials, 165–166
  after direct, positive confrontation, 166–167
  anticipating, 167–169
  discouraging weak denials, 169–171
  evaluating, 171–173
  from the guilty, 172–173
    responding to, 174–178
    strong denials, 176–178

from the innocent, 171–172
responding to, 173–174
noncontracted, 89
nonverbal indications, 168–169
responding to, 173
attempts to leave interrogation room, 178–179
guilty suspects, 174–178
(probably) innocent suspects, 173–174
during the theme, 167
verbal indications, 169
Dependent corroboration, 12
Despair and resignation, 107–108, 198
signs of, 198–200
Detail question, 206
Details of offense, relating, 213. *See also* Oral confessions; Written confessions
Diction. *See* Language usage
Direct, positive confrontation, 127–128
behavioral pause, 130–131
confrontation statement, 128–130
denials after, 166–167
transition statement, 128, 131–134
Direct questions, 67
challenging questions, 70
follow-up questions, 70–71
hypotheticals, 71–72
guidelines for asking, 68–70
memory qualifiers, 69
negative questions, 69–70
open questions, preferred, 68
responses to
deceptive responses, 85, 86–90
evasive responses, 71, 85–86
omissive responses, 72, 85
qualified responses, 71–72, 87–88
rehearsed responses, 89–90
truthful responses, 84
tagging, 69
Distractions, 29

E

Emotional condition, and behavior, 112–113
Emotional objections, 183
Emotional offenders, 119–120. *See also* Theme development
Erasure behavior, 92–93
Estimation phrases, 88
Evasive responses, 71, 85–86
Exaggeration themes, 152–154
Experts, reliance on, 15–16
Eye contact, 98
assessing suspect's veracity with, 99*t*
attention of suspect, 190
change in, 199

F

Facial expressions, 98
Fact analysis, 11–12
Fact gathering, 12–15
Fact-giver, 12
Factual objections, 183
False confession cases, 235
alternative questions, 237
corroborative information, 238
factors to consider, 238
juveniles, 235–236
mentally impaired, 235
theme development, 236
threats and promises, 236
Feet, evaluation of, 98
Flattering the suspect, 150–152
Follow-up questions, 70–71
hypotheticals, 71–72
Forced silence technique, 62–63
Formal interview, 48
introductory statement(s), 51–52
for suspects, 52–53
for victims and witnesses, 53–55
noncustodial environment, 48–50
note-taking during, 5
preparation for, 50
rapport with suspect, 50–51
Friendly/unfriendly act, 176

G

General acknowledgment of guilt, 214–216
Generalization statement, 87
Grooming gestures, 97
Guarded suspect, 82–83
Guilt or innocence, 47
assumption of guilt, 39
assumption of innocence, 39–40
feeling of guilt, reduction of, 142–143
general acknowledgment of guilt, 214–216

H

Hands, evaluation of, 96–98
Hand shrug, 96
Helpful suspect, 83
Hypothetical follow-up questions, 71–72

I

Illustrating, 96
Impertinence by suspects, 107
Implied-action phrases, 66
Informal interview, 48. *See also* Interview
Innocence. *See* Guilt or innocence
Insincere suspect, 83
Intelligence, and behavior, 112
Interrogation, 3
accusatory nature, 5
attempts to leave room, responding to, 178–179
characteristics of, 5–6
note-taking during, 6
persuasion during, 5
privacy, importance of, 25–27

purpose of, 5–6
reminders of consequences, 27–28
testimony data sheet, 239
when conducted, 6
where conducted, 6
Interrogation steps, 121–122
alternative questions. *See* Alternative questions
attention of suspect, procurement and retention of. *See* Attention of suspect
denials. *See* Denials
details of offense, relating, 213. *See also* Oral confessions; Written confessions
direct, positive confrontation. *See* Direct, positive confrontation
mood of suspect. *See* Passive mood of suspect
overcoming objections. *See* Objections
preliminary preparations, 122–124
theme development. *See* Theme development
Interruption gestures, 168–169
Interview, 3
benefits of conducting, 6–7
chair/seating arrangement, 30, 41
characteristics of, 4–5
formal. *See* Formal interview
as freeflowing and unstructured, 4–5
guidelines, 17–19
guilt, assumption of, 39
informal, 48
initial procedures, 38–40
innocence, assumption of, 39–40
investigator's demeanor during, 41–43
language usage, 43
neutral position, assumption of, 40
nonaccusatory nature of, 4
noncustodial, 29
note-taking during, 5, 42
privacy and, 25–27, 29
purpose of, 4
questions. *See* Interview questions
reminders of consequences, 27–28
smoking during, 41–42
testimony data sheet, 239
when conducted, 4
where conducted, 4
Interview room
chair arrangement, 30
distractions, 29
lighting, 29
locks, 29
noise, 30
observation room adjoining, 30–34
privacy in, 25–27, 29
setting up, 28–34
Interviewer objectivity, 40
Interviewer qualifications, 38
Interviewer traits, 37–38
Interview questions
behavior of suspect during. *See* Behavior symptoms
clarifying questions, 66–67
direct questions. *See* Direct questions
forced silence technique, 62–63
open questions. *See* Open questions
phrasing, 59–60
open questions, 62
responses to
continuity of, 92
delivery of, 91–92
direct questions. *See* Direct questions
early responses, 90–91
guidelines for evaluating, 85–90
latency in, 90
length of, 91
open questions. *See* Open questions
tone of, 42
Introductory phrase, 182
Introductory statement(s), 51–52
for suspects, 52–53
for victims and witnesses, 53–55
Investigator, 12
Investigator's demeanor
during an interview, 41–43
passive mood of suspect, 197–198

J

Juveniles
and behavior, 112
false confession cases, 235–236

L

Language usage
in an interview, 43
in confessions, 225–227
Leading question, 208
Leading questions
written confessions, 226
Leg position, changes in, 198
Lighting, 29
Listing, 89–90
Locks, 29
Lying by referral, 86

M

Manipulative crying, 199–200
Maturity, and behavior, 112
Medical examination of confessor, 229
Medications, and behavior, 109
Memory qualifiers
in deceptive responses, 87–88
in direct questions, 69
Mentally ill/impaired
and behavior, 109–111
false confession cases, 235
Miranda warnings, 222–223
custodial suspect's rights, 48
before interrogation, 122
testimony data sheet, 239

Mood of suspect. *See* Passive mood of suspect
"Moral excuse," 137
Moral objections, 183
"Morally acceptable" motivation for offense, 143–144
Most likely suspect, 16–17
Mutual gaze, 98

N

Negative questions, 69–70
Negative supporting statement, 207–208
Nervousness of suspect, 106–107
Neutral position, assumption of, 40
Noise, 30
Noncontracted denial, 89
Noncustodial interview, 29, 48–50. *See also* Interview
Nonemotional offenders, 120. *See also* Theme development
Nonverbal agreement, 198
Nonverbal behavior, 93–94
  abbreviations for, 42, 43*t*
  denials, anticipation of, 168–169
  eye contact. *See* Eye contact
  facial expressions, 98
  feet, evaluation of, 98
  hands, evaluation of, 96–98
  posture, evaluation of, 94–95, 198
Nonverbal channel, 80
Normal range, 105–106
Note-taking
  during an interview, 5, 42
  during interrogation, 6
  written confessions, 228

O

Objections, 181–182
  emotional, 183
  factual, 183
  moral, 183
  recognizing, 182
  rewarding, 182–184
  turning around, 184–185
  types of, 183*t*
Observation room, 30–34
Offenders, classification of, 119–120
Offense details, relating, 213. *See also* Oral confessions; Written confessions
Omission qualifiers, 88
Omissive responses, 72, 85
Open questions, 60–62
  clarifying questions, 66–67
  forced silence technique, 62–63
  phrasing, 62
  preference for, 68
  responses to
    deception, indications of, 65–66
    eliciting full responses, 62–63
    evaluation of, 63–66
    truthfulness, indications of, 64–65
Oral confessions, 217
  corroborative information, 216–217
  general acknowledgment of guilt, 214–216
  statement of reinforcement, 214
  witnessing, 217–219
Overcoming objections. *See* Objections

P

Paralinguistic behavior analysis, 90
  early responses, 90–91
  erasure behavior, 92–93
  response continuity, 92
  response delivery, 91–92
  response latency, 90
  response length, 91
Paralinguistic channel, 80
Passive mood of suspect, 195
  content of statements, 195–197
  demeanor of investigator, 197–198
  eye contact, change in, 199
  leg position, changes in, 198
  nonverbal agreement, 198
  posture, change in, 198
  tearing or crying, 199–200
Permission phrase, 169
Personal gestures, 97
Personality of suspect, 82
Photograph of confessor, 229
Pleading phrase, 169
Positive confrontation. *See* Direct, positive confrontation
Positive supporting statement, 207–208
Posture, evaluation of, 94–95
  passive mood of suspect, 198
Privacy, 25
  importance of, 25–27
  in the interview room, 29
Protective gestures, 97–98
Psychological withdrawal, 188

Q

Qualified responses, 71–72, 87–88
Questions
  alternative. *See* Alternative questions
  interview. *See* Interview questions

R

Range of normalcy, 105–106
Rapport with suspect, 50–51
Reformation theme, 154–157
Rehearsed responses, 89–90
Reid interrogation steps, 121–122
  alternative questions. *See* Alternative questions
  attention of suspect, procurement and retention of. *See* Attention of suspect
  denials. *See* Denials
  details of offense, relating, 213. *See also* Oral confessions; Written confessions

direct, positive confrontation. *See* Direct, positive confrontation
mood of suspect. *See* Passive mood of suspect
overcoming objections. *See* Objections
preliminary preparations, 122–124
theme development. *See* Theme development
Reinforcement, statement of, 214
Reliance on experts, 15–16
Reminders of consequences, 27–28
Resignation, 107–108, 198
signs of, 198–200
Response latency, 90
Responses to questions
interview questions. *See* Interview questions
truthful responses. *See* Truthful responses
Reticence of suspect, 106
Rhetorical questions, use of, 191–192

S

Seating arrangement, 30, 41
attention of suspect, 188–190
Self-interest, statement against, 88–89
Sincere suspect, 83
Smoking during the interview, 41–42
Social responsibility, and behavior, 112
Spontaneous suspect, 82–83
Statement against self-interest, 88–89
Statement of reinforcement, 214
Steps of interrogation. *See* Reid interrogation steps
Stop-and-start behavior, 92
Supporting gestures, 97–98
Sympathy with suspect, 141–142

T

Tagging, 69
Tearing, 199–200
Theme development, 137–138
emotional offenders, 138
approaches to avoid, 138–140
condemnation of accomplice, 146–148
condemnation of others, 144–150
condemnation of victim, 145–146
exaggeration themes, 152–154
feeling of guilt, reduction of, 142–143
flattering, 150–152
"morally acceptable" motivation for offense, 143–144
reformation theme, 154–157
sympathy with, 141–142
third-person themes, 140–141
false confession cases, 236
nonemotional offenders, 157
contact with occurrence or victim, 158–160
co-offenders, playing one against the other, 161–163
futility of not telling the truth, 160–161
lying about incidental matter, admission of, 157–158
placement at crime scene, 158–160
Third-person themes, 140–141
Threats and promises, 236
Time-gap phrases, 66
Tone of questions, 42
Transition statement, 128, 131–134
Truthful responses, 84
futility of not telling the truth, 160–161
lying about incidental matter, admission of, 157–158

U

Unconcerned suspect, 83
Uncooperative suspect, 83–84
Unhelpful suspect, 83

V

Verbal behavior analysis, 84
deceptive responses, 85, 86–90
denials, anticipation of, 169
evasive responses, 71, 85–86
guidelines, 85–90
omissive responses, 72, 85
qualified responses, 71–72, 87–88
rehearsed responses, 89–90
truthful responses, 84
Verbal channel, 80
Victim
condemnation of, 145–146
contact with, 158–160
Visual aids, use of, 191

W

Witnessing
oral confessions, 217–219
testimony data sheet, 239
written confessions, 227
Written confessions, 221
comprehensibility, 225
confessor's own language, 226
confining to a single crime, 227–228
as end of investigation, 229–230
form of, 223–225
importance of documentation, 222
language of, 225–227
leading questions, 226
medical examination of confessor, 229
Miranda warnings, 222–223
notes, preservation of, 228
personal history questions, 226–227
photograph of confessor, 229
preparation, 223
readability, 225
reading of, 227
signing of, 227
witnesses, 227